More Praise for *A Noble Madness*

"Everybody has things; some people collect things; and just a few of these people are obsessives, defining themselves through their collections. What's been thought about people like that? Are they contemptible, pitiable, or admirable? Are they perverse or pious, crazy or charismatic? James Delbourgo puts the collector right at the center of a historical story about what it means to be human. *A Noble Madness* enlightens, it provokes, and it delights."

—Steven Shapin, author of *Eating and Being*
and *A Social History of Truth*

"I've seen the inside of James Delbourgo's New York apartment, and can report that it is surprisingly orderly, even minimalist. But the inside of his mind? What a dazzling cabinet of curiosities! He shows incontrovertibly in this mesmerizing new book the parallel between people's psyches and the objects they surround themselves with. From the high-end art collector to Jeffrey Dahmer's horrifying temple of human bones, nothing puts the human soul on display like collecting. I declare from my coffee-stained couch, surrounded by dirty plates, unopened mail, and more books than anyone could ever read, that *A Noble Madness* makes a fundamental contribution to the study of human psychology."

—Justin Smith-Ruiu, author of *Irrationality:*
A History of the Dark Side of Reason

"Is a scientist plunging into a jungle in search of specimens really all that different from someone surreptitiously snipping passersby's hair to add to his very private collection? James Delbourgo has great fun tackling this question by presenting a collection of collectors in a witty dash through the history of a deeply human urge."

—Erin Thompson, author of *Possession: The Curious*
History of Private Collectors from Antiquity to the Present

"A gallery of collectors from ancient times to the present—obsessives and dilettanti, hoarders and cataloguers, emperors, scholars, and libertines. James Delbourgo's exploration of their 'madness,' whether uncontrolled passion, devious greed, or a desire to order chaos, is an exuberant and illuminating delight."   —Jenny Uglow, author of *The Lunar Men*

"This is a wonderful book: witty, erudite, and deliciously written. It has many layers, with different energies flowing and glowing across the pages, maintaining elegance and lightness of touch throughout. A rare combination of human empathy and critical insight. James Delbourgo takes us round the world and deep into history to reveal both the dark and the bright side of collecting."

—Hartwig Fischer, former director of the British Museum

A Noble Madness

ALSO BY JAMES DELBOURGO

Collecting the World:
Hans Sloane and the Origins of the British Museum

A Most Amazing Scene of Wonders:
Electricity and Enlightenment in Early America

A
NOBLE
MADNESS

THE DARK SIDE OF
COLLECTING FROM
ANTIQUITY TO NOW

JAMES DELBOURGO

W. W. NORTON & COMPANY

Independent Publishers Since 1923

For information about special discounts for bulk purchases, please contact
W. W. Norton Special Sales at specialsales@wwnorton.com or 800-233-4830

Manufacturing by Lakeside Book Company
Book design by Dana Sloan
Production manager: Louise Mattarelliano

ISBN: 978-0-393-54196-0

W. W. Norton & Company, Inc.
500 Fifth Avenue, New York, NY 10110
www.wwnorton.com

W. W. Norton & Company Ltd.
15 Carlisle Street, London W1D 3BS

10 9 8 7 6 5 4 3 2 1

To Dieter Armand Kopp (1939–2022),

an artist, not a collector

Collecting is but writing in water.

—HOLBROOK JACKSON, *THE ANATOMY OF BIBLIOMANIA* (1930)

To thine own self be true.

—HAMLET, QUOTED BY HOLBROOK JACKSON,

THE ANATOMY OF BIBLIOMANIA (1930)

*Be humble, my fellow collectors. The historian will
rub shoulders with you without even noticing you,
the philosopher will shrug his shoulders, the artist will
scorn you as a bourgeois boob and the man of the world
as a fool chasing knick-knacks; only the doctor and the
physician will tip their hat to you . . . in hopes of soon
making you one of their patients.*

—EDMOND BONNAFFÉ, *TALKS ON ART AND CURIOSITY* (1878)

Contents

Contents

A Noble Madness

LET THEM SEE
WHAT KIND OF A
PERSON I AM

Poets are always on the side of the demons.

—MICHEL LEIRIS, *PHANTOM AFRICA* (1934)

You're driving in the rain, it's late, and you're tired. You've had a strange couple of days and done something crazy: you've stolen some money. Your concentration is shaky and the rain is pelting your windshield, making it hard to see. So when you see a motel sign up ahead, you pull in and park. You honk your horn and you wait.

A young man comes out to greet you with an umbrella and shows you into his office. You decide to stay the night, so he checks you in. He's friendly and escorts you to your room, and you ask if there's any place to eat nearby. Not really, he says, but why don't you come up to the house, behind the motel, for a little supper?

The young man disappears. When he comes back, he apologizes, because his mother doesn't want anyone coming up to the house. She's unwell, he explains, and doesn't like having strangers around, so you have dinner behind the motel office instead. As you enter his parlor, the motel keeper turns on the light and you notice several large stuffed birds around the room. You sit down and take a careful bite out of your sandwich.

"You eat like a bird," says your host. "You'd know, of course," you reply. You ask about the birds and he tells you about his hobby: taxidermy. It's really not that expensive, he explains, "the chemicals are the only thing that cost anything." A man *should* have a hobby, you agree. It's all pleasant enough, though the conversation feels forced somehow and he seems melancholy. "A hobby is supposed to pass the time," he observes, "not fill it."[1]

You ask whether his time is really so empty and he tells you about his mother, more than you want to know: how she mistreats him and how he longs to be free, but can't bear the idea of being apart from her. Eventually, you make it back to your room, not noticing there are several pictures of birds on the wall. You realize your host is caught in a trap, but you don't have to be. You decide to drive home first thing in the morning and return the money you stole. You take a cleansing shower before going to bed.

Then you're murdered by Norman Bates.

Directed by Alfred Hitchcock, starring Anthony Perkins and Janet Leigh, *Psycho* was released on an unsuspecting world in 1960, though Hitchcock did try to warn viewers about the mayhem in store in his playfully macabre way. You can't trust Norman Bates, he tells us from the very beginning, even before Norman starts talking about Mother. Why? Because Norman Bates stuffs birds. Because Norman Bates is a collector. Instead of burying Mother all those years ago, he stole her corpse, preserved it, and believed he *was* his mother when he carried out a series of killings.

At the end of the film, after Bates is arrested for this string of murders, he states (mimicking Mother's voice) that he's not even going to swat the fly that has landed on his hand. "Let them see what kind of a person I am," he says. This is what Hitchcock was doing from the very start of the movie by telling the viewer that Bates is a collector: letting us see what kind of a person he is. Hitchcock later told French director François Truffaut that the birds "were like symbols. Obviously [Bates] is interested in taxidermy since he'd filled his own mother with sawdust." He feels the birds "watching him all the time" and sees "his own guilt reflected in their knowing eyes." Publicity stills for *Psycho*, which Hitchcock undoubtedly had a say in, featured Perkins with the birds.[2]

But why did it seem natural to Hitchcock to suggest that *because* Bates was a taxidermist and a collector, he was dangerous?

SHAMLEY PRODUCTIONS/Album

Publicity still from Alfred Hitchcock's Psycho *(1960)*
starring Anthony Perkins as Norman Bates, with his stuffed
birds: an early indication from Hitchcock that Bates isn't
quite himself.

In making this link between collecting and danger, Hitchcock and the
makers of *Psycho* were tapping into a long tradition of seeing collectors as
people who have something wrong with them, so wrong that they may be
a threat either to themselves or other people. This idea achieved a special
intensity in the twentieth century, after Sigmund Freud's theories of sexual
repression came to dominate perceptions of collectors as troubled, inward
and stunted. In reality, however, the idea that collectors are devious, devi-
ant, and dangerous, motivated by passions they cannot control, is far older,
stretching back centuries, albeit in many different guises.

A Noble Madness tells the story of this rather outrageous idea: that
underneath their veneer of reason and civility, collectors are febrile, volatile,
and warped. The collector turns out to be an extraordinarily diagnostic figure in our collective cultural imagination, morphing from antiquity down
to the present, constantly threatening to explode. Collectors are obsessives

who love things more than people, we like to fear, and will do anything to get and keep what they want—whether it means doing harm to themselves or to others.

When we use the word *collector*, of course, we often mean very different things. Art collectors have taste, we say: an eye for beauty and novelty or a feel for an investment. But what about people who collect plants or animals? Botanists, biologists, and zoologists gather specimens for scientific purposes. It's their vocation, and perhaps also their passion, but they collect for professional reasons and the advancement of knowledge. Collectors of ceramic hedgehogs or Liberace dolls are rather different again, off in the never-never land of the inexplicably personal.

To some, the word *collector* sounds weak and weird, suggesting people who are nerdy and reclusive—people who retreat from the real world and collect as a substitute for living a normal life, often gathering apparently worthless items from product packaging to old newspapers. Hoarders, one might think, rather than collectors—except that some of the greatest collections in history started out this way. Robert Opie's Museum of Brands in London, for example, contains one of the world's largest collections of consumer packaging, which Opie started saving in the 1960s, when virtually no one deemed cereal packets or toy boxes worthy of preservation.

To others, by contrast, *collector* is a dynamic and powerful word. It suggests ego, money, and formidable personal drive. This kind of collector can achieve almost godlike influence as a benefactor who molds the public taste, societal values, knowledge, and institutions. At their best, such collectors are noble and civic-minded servants of the public good, like the intrepid field-workers who stocked the natural history museums of the Victorian era or the dedicated philanthropists who founded art museums in the United States around the turn of the twentieth century.

From Noah stocking his ark with animals in the biblical story of the Flood to modern anthropologists and archaeologists who preserved the artifacts of non-Western cultures for posterity, this collector has often been heralded as a savior. *The Cabinet of a Collector*, dated 1617 by the Flemish artist Frans Francken the Younger, illustrates this idea. In Francken's painting, chaos reigns in the world outside the collection as donkey-headed philistines gleefully smash objects symbolizing learning, science, and the

Frans Francken the Younger, The Cabinet of a Collector *(1617): In Francken's post-Reformation vision of iconoclasm and philistinism, donkey-headed barbarians destroy objects symbolizing knowledge and the arts. Inside the cabinet, however, the collector saves and cherishes the achievements of civilization, including studies for Michelangelo's Sistine Chapel.*

arts, with an iconoclastic attack on a church in the background. Francken's collector, by contrast, is a keeper of knowledge and a guarantor of harmony and, as such, the guardian of civilization itself.

But are collectors saviors or are they travelers on the road to perdition? History reveals an infinite variety of collectors, driven by a universe of different motives. Yet, as a matter of historical fact, the story most often told about collectors is the opposite of Francken's moral allegory—not parables of heroic salvation, but dark tales of secretive thieves and crazed obsessives.

It's *because* collectors seek to turn a chaotic world into an ordered one that they make for particularly unsettling figures. Madness is never so disconcerting as when it appears in the guise of reason. Collectors can seem like the most humdrum characters in the world, but they often cross the threshold of the moral and the legal, the pious and the licit, because they dare to take what is not theirs. The consequences of doing so are often unintended; the characters who do so ambiguous.

The pages that follow present a grand portrait gallery that charts the changing image of the collector from the ancient looter and the medieval idolater to the decadent of the fin de siècle and the modern-day hoarder. *A Noble Madness* is not a social history of collecting or an exhaustive encyclopedia of all possible collectors—intriguing though such a book would be—and contains as many fictional collectors as real ones. This is because its purpose is to understand the evolution of a cultural idea, one that may or may not be true, but has exercised an enduring hold on the imagination: namely that collecting is a sign of madness. That there's something peculiar about people who love things too much has always impressed observers of the species, but their diagnosis has shifted from theories of demonic possession to accusations of superstition, obsession, sexual neurosis, and pathological greed down to the recent invention of the medical term *hoarding disorder*.

But the story in these pages goes deeper than madness and collecting. Because in order to understand how we came to see the collector as a troubled person, we have to understand how we came to believe that when we look at a collection, we see a self. We have to understand how we learned, at a particular point in time, to see a collection and ask *why? Why these things? What do they mean? What kind of person collected them? Surely a collection reveals something deeply personal about the collector?* It was not always thus. Equating the collection with the self only crystallized in the nineteenth century through the notion of a Romantic collecting self and through Sigmund Freud's invention of psychoanalysis in the 1890s. *A Noble Madness* tells the story of how this happened and asks whether we still look at a collection and see a self in 2025. Does the "why" question in collecting still matter, and, if not, why not? If we have now replaced the Romantic Freudian question about what a collection means or what it tells us about the collector's identity, what have we replaced it with, and does it matter?

This dark tale of madness and obsession has a noble twist, however. *Because* collecting has often seemed useless, obsessive, and inane if not insane, it has often been seen in a positive light. The first flickerings of this notion appeared in premodern Asia, where obsessive collectors were praised as deeply sophisticated and cultivated individuals. But it was in nineteenth-century Europe that the obsessive collector became one of the great antiheroes of modernity. Because "true collectors" were seen as resisting the brute power of fashion, utility, and profit, and collecting for personal and visionary reasons, they came to be seen as paragons of authenticity who were fundamentally true to themselves. They were authentic, not calculating; genuine, not strategic. They had integrity, almost to the point of sacrificing their lives for their collections. In the twentieth century, therefore, totalitarian regimes regarded collectors who did not conform to social and political norms as threats to their authority and tried to liquidate them, ideologically if not personally. As a result, even the most eccentric and inward private collectors became symbols of freedom, integrity, and truth to oneself. Obsessive collectors became heroes because they dared to defy society and state and to create a world of private meaning entirely for themselves. "My love's a noble madness," says Cleopatra in John Dryden's 1677 play *All for Love*, "which shows the cause deserved it." True collectors know in their hearts there *is* a cause underlying their collections, though others often cannot see it: individual self-expression, in all its noble madness.[3]

"Poets are always on the side of the demons," wrote the French anthropologist Michel Leiris, who was among the first to question the motivations behind modern scientific collecting. Leiris was right: as Milton's unforgettable portrait of Satan in *Paradise Lost* attests, evil has always proved more fascinating than good. We like Marion Crane in *Psycho*, but Norman Bates is immortal. This is why the dominant modern story about the collector features the loner who looks civilized on the surface but in whose heart lurks a passion for things so vehement it verges on insanity. And this is why notorious collectors are the most enduring in our cultural memory. At once unsettling and cathartic, they beguile us with their madness because of the sneaking suspicion we might just be them.[4]

CHAPTER ONE

STATUE LOVE

I kissed beauty itself.

—GUSTAVE FLAUBERT, *NOTES DE VOYAGES* (1845)

Many years ago, I visited the island of Capri. That singularly favored isle has played host to many illustrious guests, from stern intellectuals to pop superstars, from Vladimir Lenin and Walter Benjamin in the twentieth century to Michael Jordan and Jennifer Lopez in the twenty-first. My parents honeymooned on the island at the height of the Dolce Vita in 1959. When I visited, decades later, it was burning with heat, but no less sweet.

Capri is all about vertical motion. You arrive by boat, but from that moment on, the only way is up. You take the funicular railway up to the main square and continue to the village of Anacapri by chairlift, with commanding views of Vesuvius and the Bay of Naples as you ascend. While in Anacapri, I came upon a small museum. I don't remember its name or its precise location, but I went inside and found blessed relief from the summer sun. It was a museum of Roman sculpture. Almost no one was around, so for some reason that now escapes me all these years later, I idled up to one of the statues and stole a kiss from it.

I didn't think much about my tiny little marble tryst until, years later, I read of a discovery made by the classicist Caroline Vout when she was preparing to mount an exhibition on Antinoüs, companion and lover of the emperor Hadrian, at the Henry Moore Institute in London. Of all the sculptures Vout and her colleagues unpacked for the show, one stood out for a most unusual reason. It was a bust of Antinoüs with lipstick marks on its cheek.

Human beings have always yearned for communion with art, some more literally than others. In 2003, the artist Andrea Fraser gave this urge especially literal expression in a video entitled *Untitled*. In it, Fraser makes love with a collector who paid her $20,000 for the privilege of his amorous co-starring role. *Untitled* was meant to emphasize the financial exploitation of the contemporary art world, yet in an interview, Fraser confessed how struck she was by the sheer daring of her collaborator. On this particular occasion, the proverbially private collector proved courageous, reckless, or mad enough not merely to collect a work of art but become part of it in the most intimate way possible.

The ancient Roman world is filled with stories about people who loved art too much. One of the earliest, most searing and enduring portraits of a collector whose lust for art was so vehement it verged on insanity came in the first century BCE, when the Roman statesman Marcus Tullius Cicero prosecuted Gaius Verres for plundering the island of Sicily. Verres, Cicero insisted, was not merely driven by greed or corruption but possessed by demonic forces. A dark psychological masterpiece, Cicero's prosecution of Verres in 70 BCE, portraying him as a looter on the edge of madness, haunts the figure of the collector down through history.

First-century BCE Sicily was a wealthy province of Rome, then on the cusp between republic and empire. The island's lucrative grain trade helped feed the Roman people, but Sicily was far more than a supplier of natural resources. Sicily had been Greek, and because the Romans esteemed Greek civilization as the zenith of aesthetic achievement, copying its styles and collecting its art as much as possible, they revered the island's art and sculpture.

Some went far beyond revering it. Verres's very name was a bad omen: it meant boar or swine. In the *Verrine Orations*, which record his lengthy prosecution, Cicero explained to the jury later assembled in Rome how Verres waged a campaign of terror against his own subjects as governor. He stole grain destined for Rome and caroused with local women, bearing their love-bites on his chest. He allegedly raped a young girl. He even stole a signet ring off the finger of a man named Lucius Titius for himself and, in a tellingly transgressive outrage, ordered the execution of his fellow citizen Publius Gavius by crucifixion—a punishment normally reserved for non-Romans.

But it was Verres's plundering of art and sculpture that Cicero focused on to press home the charge of extortion. Calling a series of witnesses, Cicero told the jury how Verres ordered his men to ransack Sicily's illustrious Greek temples. They seized statues and works of art, furniture and cloth, gold and silver vessels. Many of these were devotional objects, held sacred by the Sicilian people. Verres commandeered ships to haul his booty back to Rome, disrupting the island's trade, and shamelessly displaying them in his home in the capital.

Summoning an array of carefully chosen epithets, Cicero denounced Verres as a bandit, a pirate, and a predator. But, he told the jury, Verres was more than a criminal. In one resonant phrase, worth quoting in the original Latin, Cicero spoke of Verres's "amentiam singularem et furorem": his singular and furious madness. *Amens* literally means to be out of one's mind, while *furor* carries connotations of rage, plunder, and rape. Underlying Verres's looting, in other words, was violent sexual desire. He was "covetous," Cicero explained to the jury, and driven by "cupidity." He also denounced Verres for having "perverted desires" and sporting an effeminate Greek shawl, symbolizing the accused's wanton lasciviousness and his yearning for luxury.[1]

Cicero's portrayal of Verres marks a beginning of the idea that collecting and sexuality are linked, though in the opposite manner modern writers would claim two millennia later. At the end of the nineteenth century, psychologists—most notably Sigmund Freud and his followers—came to view collectors as sexually repressed. Freudians saw collecting as the absence of sex; the love of objects substituted for the love of people. Cicero, by contrast, portrayed Verres's lust for art as an extension of sex and an overflow of dangerously lascivious drives. Cicero saw Verres's looting not just in individual terms, however, but as threatening the collapse of Roman society as a whole. Why?

The Roman Republic had been founded four centuries earlier in 509 BCE. But by Cicero's time, despite its lucrative imperial expansion, Rome was riven by political division. After defeating the Punic Empire in Carthage in 146 BCE—absorbing Sicily in the process—Rome's domination of the Mediterranean world went increasingly unchallenged. Soon, the general Octavius would vanquish Mark Antony and Cleopatra in Egypt and become Rome's first emperor, Augustus, presiding over a bountiful trade to the East.

Rome's conquering generals took to displaying spoils from their conquests on grand triumphal marches. These included weapons, statues, plants, animals, and even models of conquered cities. The spoils were to be divided among the soldiers, with art and sculpture to go on public display, in theory viewable by all and a boon to all of Rome. The *triumphator* was the centerpiece of the occasion, godlike in his magnificence, though he sometimes arranged for someone to walk behind him to remind him that "you are not immortal." One historian refers to Rome itself *as* a museum because Augustus established so many new monuments, including prized obelisks from Egypt. Plundering enemies in war was deemed entirely legitimate when seen to serve the public good.

Individual Roman citizens also amassed major personal collections, and a thriving market for private collectors developed. Both Verres and Cicero were among them. It is thought Verres himself may have been an art dealer and may even have persuaded his lawyer Hortensius to take on his case by paying him in art. Cicero's is among the very best documented of Roman lives, and his surviving letters include notes to the brokers who assisted him in decorating his houses with many fine pieces, including his villa at Tusculum outside Rome. Pride of place naturally went to Greek art.

Even private collecting was animated by a public ethos, at least in theory. Statesmen of Cicero's stature were keenly aware that collections could burnish their reputations as men of virtue dedicated to the common good. Collectors, therefore, often displayed art in semipublic fashion to visitors in their homes. In fact, Cicero informed Verres's jurors that he had seen stolen works of art in Verres's home, adding for effect that visiting Sicilian envoys had wept when they laid eyes on them. The Romans believed that to the victor went the spoils, but for a peacetime governor to loot his own people was villainous.

Whether they were discussing Greek sculpture or silks imported from Asia, Roman commentators tended to agree that the adoration of physical finery was a potent and dangerous contagion that spread at Rome's peril.

All surviving Roman sources that come down to us were written by men and lay great stress on the corrupting love of luxury as an allegedly female trait. Roman men tried to break Roman women's addiction to fashion and beauty but, they lamented, they never succeeded in doing so.

In 195 BCE, for example, the senator Cato deplored the role that women's lobbying played in repealing sumptuary laws, notably the *Lex Oppia*, which aimed to limit the amount of jewelry and clothing women could wear. In his first-century CE *Natural History*, Pliny the Elder railed against the rage for luxuries draining Roman coffers to the tune of 100 million sesterces per year—half of all the money Rome minted annually. The possibilities for compulsive acquisition seemed infinite. There was the so-called table madness, an obsession which, Pliny claimed, afflicted even eminent statesmen from Cicero to the emperor Tiberius. In his satirical *Epigrams*, also written in the first century CE, the poet Martial savaged collectors as avaricious and vain. Among many tales of delusional greed, he recounted the folly of a woman named Gellia who loved her pearls more than her own family or the gods.

The trouble was that new money hankered after social status and collecting was one way to buy it. Petronius's grotesque first-century satire *Satyricon*—imaginatively filmed by Federico Fellini in 1969—mocked the shallowness of its nouveau riche protagonist. Trimalchio is notorious for staging a fantastically opulent banquet, but he was also a profligate collector who hungered for luxuries such as prized Corinthian bronze. While Rome's trade with Egypt, India, Africa, and Persia promised untold bounty, expanded commercial relations portended that greatest of all Roman themes, repeatedly emphasized by Enlightenment historians from Montesquieu to Edward Gibbon: moral decadence would lead to decline and fall.

This is why, according to the prosecution, Verres's looting was so significant. Cicero insisted that letting him go free would undermine faith in Roman legal institutions as a whole. And there was political danger too. The Thracian gladiator Spartacus was leading a momentous slave uprising against Rome at that very moment, and so to condone the plunder of a Roman province by its own governor would likely provoke fresh rebellions. For this reason, Verres the "tyrant" had to be made an example of.[2]

Cicero went further still. In plundering sacred objects from Sicily's temples, Verres had deprived an entire people of their means of worship and, therefore, a fundamental source of their very identity as Sicilians. As such, his crimes rose beyond the merely legal or political to the disturbing level of sacrilege. Looting for the good of Rome was one thing. But pillaging sacred sites was an affront to the gods: it courted divine displeasure, damnation, and retribution. Verres, in other words, exposed the civilization of Rome to the logic of the curse and the possibility of devastating divine punishment.

The act of placing a curse on perpetrators of sacrilege was immemorial. Fully 2,000 years before Cicero tried Verres, for example, monuments in ancient Mesopotamia bore threats of annihilation carved on stone against any who would remove or damage them. Perhaps because Roman religious culture was so transactional—it involved procuring good fortune through various conventions for appeasing the gods rather than virtuous personal conduct as stressed in Christianity—the Romans were especially vexed by the specter of supernatural vengeance. The historian Livy decried Marcus Fulvius Flaccus's looting of temples in Calabria as a barbarous act of sacrilege. Pausanias saw the general Sulla's looting of Greek cities as an expression of madness, for which the gods punished him with a hideous death by lice. And when the emperor Caligula's men sought to remove a statue of Zeus from Olympia, the statue miraculously burst into such violent laughter, the scaffold they were on collapsed. This, the historian Suetonius insisted, was a clear omen of Caligula's later assassination as a punishment for his impious depredations.

Many regarded the dangers of sacrilege with the utmost concern. Both Julius Caesar and Augustus reputedly sought to avoid looting temples. The Romans even made restitution to conquered peoples: Scipio Aemilianus, for example, restored plundered sites in Sicily in the second century BCE. Such men sought to embody an ideal of the humane conqueror and earned praise from contemporaries for being magnanimous in victory.

When Verres stole from the temple of Athena and the Heius family chapel in Sicily, therefore, Cicero deemed it a heinous crime. Verres was "an insane and immoral scoundrel [who] has openly waged impious and sacrilegious war" against everything sacred, he told the jury. His impiety was a reckless provocation of the gods and thus proof of his insanity. He was not even fully human, Cicero reckoned, but beast-like, calling him "another Orcus"—a reference to the lord of the underworld, synonymous with unnatural evil. Verres *must* be found guilty to save Rome itself from divine retribution.[3]

Found guilty he was. But Verres was never punished because he never attended his own trial. He fled to Marseilles as soon as he was charged, so Cicero prosecuted him entirely in absentia. As a result, we do not know Verres's side of the story, because he mounted no defense. Did he die a poetically just death when, as one story has it, twenty-seven years later while still in Marseilles, the Roman general Mark Antony is said to have killed him after Verres refused to give him some of his Corinthian bronze? Perhaps, though the justice seems rather too poetic.

Verres has certainly not been forgotten, however. He lived on in the annals of looting for his legendary rapacity. The Irish politician Edmund Burke invoked his greed in a speech discussing Warren Hastings, who was impeached for corruption as the British governor general of India in 1787. And a generation later, the Duke of Wellington also recalled Verres's looting when, in 1815, he returned to Italy the antiquities Napoleon had stolen at the end of the eighteenth century.

The modern Verres that Burke and Wellington spoke of was an unprincipled bounder, not a demonic monster; a criminal, not a madman. But Cicero's Verres casts the longer historical shadow. A man so beholden to art and beauty, so consumed by his lust to possess it and so willing to flout convention to do so, he lost his humanity to his own desire. In the end, Cicero judged, Verres wasn't a real collector at all. His passions were so twisted, he couldn't actually value anything he stole, plundering out of mere compulsion. An early embodiment of the peculiar fear that a single person's demonic desire for fine objects might rain destruction down upon an entire civilization, he haunts us to this day.

From the start of recorded history, humanity has been obsessed by the idea of the obsessive collector. Countless ancient writers breathed life into this figure, as though the obsessive collector somehow constituted a single shadowy presence, constantly regenerating from one incarnation to the next.

The notion of falling in love with art has a more literal history than the litany of Verres's crimes would suggest, however. Its roots lie in classical mythology and its most celebrated fable is that of Pygmalion. The Roman poet Ovid tells the tale in his first-century narrative poem the *Metamorphoses*. Pygmalion is king of Cyprus and a sculptor who falls in love with a female figure whom he has carved out of ivory, later identified as Galatea. When Pygmalion kisses Galatea's lips, they turn warm and she comes to life as a gift to the king from Aphrodite, goddess of love. Galatea is perfection itself; she marries Pygmalion and they have children.

The legend exhibits one of the supernatural assumptions of ancient mythology, that gods and mortals can interact. But it also reflects the ancient belief that artistic representations of living beings can be so realistic as to appear almost breathing. The notion of a living statue, likely encouraged by the production of early mechanical automata in the ancient world, fostered a beguiling confusion. Astonished onlookers observed that real birds sometimes flew toward painted ones. But was this because the power of art to mimic nature was so strong or because paintings actually came to life? The idea that people could fall in love with statues posed a similar problem. Was it because the statues were so beautiful or because those who fell for them were suffering some form of insanity?

As Rome became an empire, stories of statue love became a way for critics to warn their fellow citizens about the dangerous passions of increasingly tyrannical rulers. Both Pliny and Suetonius recounted stories about the emperor Tiberius and his collection of erotic books and paintings. One told of the painting of a high priest of the fertility goddess Cybele: Tiberius loved this portrait so that he bought it for the sum of 6,000 sesterces, taking it into the bedchamber of his villa on Capri. Back in Rome, Tiberius was so taken with Lysippus's statue of the athlete Apoxyomenos that he had it removed from the Baths of Agrippa and taken to his private home, replacing it with a copy.

Pliny repeated similar tales in his *Natural History*. He told the story of a Greek man who visited the shrine of the goddess Aphrodite at Knidos (in present-day Turkey) and was "overcome with love for the statue." The man embraced it, leaving "a stain, an indication of his lust." The satirist Lucian recorded a rather darker folly in which a young boy left a small deposit of semen on a statue and then committed suicide. There were stories of semen stains on statues at Parium, Samos, and Delphi in the Greek islands, as well as of Syrian soldiers leaving stains on the statues of the general Agrippa's daughters. There were stories of women who enjoyed carnal knowledge of stone, too. The poet Juvenal mocked Roman wives who, he claimed, liked to ride likenesses of the goddess of female chastity Pudicitia. The Jewish Talmud also speaks of a queen who pleasured herself on a phallic statue.[4]

It's hard to know quite what to make of such interesting tales. They're moral fables of a sort, to be sure; dark warnings of unnatural lusts; and quite possibly, politically motivated character assassination. However true or exaggerated they may be, the idea of statue love fascinated the ancient imagination, and rivers of ink flowed to dramatize these sensational derangements. According to Suetonius, Tiberius romped through orgies with minors, once had a man's genitals tied to prevent him from urinating, and ordered his enemies thrown from cliffs into the sea. These, Suetonius meant his readers to understand, were all appalling manifestations of Tiberius's tyranny. And when it came to statue love at least, resisting the tyrant wasn't always futile. When Tiberius seized the statue of Apoxyomenos, the ensuing uproar compelled him to return it from his home to the public baths. Even tyrants stole from the public at their peril.

According to ancient sources, Tiberius's successor Caligula was the most infamous tyrant of all. Suetonius's account of him is the classic Roman portrait of dictatorship and insanity. Caligula seized the private property of Roman citizens; committed incest with his sisters; set wild animals to attack aged gladiators; executed enemies gradually so as to increase their agonies; and once commanded that his horse Incitatus be given his own house and servants and made consul. Caligula, Suetonius wrote, was a nightmarish combination of overconfidence and fearfulness bred by chronic infirmity. He had fainting fits as a youth, suffered from insomnia, and was visited by terrifying apparitions, yet insisted on being revered like a god.

Caligula was also obsessed with art and sculpture, seizing statues from Roman and Greek territories for his private collection. Once, infuriated by the thought that anyone might enjoy fame to equal his own, he ordered a series of statues which Augustus had assembled on the Capitoline to be smashed. He also commanded Greek statues to be decapitated so that their heads could be replaced with his own. As a further example of his alleged insanity—one restaged in the 1970s BBC drama *I, Claudius,* based on the novel by Robert Graves—Caligula once reputedly instructed his soldiers to "gather up seashells" for him. Lavishing praise on these "spoils of the ocean," he told his troops to "fill their helmets, and the folds of their dress with them."[5]

Scholars insist we would be unwise to take these dramatic stories of madness and tyranny at face value. Writers like Suetonius were critics, after all, not objective reporters. In all probability, their attacks on Caligula and others reflect the bitter power struggle between the emperor and the aristocracy in Rome at the time. Take, for example, the idea that Caligula demanded to be treated like a god. This might sound delusional if not unhinged, yet Roman emperors often claimed to possess divine status as a play for enhanced political power over their rivals and enemies. Few if any Romans took such claims literally. Similarly, Caligula awarding his horse both servants and political office may have been intended as a symbolic insult to the aristocratic class and not the fantasy of a madman it first appears. And rather than actually ordering his troops to collect shells, believing they were real treasures, Caligula may have been referring to enemy ships met-aphorically *as mere shells* for the taking. Even feigning madness in order to resort to political violence was far from unheard of as a populist tactic. Emperors loved to curry favor with the plebeian class by humiliating the elites whom commoners resented.

If the madness of Roman tyrants is an exaggeration or even a fiction, however, it still reveals two vital things. It demonstrates the power of stories about obsessions with objects to define people as mad and dangerous. Suetonius understood this power: accurate or not, his portraits of Tiberius, Caligula, Nero, and others have lasted down the centuries and still seize the imagination today. Second, the idea that Roman tyrants were insane also reveals how later concepts of madness have often been imposed on the ancients, especially ideas and terms borrowed from modern psychology.

The lore of statue love did not fade with the centuries but came into sharper focus with the passage of time. In the seventeenth century, while traveling in Italy, the English virtuoso John Evelyn recorded tales of the collector Hippolito Vitelleschi kissing the statues in his collection. In 1845, the great French novelist Gustave Flaubert recorded his own dalliance with marble when he sneaked an intoxicated kiss from the armpit of Antonio Canova's rendition of the goddess Psyche in his sculpture *Eros and Psyche*. "It was my first sensual kiss in a long while," Flaubert wrote, and "it was also something more; I kissed beauty itself." In 1890, the artist Jean-Léon Gérôme painted *Pygmalion and Galatea*. In it, Gérôme depicted Galatea's white marble body turning to living flesh as Pygmalion kisses her. It were as though modern artists were making love to the Greco-Roman past itself.[6]

Modern psychiatrists diagnosed such reveries not as neoclassical flights of fancy, however, but the product of sick minds. In the late nineteenth century, the new science of sexology recast the long and tortuous history of human sexuality. In his groundbreaking 1886 book *Psychopathia Sexualis*, the Viennese physician Richard Krafft-Ebing dedicated an entire section to

Held in the Metropolitan Museum of Art

Jean-Léon Gérôme, Pygmalion and Galatea *(1890): Inspired by Ovid's* Metamorphoses, *Gérôme shows Galatea coming to life as she is kissed by King Pygmalion, a story that symbolizes ancient obsessions with the idea of falling in love with statues.*

individuals in the peculiar habit of defiling statues. Krafft-Ebing drew on French psychologist Paul Moreau's book *Des Aberrations du sens Génésiques* (1880), which in turn drew heavily on Suetonius and other ancient texts, treating those texts as reliable source material from which to diagnose the Romans as though they were modern psychiatric patients.

The Romans' own explanations of insanity ranged from divine punishment to more naturalistic accounts of mental infirmity, which they accounted for through imbalances of the four humors. But the modernizing Moreau swept all such notions aside. Taking his sources at face value, he used his reading of them to declare that Julius Caesar was an "epileptic" and Tiberius an "alcoholic." The madness of Caligula and Nero he redefined as "psychic aberrations," which originated in their "pathological" organs.[7]

Following Moreau, Krafft-Ebing transformed the cultural meaning of statue love from a political warning sign to a psychological one. In the modern psychiatric imagination, making love to marble was no longer a manifestation of tyranny—let alone the elite foible of mortals consorting with gods—but a medical symptom of base sexual perversion that might now be identified in anyone, no matter their position in society. Krafft-Ebing documented several relevant cases, such as that of an ordinary gardener "who fell in love with a statue of the Venus of Milo and was discovered attempting coitus with it." His diagnosis? The gardener was suffering from "abnormally intense libido" combined with "defective virility." Referring back to classical mythology, Krafft-Ebing's fellow sexologist in England Havelock Ellis aptly glossed such urges as *Pygmalionism*.[8]

Like Moreau before him, Krafft-Ebing rediagnosed the ancients in resolutely modern terms that would have made no sense to the people he was discussing, tearing them from their own context and transposing them to his own. For example, he labeled a Greek man who defiled a statue of Cupid at Delphi as "perverse," a word that in the nineteenth century carried connotations of homosexuality, a term that itself did not exist in the ancient world and had just been invented as a legal and medical construct in the 1860s.

Krafft-Ebing saw statue defilers everywhere. He included men who got erections just by looking at statues in museums. In documenting these cases among ordinary men of all kinds, he dramatically lowered the cultural status of statue love. Frightening acts of sacrilege committed by tyrants in the style of Verres or Tiberius were reduced to a common sexual pathology. Anyone could now be a pervert, from an emperor to a gardener.

Moreau and Krafft-Ebing were by no means unique in "translating" the ancients into modern terms; such "translations" are a recurrent theme in modern classical studies. In his 1957 translation of Suetonius, Robert Graves diagnosed Caligula as an "epileptic," even though this term was first used in the sixteenth century according to the *Oxford English Dictionary*, and did not even exist as a medical concept in ancient Rome. In 1989, one classicist published a scholarly paper insisting that Caligula's madness was really the result of interictal temporal lobe epilepsy. "We moderns can almost pity one so ill," the author wrote, "before the discovery of drugs like Dilantin." If only the Romans had invented Big Pharma.[9]

Kissing stone has a long history—in Rome, Capri, and beyond. So, too, does the dream of loving, possessing, even merging with art. The meaning of this dream has changed dramatically, but if we set modern-day assumptions aside, we can begin to see why the fear and desire surrounding works of art was so charged and so meaningful to the ancient mind. This commingling of fear and desire regarding physical objects was by no means confined to the realm of the political, however. It permeated premodern religious thinking just as much, although with one crucial difference. As monotheism swept the medieval world after the fall of Rome, the person who loved objects too much embodied not the danger of tyranny, but the sin of idolatry. Exit the tyrant, enter the idolater.

CHAPTER TWO

THE IDOLATER'S FOLLY

The finite cannot contain the infinite.

—ATTRIBUTED TO JOHN CALVIN

The German city of Halle possesses several interesting museums, a zoo, a botanical garden, and a most historic church. In the twin-spired Protestant Market Church in the Old Town, you can still see the baptismal font used to christen the composer George Frederick Handel, who played the church's organ at the end of the seventeenth century before he moved to London. The Market Church is also home to the death mask of Martin Luther and a cast of the great reformer's hands—the hands that wrote the ninety-five theses denouncing Roman Catholicism, igniting the Reformation in 1517.

That Luther's death mask and hands survive in physical form is a rather ironic reminder of a life dedicated to the idea that Christians should worship God through His Word, not images or objects. Protestants, as the new Christians became known, insisted that the veneration of relics, whether remnants of Christ or the saints, or icons featuring God the Father or the Virgin Mary, was a form of religious delusion. They insisted that the clerics who promoted them were frauds: idolaters who worshipped things, not God.

The specter of idolatry is a fixation that has bedeviled the religious imagination in waves of consternation across history. Campaigners of many stripes have crusaded to banish false gods and stop people from loving things too much—sacred-seeming objects they mistake for God Himself.

Yet, as the philosopher Bruno Latour observed, human beings very often create new images and objects to revere in place of ones they have banned or destroyed.

Galileo Galilei fought to establish the scientific truth of a sun-centered universe against the dogmas of the Catholic Church in the seventeenth century, yet today the Science Museum in Florence proudly displays one of his fingers as if it were the relic of a Christian saint. In his singular 1877 story "A Simple Heart," Gustave Flaubert told the tale of a humble servant named Felicité who worshipped the corpse of her pet parrot Loulou, who appeared before her in the guise of the Holy Spirit. And in recent years, the Chinese Communist Party has removed pictures of Christ from churches and replaced them with photographs of Mao Zedong and President Xi Jinping.

If the problem of idolatry seems perennial, so does the quest to reform the idolater. Why do people crave images and objects to worship so much, and how can they be shown the error of their ways? Luther's nemesis— his ideal idolater, if you like—was Cardinal Albrecht von Brandenburg. Albrecht was the Catholic archbishop of Magdeburg and Mainz, one of the highest officials in the Holy Roman Empire and a devout relic collector. Albrecht's church, the Church of Saint Maurice and Saint Mary Magdalene, was also located in Halle and possessed a notable distinction. It housed an enormous collection of relics in what was known as the Halle Sanctuary, including more than 8,000 objects and the remains of 42 saints.

These relics were important instruments of faith. Catholics believed that before entering heaven, sinners had to endure a period of time in the state of purgatory; just how long depended on how much they had sinned. Accumulating and contemplating relics was one way to procure an indulgence from the pope, reducing one's time in purgatory and expediting one's passage to heaven. Luther railed against indulgences as bribery and extortion. But to Albrecht, the careful accumulation of relics was highly meaningful. He calculated that the relics in Halle would bring down his own time in purgatory by a not inconsiderable 39 million years.

It has been said that the Middle Ages was an era of collections without collectors. There were palace collections and royal treasuries, armories and reliquaries, but these were institutional rather than personal holdings. Yet, as Albrecht's example shows, this is not entirely true. The medieval era is

Held in the John and Mable Ringling Museum of Art, Sarasota, Florida

Lucas Cranach the Elder, Cardinal Albrecht of Brandenburg as Saint Jerome *(1526): The Halle church of Cardinal Albrecht von Brandenburg (1490–1545) housed an enormous collection of relics, which he believed would reduce his time in purgatory—a view rejected as idolatrous by Luther and the Protestant reformers.*

crucial, moreover, to understand the evolution of the idea that amassing physical objects imperils the soul of the person who loves those objects too much, believing they will save them. With the rise of monotheism, fear of idolatry seized the theological imagination, convincing it that the idolater was on the path to damnation, not salvation.

Fear of idolatry was ancient. "Thou shalt not make unto thee any graven image," reads the second of the Ten Commandments that Moses conveyed to the Israelites, as recorded in the book of Deuteronomy, composed around the seventh century BCE. While Moses was receiving God's law, however, the Israelites, fearing he would not return, built themselves a golden calf to worship.[1]

Several centuries later, *The Wisdom of Solomon*, a Jewish text from the year 15 BCE, attempted to explain exactly how and why the first idolater emerged. Assuming the voice of the wise King Solomon, the text's anonymous author recounted how humanity had once lived in a world without any sacred pictures, objects, or statues, in an ideal aniconic past. But this era of true faith did not last. The world fell into polytheism and idol worship.

Pseudo-Solomon told the story of a father who became so distraught at the death of his son that he built a statue in his memory and began to worship it. This kind of love was a tragic mistake, Pseudo-Solomon warned. People who worshipped icons and idols—terms that derive from the Greek *eikon* and *eidolon*—were fools who tricked themselves into adoring mere matter. Their desire was almost carnal, originating in a deep longing for someone beloved but no longer present. From the beginning, therefore, statue love and idol worship were not only a pagan dilemma or a political warning but also a problem that haunted the religious imagination. Thus it was that a seventh-century Hebrew text, entitled *The Apocalypse of Zerubbabel*, told how the false messiah Armilus had been spawned by an act of intercourse between Satan and a statue of the Virgin Mary. The love of things was impious, unholy, and dangerous.

Hostility to human desire for objects was by no means limited to pagans or Judeo-Christians in the ancient world. In China, there was no monotheistic tradition, so ancient Chinese philosophical traditions were not preoccupied with idolaters, though they did emphasize the importance of moderation in one's personal possessions. According to Confucius (551–479 BCE), whose teachings were adopted by the Han Dynasty after the second century BCE, the accumulation of material things was not in itself wrong, and the neo-Confucian Mandarins of later centuries enjoyed considerable material comfort in their lives. Neo-Confucian scholars did warn, however, that excess profit-making would foster social division and unrest, so the state should regulate wealth to preserve social stability. At one point in the *Analects*, a collection of sayings attributed to Confucius, the businessman Zigong asks whether he should store a piece of precious jade or sell it. Confucius tells him to sell it, encouraging him to circulate wealth for the good of society. The person who values possessions is not sinful or idolatrous, but the wise do not hoard.

Buddhists challenged such thinking with a new ethos of zealous self-denial, renouncing worldly satisfactions. They took their inspiration from the Indian spiritual teacher Siddhārtha Gautama (ca. 563–ca. 483 BCE), whom they called the Buddha, meaning *enlightened one*. Siddhārtha was a Hindu who rejected India's hierarchical caste system, rituals, and ostentatious temples. He stressed instead that life in the material world is an illusory dream calling for meditation in order to transcend it by attaining a state of nirvana.

Like Judaism, Buddhism is thought to have had aniconic beginnings without divine images, but its adherents soon began using objects to promote their creed. Sculptors crafted statues of the Buddha's likeness from gold and gemstones and other precious materials. The monks who looked after them lived lives of poverty, but they justified such opulent statues as expressions of the Buddha's spiritual magnificence. Objects, the monks found, made better tools than words for persuading people to follow the Buddha's example. Like premodern Christians, therefore, Buddhists collected and venerated relics of famed monks' remains, even entire corpses. Likenesses of the Buddha and *bodhisattvas*—saints on the path to nirvana or those who had already achieved it—circulated in large numbers. Buddhists considered them to be alive with divine presence.

By the ninth century, however, the Chinese authorities engaged in a series of campaigns to suppress Buddhism. These were some of the first orchestrated efforts to target those who amassed objects that rivaled the authority of state doctrines. Because Buddhism promised spiritual independence and equality for all believers, no matter what one's station in society, the Chinese state regarded Buddhists as competitors for the loyalties of ordinary people and a threat to traditional family structure. Beginning in 842, therefore, the Tang emperor Wuzong initiated efforts to strip the Buddhist temples. This was an early wave of iconoclasm: eliminating the false religion of things by removing, selling, or destroying those things. It proved profitable, too. The Chinese authorities confiscated and demolished Buddhist statues, seized monks, levied new taxes on them, and sequestered their land.

These were some of the first iconoclastic campaigns in recorded history, but not *the* first. In the year 312, the Roman emperor Constantine converted to Christianity, and the empire was divided into two. Rome nominally remained the capital, but Constantinople (Istanbul) became the preeminent city of Byzantium. An eager Christian convert, Constantine repurposed pagan statues and Greek temples, as Christianity was to be a religion of deeds, not things. And yet, the production of icons flourished, emblazoned with gilt and images of Christ and the Virgin Mary, the saints and the angels, and scenes from the Bible. As in China, conflict centered over the ambiguity of such objects. Was God literally present in pictures of Christ, as devotees claimed, or was such belief heretical? Many Christians insisted icons provided direct access to the divine and derived great personal comfort from keeping them in their homes.

The independence from church authority this behavior implied vexed the clergy because, if the faithful could enjoy direct access to God through icons, was clerical guidance irrelevant? In response to this dilemma, the Byzantine emperor Leo III, followed by his son Constantine V, issued a series of edicts against the use of icons. Worshipping images of Christ became heresy. In 754, the Synod of Hieria judged it unlawful to depict Christ and other holy figures on the grounds that doing so reduced the sacred and immortal to the material and perishable. Prayer led by ministers in church, they asserted, was the best form of worship. The only physical objects with supernatural meaning were the wafer the and the wine of the Eucharist. According to the doctrine of transubstantiation, they miraculously turned into the body and blood of Jesus. Icons were just painted pieces of wood.

By most indications, this iconoclastic campaign appears to have failed. Faith in icons was not stamped out but remained an enduring facet of Byzantine culture. Icon worshippers did not part easily with their pictures. Even more intriguingly, scholars cannot be sure whether their attempts to enforce these iconoclastic edicts were in fact substantial or not. The Byzantine authorities may have hoped their pronouncements alone would suffice. But they may also have realized it would be difficult, if not impossible, to seize all devotional objects from the devout.

In the medieval Islamic world, Muslim theologians were preoccupied by similar concerns. Islam is often regarded as the world's most iconoclastic faith, shunning sacred objects in favor of understanding the will of Allah through His words alone, as revealed to the prophet Muhammad. Keeping and worshiping objects and images was, therefore, denounced as a form of idolatry, or *shirk* in Arabic. Muslim attitudes to the production and worship of sacred objects have, however, varied over time.

Initially, the Islamic caliphates that rose in place of Byzantium and Sasanian Persia (Iran) after the seventh century preached a message of religious toleration. Despite theological injunctions against visual representations of the divine, early caliphate coins featured likenesses of Muhammad. Peoples and faiths commingled through extensive commercial ties. Abbasid coins in Sindh (now in Pakistan) sometimes bore images of the sacred bull of the Hindu god Shiva and inscriptions in both Arabic and Sanskrit.

But as time passed, Islamic authorities insisted on stricter interpretations of Muhammad's revelations. Muslims removed Christian art and sacred objects from the cube-shaped stone building in Mecca called the Ka'ba, transforming it into a "House of Allah." The Qur'an described idolaters as dupes of corrupt priests and warned that "those who hoard gold and silver instead of giving in God's cause . . . will have a grievous punishment" and be branded by their own bullion in hell. Some Islamic authors conceded that those who were illiterate would inevitably worship God through objects because they could not understand abstract notions of piety. But clerics agreed that divine images were distractions from true faith.[2]

When it came to war, Muslim commanders acted like Roman ones: they looted. After conquering Sindh in the eleventh century, Mahmud of Ghazni took a captured *linga*—a symbolic representation of the Hindu god Shiva—and set it in the threshold of a mosque so that Muslim worshippers could trample on it as they entered to pray. Like a Roman triumphator, Mahmud paraded his spoils, as Muhammad said conquering Muslims should. But Islamic spoils were mainly intended for use, not accumulation or display, so Mahmud ensured that precious metals were melted down and put into circulation to contribute to the economy.

The material culture of Islamic societies was nonetheless extraordinary in its splendor. The caliphates became the richest region in the medieval world and their capital, Baghdad, the world's largest city and a vast hub for markets and bazaars, goods and objects. By the early ninth century, the treasury of the caliph Harun al-Rashid alone was said to contain thousands of turbans, porcelain vessels, lances, shields and boots, gold and silver, as well as mechanical automata and gifts from potentates, most notably the Holy Roman emperor Charlemagne.

Muslim princes excelled as patrons and collectors during the "Golden Age" of Islamic civilization. They established numerous libraries where Greek and Roman manuscripts were translated to promote science and medicine, legal administration and the art of government. Muslim collectors sponsored encyclopedic projects, for example the *Ultimate Ambition in the Arts of Erudition*, a gargantuan thirty-volume work compiled by the fourteenth-century Cairo scholar Shihab al-Din al-Nuwayri. Just as Pliny cataloged the trade of the Roman Empire, al-Nuwayri held forth on the riches of learning and commerce, from astronomy and the human body to wine and livestock, fish and fruits.

Despite the aniconic thrust of Islamic doctrine, the religious practices of many Muslims retained the use of sacred objects. Amulets were condemned by Muhammad in the Hadith, the record of his words and deeds. But they remained popular among the faithful as instruments of protection from illness and evil spirits called the *jinn*. Magical objects remained a vital presence in Middle Eastern popular culture, as immortalized in medieval folk tales, most famously the *Arabian Nights*.

So was there something wrong with the hoarder of treasures and talismans in Islamic thought or not? Different regimes arrived at different answers. Take the example of Mughal India during the sixteenth and seventeenth centuries, a later Islamic empire centered on the Indian Ocean and which achieved enormous wealth and power. In the 1520s, the armies of the Central Asian conqueror Babur swept down through the Indian subcontinent. As they placed India under Islamic control, they defaced the religious sites of those they subjected. Subsequent Mughal emperors, however, such as Akbar, Jahangir, and Shah Jahan, adopted policies of religious toleration instead. They also spent fortunes on collecting and amassing great libraries, which they stocked with manuscripts and fabulous treasuries of art, gems, and curiosities.

These emperors celebrated themselves as great collectors and learned connoisseurs in sparkling portraits they commissioned. During his time in South Asia in the early seventeenth century, the Flemish traveler Jacques de Coutre compared the emperor Jahangir to a great bejeweled idol. When Aurangzeb became emperor in 1658, however, he recoiled at ostentatious collecting and display as gross impieties. Aurangzeb turned away from the path of religious toleration, raised taxes on his Hindu and Sikh subjects, and eliminated exhibitions of gold and silver as violations of Islamic law. Muslims' attitudes to getting, keeping, and showing objects kept changing.

In medieval Christendom, as in Asian and Islamic societies, attitudes to amassing fine objects were ambivalent. Once again, a vibrant popular culture in which physical things possessed magical and mystical meaning vied with religious objections that hoarding finery and devotional objects was sin and folly—an objection destined to culminate in the Protestant Reformation.

Popular memory of the European Middle Ages is dominated by the idea that the Goths, Vandals, and Huns who defeated the Romans were barbarians who destroyed a superior civilization. The figure of the looter is central to this narrative. The Visigoth Alaric, who sacked Rome in the fifth century, and Attila the Hun were experts in destruction, it insists, yet incapable of building great civilizations of their own. Medieval Europe entered the "dark ages," characterized by the loss of knowledge, reason, and political stability. Religious fundamentalism filled the void.

In the eighteenth century, leading Enlightenment thinkers led by Voltaire would label medieval military conquerors such as the Mongols irredeemable barbarians; in the nineteenth, Westerners reviled them as alien "Mongoloids." The achievements of the Khans in Asia, however, show how distorted such notions are. When Kublai Khan (grandson of Genghis) led his Mongol fighters to triumph over China's Southern Song Dynasty in the thirteenth century, the ultimate result was not destruction, but creation, with an important role for the gentler art of collecting. Kublai Khan established the Yuan Dynasty that ruled China after 1279 and proved himself one of history's great civilization builders. He molded Beijing into a grand capital city where the so-called barbarians adopted Confucian manners, patronized the arts, and encouraged courtly collecting, especially of calligraphy and antiquities. In 1323, the Yuan princess Sengge Ragi hosted a famed "Elegant Gathering," where she and her refined guests pored over works of art and calligraphic scrolls, adding their colophons (personal seals) as ceremonial marks of distinction.

Yet the specter of loss haunted the medieval European mind, especially the loss of sacred objects to enemies. As a result, Christians became obsessed by quests for missing relics and revered those who hunted after them as spiritual crusaders. The Quest for the Holy Grail appears to have originated in Celtic mythology, but by the twelfth century it had become thoroughly Christianized, reimagined as an attempt to recover a dish or cup from Christ's Last Supper. And when Christian fighters launched their Crusades against the Muslim peoples of the Near East, relics formed a significant part of the booty they took. At the siege of Antioch in 1097–98, Crusaders are said to have seized the Holy Lance used to pierce Christ during the crucifixion. After Constantinople was sacked in 1204 during the Fourth Crusade, retaken relics were distributed all around Christendom, from Byzantium and Venice to Flanders and France. Those who died in the cause were cheered as martyrs.

Even in peacetime, those who got relics back by trading for them, or stealing them outright, were fêted as heroes and regarded as enactors of sacred thefts. Technically, these thefts were crimes, referred to in Latin as *furta sacra*, or holy robberies, but they inspired narratives that glorified the derring-do of the robbers as valiant Christian criminals. In reality, some of these "heroes" were merchants who stole relics in order to sell them for a profit, as the relic trade was highly lucrative. But their apologists insisted that relics yearned to be taken to zealous parishes. Those who rescued them were neither mercenary nor sacrilegious. They were devout.

Catholics believed that relics possessed magical potencies. Contemplating them could heal the sick, inspire the faithful, and atone for one's sins—as Cardinal Albrecht believed. Idolatry was, of course, a sin, but because the vast majority of parishioners could neither read nor write, many accepted that objects helped make Christian worship tangible and intelligible. Like icons in Byzantine culture, relics remained charged with awe and mystery owing to the belief that God was physically present in the object.

The accumulation and possession of relics was therefore vital. On occasion, parishioners would hold Eucharist wafers in their mouths without swallowing them, in order to bring them home where they might bring favor on their households. Relics took many forms: from miraculously bleeding statues and the remains of saints' bodies to remnants of the True Cross and even Christ's foreskin—the so-called Holy Prepuce. Virtually any kind of object could attain blessed status. "I exorcize you, creature radish, in the name of the Father, Son, and Holy Spirit," reads a fifteenth-century blessing from Breslau (Wrocław in Poland), "that wherever you are dispersed, every unclean spirit is driven from the place."[3]

The more relics a church gathered, the greater its perceived stature. Noted relics could do wonders for a congregation's spiritual confidence, not to mention its treasury, drawing in pilgrims and financial contributions, as well as affording parishioners a sense of protection in times of war and disease. This may explain why clergymen tolerated relics and icons as much as they did, preferring to court popular fervor for magic rather than resist it. Churches put relics on display for common parishioners, at least some of the time, and even published relic catalogs to entice pilgrims from afar. As long as relics remained inside churches, clerics could hope to control their use and meaning as part of a regulated system of worship.

But in time relics drew more and more ire. In 1120, a feisty Benedictine abbot named Guibert of Nogent, a small town east of Paris, penned a withering assault on relic culture entitled *On the Relics of Saints*. In it, Guibert dismantled what he took to be the colossal mendacity of clerical claims about the miraculous powers of sacred artifacts from the Christian story. How, for example, could the monks of St. Médard possibly claim to be in possession of Christ's tooth? Just how, for that matter, had Christ been so careless as to overlook his own tooth? Perhaps, Guibert speculated, Jesus would one day open his mouth wide to welcome back said wandering tooth? Any who claimed such stories were true were nothing but swindlers.

Then there were the *two* churches claiming ownership of the head of John the Baptist. "Could there be anything more preposterous said of such a man, other than both groups in effect claiming he was two-headed?" Guibert excoriated the "sacrilege" of such charlatans; like Cicero in his prosecution of Verres, he used the Latin term *sacrilegium*. "What is more sacrilegious," he asked, "than worshipping as divine that which is not?" Amassing such objects was pointless, Guibert concluded, even if they

proved authentic, because physical things were irrelevant to eternal salvation. There was no access to the inner world of God through the material
grossness of tangible objects. Faith alone could save; faith in objects was
"extreme folly."[4]

While Guibert railed against relics, clerics continued to amass them and
to decorate their churches in jewels, turning some of them into spectacular
treasuries. In Paris, the Abbé Suger transformed the church of St. Denis
into one of the most stupendous palaces in Christendom. Suger employed
artists to "glorify the venerable cross," as he put it, repairing St. Denis's pul-
pit and embellishing its altar, while overseeing the acquisition of gold, sapphires, rubies, emeralds, and pearls to beautify the house of the Lord. "The
beauty of the house of God," he liked to say, "called me away from external
cares." Not unlike the Buddhist monks who defended the proliferation of
golden statues of their master, Suger insisted that sumptuous ornamenta-
tion would foster greater attention to the "sacred virtues" by "transferring
that which is material to that which is immaterial."[5]

But Suger's arguments faltered. The Catholic Church became synonymous with corruption. In the *Canterbury Tales* (1387–1400), the London
diplomat Geoffrey Chaucer painted a scabrous portrait of The Pardoner as
a pious hypocrite who preyed on sinners' gravest fears. The Pardoner carried
a bag "brimful of pardons, all come hot from Rome," Chaucer wrote, "rags
and bones," which the common people believed to be true relics. "Money is
the root of all evil," the Pardoner counseled his wards, yet conceded to his
reader: "all my preaching is about avarice / and such cursed sins, in order to
make [people] / give freely of their pennies." The figure of the pious cleric
thus became associated with the cynical manipulation of baubles for graft.
In his macabre series of woodcuts *The Dance of Death* (1523–25), Hans Holbein depicted a number of luxury-craving clergymen meeting their doom.
In one, a cardinal is selling an indulgence to a gentleman, when the Grim
Reaper shows up to take his life.[6]

Christianity had become perverted in the eyes of many, but what exactly
had gone wrong? The humanist scholar Desiderius Erasmus of Rotterdam
wrestled with the question in his satire *In Praise of Folly* (1511). Erasmus
thought it absurd to accumulate sacred treasures like Suger did in Paris,
but acknowledged that "the power of folly," especially when it came to

commoners' belief in the spiritual power of objects, was considerable, if not inevitable. Using the French term *folie*, he meant foolishness, rather than the raging insanity of the Furies—evil spirits from the underworld thought to cause madness through demonic possession. But just why *were* people so credulous? Why did they love things so much and cling to objects as vehicles of salvation?[7]

Erasmus's answer was that such delusions were simply irresistible because many preferred the succor of physical comforts to the spiritual struggle for piety. He agreed with Guibert that relics were a fraud, but Erasmus was more tolerant, even indulgent. "It is quite clear," he concluded, "that the Christian religion has a kind of kinship with folly," citing the aged, women, and those simpletons who "take the greatest delight in sacred and holy things . . . by their natural instinct." At times, he mocked those who kissed and handled sacred objects. But, like Buddhist and Muslim commentators before him, he acknowledged that the illiterate needed images to focus their piety; they could never rely on the word of God alone. That was far too rationalistic. Christian humility demanded accepting a certain amount of human folly, he suggested, playfully. None of us are *that* wise.[8]

Erasmian irony could not stem the rising tide of anticlerical animus, however. As the Reformation erupted after 1517, iconoclasts stripped altars and dissolved monasteries across northern Europe, defacing sculptures and burning sacred images in a direct assault on Catholic worship. Like Guibert, most Reformation theologians focused their wrath on clerical fraudsters, not the ordinary worshipper. But some did attempt to probe the question of what was wrong with the idolater.

Martin Luther judged that all objects were irrelevant to Christian piety. In "the proper worship," he wrote, "a person needs . . . no paintings or images . . . for these are all human inventions." The Wittenberg theologian Andreas Karlstadt, a close associate of Luther's, likened the appurtenances of Catholicism to self-harming gewgaws. One seizes a knife from a child, Karlstadt explained, in order to protect the child—one should therefore seize relics because parishioners need protection from their own childish cravings.[9]

The Swiss theologian Ulrich Zwingli also analyzed the idolatrous mind. The idolater's great error, he was convinced, was to try to reduce

God to material objects. Like Karlstadt, Zwingli reasoned that human beings were corrupt at heart, both spiritually and cognitively compromised by their fallen nature. People were naturally beholden to treacherous inner idols that made them yearn for physical things as a means to attain immortal life. Ironically, after Zwingli's death, his Catholic opponents cremated and scattered his remains, so that his Protestant followers would not be able to venerate them as relics.

These attacks were driven home by the Geneva reformer John Calvin. "The finite cannot contain the infinite," Calvin reminded his readers. Relics or icons could never contain Almighty God in his infinitude, for God is entirely other. Striving to make him physically intelligible was, therefore, a grievous sin. In his *Treatise on Relics* (1543), a satire of the relic catalogs published at the time—and in some ways a precursor to modern museum catalogs—Calvin poured scorn on those who amassed relics as mere collectors piling up meaningless junk. The idolater, Calvin insisted, was someone who tragically mistook hoarding relics for genuine spiritual action, when such hoarding was in fact a path to spiritual death. It was one of the first instances of the argument, destined to be repeated in secular form in the modern era, that collectors are people who waste their entire lives by mistaking collecting for living.

The Reformation changed the course of Christianity, but Cardinal Albrecht, keeper of the Halle Sanctuary, withstood its reforming assaults, some of which landed at his own door. Albrecht stood accused of selling indulgences to help pay for the reconstruction of St. Peter's in Rome, prompting Luther to issue his ninety-five theses against the Catholic Church. The fear of genuine faith was far preferable to the "false security of peace" offered by indulgences, the great reformer lectured the archbishop.[10]

Halle became Protestant and Albrecht withdrew to the reliably Catholic hinterlands of Bavaria. He remained unmoved by Luther's attacks, however, continuing to collect and compute the spiritual value of his reliquary. And while the Reformation promised to create a new kind of Christian— one who worshipped God without things—the survival of Luther's death mask and hands in Halle's Market Church remind us how even its champions come down to us in the form of relics.

From ancient Rome to Reformation Europe, loving things too much raised the specter of sacrilege. The Reformation was an attempt to solve this problem by eradicating a certain kind of religious collector: the idolater. At virtually the same time, however, the idea that it might be *good* to love things too much was emerging on the other side of the world. Writers in Asia began to describe collectors as obsessive and not entirely rational. Yet, this obsessive collector also became an object of praise as a charismatic, sophisticated, and authentic kind of person. The emergence of the figure of the obsessive collector is sometimes traced to Western Europe during the nineteenth and twentieth centuries. But an earlier beginning can be found in China during the Ming Dynasty. What was "wrong" with these Chinese collectors? To any sensitive and intelligent observer, the answer was obvious. They were suffering from *pǐ*.

CHAPTER THREE

BEWARE THE UNOBSESSED

Dallying too much with objects kills one's will.

—ATTRIBUTED TO CONFUCIUS, *THE BOOK OF DOCUMENTS*

In Mandarin Chinese, the character 癖 is pronounced *pǐ*. The sound resembles the English word *pea*, but dips in the middle. The most important clue to the meaning of 癖 is its root symbol 疒, which means sickness. In premodern Chinese sources, *pǐ* is sometimes also written as 僻. This variation signifies things or people that are off-center, leaning to one side or in some way awry.

The Chinese have used these characters for centuries, but their meanings have changed with the times. Looking up *pǐ* today, one finds a bewildering array of translations and connotations: habit, hobby, craving, weakness, indigestion, obsession, eccentricity, addiction, alcoholism, fetishism, nail biting, compulsive cleanliness, sadism, exhibitionism, homosexuality, transvestitism, pedophilia, pica (eating soil or paper), necrophilia, and Munchausen syndrome—pretending to have a physical or mental illness when one does not.

A related character 痞, also pronounced *pǐ*, signifies constipation, a lump in the abdomen, dyspepsia, spleen infection, or a rogue. It again uses the sickness radical 疒 in combination with 否, the latter character meaning something clogged or evil.

Historically, these characters have also been used to describe collectors as obsessives who suffer from a mental fixation so strong it's akin to a physical obstruction. The very idea of the obsessive collector, in other words, appears to find its earliest expression in premodern China. This figure marked a significant departure from ancient and medieval preoccupations with the greed of the looter and the folly of the idolater: first, because the obsessive collector was seen to be a psychologically complex individual, rather than a proverbial mad emperor or generic gullible parishioner; and second, because that complexity was regarded in a positive light as a desirable form of personal sophistication.

Beginning with the Xia, China's earliest recorded dynasty, which dates to 2070–1600 BCE, prestigious objects conferred power and legitimacy on successive regimes. The Nine Tripods were ceremonial cauldrons cast in bronze and thought to endow their possessors with the divine mandate of heaven, giving them the authority to rule. Forged under the Xia, the Tripods were then claimed by the Xia's successor dynasty, the Shang, but they were lost by the advent of China's first imperial dynasty, the Qin of the third century BCE. It was the beginning of a pattern destined to recur across centuries of Chinese history: the building then losing of collections marking the rise and fall of different dynasties.

Collecting and cataloging art, antiquities, and calligraphic scrolls became enduring pursuits of the Chinese emperors and the literati class of scholar-bureaucrats known as Mandarins. Over time, private citizens began to collect more as well, even though Chinese culture resounded with warnings about loving things too much. "Dallying too much with objects kills one's will," warned Confucius in *The Book of Documents*. The ancient Taoist text *Zhuangzi* advised people to "thing and not be thinged": use material objects, in other words, don't let them use you. The eleventh-century poet Su Shi said it was fine to spend time gazing at beautiful things, but don't fixate on them, or your soul will be burdened by anxiety for *their* well-being instead of your own.[1]

Official collections could project magnificence and authority, but their loss signaled political and personal calamity. When the collections of the emperor Yuan, who reigned at the end of the Liang Dynasty, were burned by the rebel Hou Ching, Yuan reportedly tried to throw himself into the fire. The collections of the Sui Dynasty's hedonistic Emperor Yang perished on a touring boat that sank at Yangzhou. The emperor Huizong lost his collections when the Northern Song were defeated at Kaifeng in 1127 by Jin invaders, who seized them and brought them to Beijing. The poet Li Qing-zhao wrote poignantly of her travails during this upheaval. Li's husband was an antiquarian who asked her to protect fifteen boatloads of books. She lost both her husband and the books and came to lament his passion for them as a tragic mistake.

The Ming Dynasty witnessed a vibrant renaissance in collecting. Despite a brief period of naval supremacy in the Indian Ocean under Admiral Zheng He in the fifteenth century, the Ming never became a great maritime power. However, a thriving internal trade in grain, rice, porcelain, cotton, cloth, tea, and sugar, facilitated by the infrastructure of the Grand Canal, brought China great new commercial wealth. The word *Ming* (明) is made up of the characters for sun and moon and means great brightness, and by the sixteenth century, Chinese society seemed richer and brighter than ever.

Traditionally, Chinese culture drew a moral distinction between agriculture as the honest bedrock of civilization and the corrupting influence of commerce and luxury. But under the Ming, commerce became newly prized. Confucian homilies were eclipsed by a burgeoning taste for fine furniture, clothing, and more. As in ancient Rome, the authorities passed sumptuary laws, but they were flouted. The genteel classes enjoyed more material comforts and so too did the peasantry, who developed a new passion for decorating their homes and wearing jewelry. The Jesuit Alvaro Semedo, one of many Catholic missionaries who traveled to China to make Christian converts, went so far as to observe that his hosts were "naturally inclined to be merchants." To others, the circulation of goods in China inspired a cosmopolitan philosophy of commercial life as a model of cosmic harmony. "If everything remained permanently where it was," the scholar Song Yingxing asked in 1637, "how would each find its proper place?"[2]

Ming prosperity was a boon for collectors. Entrepreneurs and the merchant classes emulated the emperors. Middling folk with new fortunes swelled the ranks of courtly and literati collectors, buying up the new guidebooks increasingly published on every possible collectible: musical instruments, fans, paper, ink, inkstones, brushes, chess sets, seals, wine, wine bottles, rocks, tea, incense, flowers, vases, canes, and swords—as well as elite favorites calligraphy, paintings, antiques, and even foreign luxuries including lacquer boxes from Japan.

In early eighteenth-century England, Daniel Defoe penned epic yarns of social mobility renowned for their dramatization of the promises and perils of the commercial way of life. His stories featured changes of identity, reversals of fortune, and boom and bust, probing the question whether the nouveaux riches who achieved wealth and status in the most sudden fashion were ever as genteel as they strived to seem. A full two centuries before Defoe's bodice-ripping sagas of greed and glory, however, Ming China confronted the exact same question. Were new collectors *true* collectors or were they hollow frauds like Trimalchio in Petronius's *Satyricon*? Antiques, for example, straddled the status fence between fashionable consumption and learned connoisseurship. Did owning them make you a collector or just a superior shopper? Forgeries became widespread, so collectors' manuals became more important than ever, advising visitors to the markets of Beijing how to tell the difference between fakes and the genuine article.

Would that it were so simple. "Sons of the rich and a handful of the ignorant, uncouth and stupid," wrote the scholar-painter Wen Zhenheng in his *Treatise on Superfluous Things* (1620–27), "no sooner open their mouths at a meeting of connoisseurs than they spew forth vulgarity." Wen could not contain his irritation at the galling spectacle of false refinement. "Their handling of objects is clumsy, they indulge in exaggerated gestures of appreciation [and] they are full of insult for the refined." Things had come to such a shocking pass that "gentlemen of true taste, talent and sensibility [now] avoid discussion of matters of style and elegance."[3]

As in Rome, the specter of profligacy gripped the Ming imagination. Critics began decrying collections of rarities and deriding the rise of the merchants as an omen not merely of personal disgrace but civilizational ruin. A scandalous novel, in whose tradition Defoe followed, captured the titillating hazards of the new hedonism in all of their alarming sensuality. Its Chinese title was *Jin ping mei* (金瓶梅), published in 1618 under the pseudonym The Scoffing Scholar of Lanling, and has variously been translated as *The Plum in the Golden Vase*, *The Golden Lotus*, and *The Glamour of Entering the Vagina*. Its protagonist is a merchant named Ximen Qing on the eve of the defeat of the Northern Song by the Jin forces in the early twelfth century. Qing is a nouveau riche with carnal passions who hankers equally after possessions and flesh. In one typical scene, he cannot resist fondling his maid after being aroused by her silk blouse. A serial adulterer with several wives, Qing also enjoys encounters with boys but dies prematurely when he overdoses on aphrodisiac. The author's message? The Confucian ideal of moderation was long dead, decadence ruled the Chinese soul, and disaster was at hand.

But were the Ming really so decadent as such stories made out? Some scholars argue that the very notion of Ming decadence is a European import, borrowed from modern narratives of the decline and fall of the Roman Empire that became prominent after the eighteenth century thanks to the likes of Edward Gibbon. Yet when the Ming did fall to invading Manchu armies from the north in 1644, their defeat naturally prompted the question *why?* The idea that proudly amassing collections courted a cosmic correction resonated in Chinese culture and China's Manchu conquerors wasted little time in using it to justify their domination. Indeed, Manchu writers were the first to spread the idea that the Ming fell *because* they had become vitiated and corrupt. The conquerors decided to distinguish themselves from their predecessors by adopting the name *Qing* (清) for their regime, meaning clear or pure. By doing so, they reinforced the idea that those who loved things too much brought disaster on their society, while those who possessed greater moral discipline were destined to prevail.

Despite their misgivings about material possessions, the Ming appear to have been the first to heap a strange yet significant kind of praise on people who were obsessive collectors. According to Ming commentators, these collectors were suffering from an illness known as *pǐ*. *Pǐ* was highly unusual, however, because its sufferers were thought to be distinguished by their possession of rare charisma, superior sophistication, and uncommon personal authenticity.

The earliest references to *pǐ* long predate the Ming. One of its first known mentions comes in the third-century *Classic Materia Medica*, a compendium of herbal medicine and agriculture said to have been compiled by Shen Nong, the mythological divine farmer. Here, *pǐ* was used to signify a physical obstruction that caused indigestion. A seventh-century dictionary further explained that *pǐ* could mean a painfully hard substance forming in one's insides. A medical dictionary a century later warned that a *pǐ* could become as hard as a stone.

Collecting, meanwhile, became increasingly identified with obsession. Consider the case of Zhang Yanyuan, a ninth-century calligrapher and art historian. Zhang was a devoted collector of rarities. He would sell his old clothes and eat sparingly so he had enough money to add to his collection. His family took him to task for lavishing attention on useless pursuits. But he hit back at all such cavils like a true philosopher. "If one doesn't do such useless things," Zhang wrote, "how can one take pleasure in this mortal life?" In Europe, Protestant reformers would insist that finite things could never contain the infinite. But Zhang praised the act of collecting precisely because it was a noble attempt to wring meaning from the infinite variety of the physical world. Trying to bring order to the chaos of existence was not madness but, rather, taught a valuable lesson of profound humility in the face of the absolute.[4]

Zhang was also one of the first writers to venerate the collector as a happy recluse. Only someone who has withdrawn from the pressures of human society, he believed, can truly express themselves. The collector's obsessions were no burden, therefore, but a means of self-realization, if not liberation, and contemplative transcendence. A thousand years before Freud popularized the idea that when we look at a collection, we see the outward expression of a hidden inner self, Zhang embodied the notion that collecting is not something you do, it's what you are. A true collector *is* their collection.

Like Zhang, the Ming scholar and poet Yuan Hongdao considered obsession noble because it transcended self-interest and inspired sacrifice. In his *History of Flower Arranging* (1599), Yuan lauded those ancient plant-hunters who braved mountains, searing heat, and torturous cold to capture rare blossoms. Doing so required selfless dedication, a purpose beyond oneself, and singular integrity. A true gentleman, Yuan observed, "worries only about having no obsession." Whether the object was a flower or a rock, collecting involved "the self loving the self," he wrote in a signal phrase. Obsession wasn't derangement or illness; it was a sign of depth and truth to oneself. "One cannot befriend a man without obsessions," the seventeenth-century essayist Zhang Dai echoed Yuan, "for he lacks deep emotion." Beneath the seeming strangeness of their almost fanatical devotion to material objects, the obsessive collector was heartfelt, trustworthy, and a person worth knowing, because such individuals were authentically themselves. Those not truly obsessed, by contrast, lived for mere gain and fame, and were callow and insipid, driven by fashion and only the superficial considerations of the moment.[5]

To understand the nature of obsession, the Ming fused notions of physical obstruction and mental fixation to redefine *pǐ* as the collector's malady. Li Shizhen was a physician at the turn of the seventeenth century, whom Chinese Communists under Mao later rebranded a hero of the common people they called the Barefoot Doctor. Li compiled an encyclopedic work of *materia medica* called the *Bencao Gangmu* (1596), intended as a monumental correction of popular errors and superstitions even though, like Pliny and other encyclopedists before him, Li himself combined both empirical observation and fantastical lore.

Pǐ was a case in point. "There are people," Li explained, "who concentrate on something until it becomes an obsession." This could lead to the formation of a *pǐ* stone, which Li compared to the bezoar stones that form inside animals and were often used medicinally in the premodern world. Thoughts and feelings possessed this power of petrifaction, too. Li recounted the most unusual story of how a heart discovered inside the corpse of a girl was found to contain within it the figure of that same girl gazing at a landscape. Li explained this strange phenomenon through the power of obsession: the girl's love of landscape produced the petrifaction in her heart as a memorial of that love. This was why the petrified form of the Buddha had likewise sometimes been discovered in the hearts of dead Buddhist monks. Human longing was so powerful, it could produce tangible effects in the most sacred places of the external world.[6]

The Ming cult of obsession extended to collections of many kinds: books and paintings, calligraphy and musical instruments, rocks and plants, flowers and animals, tea and wine. It generated curious legends about intense bonds between people and things. A belief that physical objects were dynamic and capable of change, rather than immutable and fixed, together with a faith in the extraordinary depth of feeling they could inspire, fostered an animistic view of objects as living entities. If you loved things, things would love you back.

This was the idea behind "The Ethereal Rock" by master seventeenth-century storyteller Pu Songling, compiler of the renowned *Strange Tales*, a rich compendium of oddities and the bizarre. In it, Pu tells the tale of a man named Xing Yunfei who falls in love with a rock he finds in his fishing net one day. The rock is beautifully shaped in the form of a mountain and even possesses its own clouds. Xing simply must have it. But a series of misfortunes plagues him as a consequence of his desire for the rock. Thieves and government officials claim the rock for themselves. Xing vows to give up three years of his life in order to keep it himself, but a corrupt official deprives Xing of the rock before he dies. The rock, however, is still alive. It escapes and smashes itself into pieces, allowing Xing's son to gather its remains and bury them in his father's grave. The rock loved Xing as much as Xing loved the rock—deliberately making itself attractive to Xing from the start and jumping into his net on purpose. In the end, it matched Xing's love with its own sacrifice, destroying itself so they can be reunited in death.

Xing's story is strange and moving. Even if he may have been deluded in his obsession with the rock, Xing lived a more meaningful life as a result. That was the thing about *pǐ*. It was an illness that made you *better*.

Pǐ was a patrician malady and an ailment of the literati, the educated, and the aristocratic. But the allure of obsessive collecting proved too seductive to contain. Soon enough, the figure of the obsessive collector took the boat and crossed the East China Sea to Chosŏn Korea, and began to appear in different social classes.

Chinese influence shaped Korea in many ways, not least in the realm of religion and philosophy, including Buddhism and Confucianism. Excessive materialism was, therefore, to be guarded against because as Confucius taught, "superfluous" things destroyed the will. But by the waning decades of the Chosŏn Dynasty, Korean attitudes were changing, again under the influence of their powerful neighbor. By the 1700s, Korean merchants were engaging in trade for commercial goods in Beijing's Liulichang district.

They brought back both Chinese and Western commodities: books, games, optical lenses, and toys. Formally, Korea was closed to European commerce, but Western goods entered by way of China and proved especially enticing in the era of the early Industrial Revolution. By the eighteenth century, therefore, Korean collectors were accumulating calligraphy and art like the Chinese literati but also new European luxuries such as clocks.

New commerce gave rise to new identities. Korea had its own class of propertied literati, known as the Yangban, at the apex of the social hierarchy. But the new possibilities brought about by a commercial way of life emboldened the class of rising professionals known as the Chungin. And, by the eighteenth century, one of the ways the Chungin came to assert themselves was by consuming, collecting, and displaying their *pyŏk*. Korean *pyŏk*—pronounced *pea-oh*—derived from the Chinese concept of *pi*. Like *pi*, *pyŏk* signified obsession and was originally a term of opprobrium. People with *pyŏk* had something wrong with them: they flouted Confucian wisdom by loving things too much. But like its Chinese counterpart *pi*, *pyŏk* became a way to revere certain "addictions" as a form of cultural sophistication and validate obsessiveness as the mark of charisma and authenticity.

Like Yuan Hongdao in China before him, the early nineteenth-century Korean artist Cho Hŭiryong reasoned that obsession taught humility before the infinite. "I have a *pyŏk* for sightseeing," Cho wrote, "every time I read the travel records, I realize how small I am, just like a frog in a well, and how vast the world is, like a great misty ocean." The object of one's *pyŏk* might be calligraphy or art, rocks or plum trees, mourning dresses or swords. It didn't matter too much, although some objects might be more significant than others. Cho praised the *pyŏk* of Kim Ŏk, for example, a man who collected swords: one for every day of the year. Kim kept his swords sheathed, however, and, as such, they aptly symbolized the historic frustrations of the Chungin class.[7]

In this respect, *pyŏk* differed from *pi*. The social significance of obsessive collecting changed as it traveled. In Ming China, *pi* was a badge of eccentric sophistication among individual members of the literati class. But in Chosŏn Korea, displaying one's *pyŏk* became a way for the professional Chungin class to challenge the hierarchies of their time by claiming to be just as sophisticated as the elite Yangban class—just as obsessive.

For Chungin who were determined to show off their *pyŏk*, one of the most striking ways to do so was to commission minutely detailed paintings of their collections to showcase their possessions—and their selves. These paintings, which proliferated after the eighteenth and nineteenth centuries, were called *ch'aekkŏri* or *munbangdo*, terms signifying a scholar's study paintings. We might also see them as some of the earliest self-portraits through objects in the history of art, as collectors started to define themselves through pictures of their collections—not merely displaying their wealth and taste but suggesting the charismatic individual personality that lay behind them.

To Western eyes, the *ch'aekkŏri* appear a combination of the cabinets of curiosities of the European Renaissance and the still-life tableaux of the Dutch Golden Age. They're quietly contemplative luminous micro-panoramas, where the viewer's eye roams over many objects, both Asian and Western, packed onto the neatly geometric shelves of elaborate cabinets: vases, books, and clocks; corals, flowers, and scrolls; pictures, microscopes,

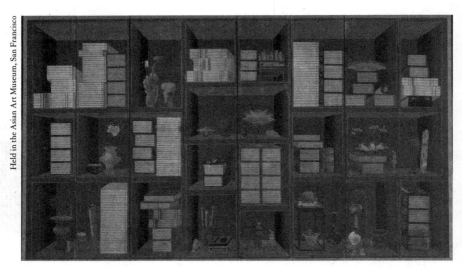

Held in the Asian Art Museum, San Francisco

Yi Eungrok, ch'aekkŏri painting, Chosŏn Dynasty (ca. 1860–74): Paintings of individual collections like the court painter Yi Eungrok's asserted the status of Korea's rising professional class, the Chungin, emphasizing their cosmopolitan taste (they owned both Western and Chinese goods) and their obsessive cultivation, which they referred to as their pyŏk, *a derivative of the Chinese concept of* pǐ.

and sculptures; figurines, eyeglasses, and teapots. They are visual messages from the Chungin that seem to say *I am what I collect. I am my pyŏk. I am my obsessions. Aren't I remarkable?*

The *ch'aekkŏri*, that is to say, mark an early phase in the democratization of the figure of the obsessive collector, as well as the idea that obsessiveness was a positive badge of cultural sophistication. In Korea, the strange glory of being obsessed was no longer an aristocratic privilege as in China but a malady that might potentially afflict anyone—and that was a *good* thing. This notion was to find its most vivid expression in the Romantic culture of modern Europe and America, through the evolution of a Romantic collecting self and above all in the decadent collecting culture of the fin de siècle, but it emerged first in China and Korea.

The same centuries that witnessed the rise of Ming and Chosŏn collecting also saw the making of vast European fortunes through global trade and colonization. This unprecedented wealth meant that Europeans of different social classes began to amass collections of many kinds. It heralded the emergence of the European collector: in art, science, antiquarianism, and curiosities. Astonishing treasures flowed into European ports. But how exactly were Europeans to make sense of these fabulous new worlds they were now collecting? The question mattered because European knowledge was in a state of flux between magical and scientific belief systems. Was nature a mystical code written by God to be divined by the adepts of occult knowledge or a mere machine to be managed by technical experts for practical benefit and economic gain? Who, in other words, made the better collector: the magus or the merchant?

CHAPTER FOUR

THE MAGUS AND
THE MERCHANT

This kind of man thinks philosophy is a sort of
book . . . and that truth is to be found out not in the
world or nature but in the collection of texts.

—GALILEO TO JOHANNES KEPLER (1610)

The Museum of Jurassic Technology in Los Angeles is a ramshackle masterpiece. A collection of throwaway oddities behind a grungy façade on Venice Boulevard in Culver City, its curiosities wink at you like a homemade *Ripley's Believe It or Not*. A pair of decaying dice labeled *Rotten Luck*. A pair of white mice on toast (an ancient medical remedy, apparently). The sound of a barking dog that turns out to be a manic human mimic. A portrait gallery of actual canines nobly launched into space by the Soviet Union. And the *Deprong Mori*—a winged creature, quite possibly a bat, able to fly through solid objects.

Dark passages wind mysteriously around the museum's homemade displays. Visitors lift telephones off the walls that look like they've been there since the 1970s to listen to descriptions that crackle down the line. A flight of stairs leads up to a disarmingly peaceful drawing room where you can take tea and read, before you come to an ethereal columbarium, where doves perch and coo in your ears.

Created in 1988 by David Wilson, the Museum of Jurassic Technology was one of the first modern-day reworkings of the Renaissance cabinet of curiosities, or *Wunderkammer*. As the name *Wunderkammer* suggests, what Wilson offers his visitors is not the scientific authority of the modern museum but a rather deeper, more ancient and mystical journey into awe and wonder. He takes us back to the world before the nineteenth century, when no clear division existed between the art gallery and the science museum, when objects were mysteries that posed the question: What *is* this?

A singular guiding spirit animates Wilson's museum, although *whose* is not immediately clear. A clue floats in the air: the sound of tinkling bells that draws visitors into a darkened room. Their source turns out to be a prize piece of Jurassic tech: a rotating wheel of metal bells. It is the re-creation of a machine designed by the seventeenth-century Jesuit priest and polymath Athanasius Kircher. Kircher curated a cabinet of curiosities at the Collegio Romano in Rome and was convinced that nature comprised a secret code to be deciphered by the learned—not using the methods of the modern scientist but the hallowed and hoary wisdom of the magus. Kircher's museum was not a laboratory, it was a temple.

The figure of the magus dominated the image of the Renaissance collector. The most storied collector of the era is not Kircher, however, but Rudolf II (1552–1612). He was undoubtedly also the most notorious. Was Rudolf mad, people wondered, or even possessed by the devil, and what did his collections reveal about what was wrong with him?

Rudolf was king of Bohemia, Hungary, and Croatia, and archduke of Austria. In 1576, during a time of great spiritual and military turbulence, he became the Holy Roman emperor. A member of the House of Habsburg, he reigned as a Catholic during the Counter-Reformation, when the Catholic Church sought to roll back the advance of Protestantism, while facing down the military might of the Ottoman Empire on Europe's eastern frontier. Rudolf, however, was not a zealous crusader. He spurned religious dogmatism, extended a policy of toleration toward his Protestant subjects, and, after fighting the Ottomans in the 1590s, strived for peace and reconciliation.

Deeply learned, Rudolf immersed himself in the rigorous textual studies of the humanists and embraced their devotion to the recovery of ancient learning through the mastery of original Greek and Roman manuscripts.

To this end, he hosted a sparkling court at Hradčany Castle in Prague, where he invited some of the leading intellectuals of his time, including Tycho Brahe and Johannes Kepler. In time, Brahe and Kepler would redefine astronomy by replacing the Aristotelian view of an earth-centered cosmos with a sun-centered model of the universe. This achievement drew on the work of Galileo Galilei in Italy and culminated in Sir Isaac Newton's formulation of his three laws of motion in the *Principia Mathematica* (1687), becoming known as the "new science" and, to modern scholars, the Scientific Revolution—with mathematics gradually eclipsing magic as the most authoritative explanation of the workings of the natural world.

Mathematics and magic, however, presented no contradiction for Renaissance thinkers. Natural philosophers, as they called themselves, believed nature was a baroque puzzle that required occult forms of knowledge to penetrate its secrets. Rudolf took great interest in sponsoring experimental philosophers, most notably Giambattista Della Porta, renowned for designing daring technological projects in optics, engineering, and hydraulics. But Rudolf was also drawn to the esoteric writings of the Christian Cabbala and brought the alchemists John Dee and Edward Kelley from England to Prague to crack the secret of the philosopher's stone in a quest to manipulate matter and achieve immortality.

Collecting undergirded Rudolf's attempt to reveal the truth of nature's mysteries. Among the enormous holdings he amassed were paintings by Albrecht Dürer, Hans Holbein, Pieter Bruegel the Elder, and Paolo Veronese; ornate metalwork by the master artisan Wenzel Jamnitzer; drawings of natural history specimens commissioned from the draftsman Joris Hoefnagel; a celestial clockwork globe mounted on the shoulders of the mythological horse Pegasus; countless scientific instruments; thousands of books and manuscripts, including mystical Christian writings and an Arabic Bible; and thousands of coins and minerals from regional mines. Rudolf also enjoyed access to a deer park and aviary around Hradčany Castle. He was voracious in all things. "What he knows," it was said, "he feels obliged to have."[1]

Rudolf aspired to assemble the world in microcosm as a *theatrum mundi*, or theater of the world, emulating God's creation in miniature. A lover of marvels, he strove to comprehend what all things were made of and how they functioned, from plants and animals to technology. But his curiosity was also deeply religious. He owned a mandrake root in the shape of a crucifix and relics including, so it was said, nails from Noah's Ark. The collector as magus was thus heir to the tradition of the medieval Christian reliquary, even as he pursued practical power through scientific and technological means.

So sublime was Rudolf's sense of purpose, he commissioned Giuseppe Arcimboldo to paint his portrait, in what has become one of the great works of mannerist art. In it, Arcimboldo depicts Rudolf as Vertumnus, Roman god of the seasons, rendering the emperor's face as a dancing concatenation of fruits, flowers, and vegetables—as though nature itself were animated by Rudolf's encyclopedic curiosity.

Held at Skokloster Castle, Sweden

Giuseppe Arcimboldo, Vertumnus *(1591): Previously mistaken as an indication of mental infirmity on the part of Rudolf II (1552–1612), this depiction of the Holy Roman emperor as a concatenation of fruits, flowers, and vegetables celebrates his mastery of the natural world by portraying him as Vertumnus, Roman god of the seasons.*

Witnesses insisted, however, there was something terribly wrong with the great collector. Court observers gossiped about the emperor's dark moods and inscrutable behavior. The ambassador of the Duke of Savoy reported that sometimes Rudolf spent "two and a half hours sitting motionless, looking at the paintings of fruit and fish markets sent by your highness." Some regarded the emperor's intense studiousness with foreboding. There was a growing consensus, Cardinal Filippo Spinelli informed Pope Clement VIII in 1600, that Rudolf was "bewitched and is in league with the devil." Spinelli even claimed to have seen "the chair in which His Majesty sits when holding conversations with the Prince of Darkness himself. I have seen the little bell His Majesty uses whenever he wishes to summon the spirits of the departed to do his bidding." Spinelli added that Rudolf trembled in chapel and winced at the sign of the cross, forbidding it in his presence. "I am a man possessed by the devil," he was reported to have said.[2]

Rudolf's accusers may well have thought him bewitched because, to the Renaissance mind, demons, witches, and the devil were real entities who consorted with mortals. But spreading the idea that the emperor was possessed may also have been a way for Catholics to express disappointment in a ruler they believed had failed to prosecute the Counter-Reformation with the proper zeal. To critics, Rudolf's entire reign was a calamity. His dreams of mastering the magical and alchemical arts came to naught, and his vision of universal peace crumbled. He was forced from his kingship by his brother Matthias in 1611, and, a few years after his death, Protestants removed Rudolf's surviving officials by hurling them out the windows of Hradčany Castle. The Defenestration of Prague, as it was known, helped trigger the Protestant-Catholic turmoil of the Thirty Years' War.

Could Rudolf's absorption in his collections have somehow brought on these disasters? Several have suggested so. In the 1960s, the brilliant historian Frances Yates, who pioneered the recovery of magic as central to Renaissance thought, saw Rudolf as "hiding" from the world in his collections, where he "withdrew in alarm" from the storm gathering round his kingdom. In his 1988 novel *Utz*, Bruce Chatwin described a fictional journalist's fascination with the "gloomy palace-fortress" where the emperor "shut himself away" and "would, for weeks on end, neglect the affairs" of his realm. In his 1994 history of collecting, the psychoanalyst Werner

Muensterberger diagnosed Rudolf as an "anal-obsessive" and "melancholic voyeur" who used collecting as a fix for his "depression."[3]

Just as nineteenth-century writers rediagnosed ancient Roman collectors to fit the preoccupations of the modern era, these later views of Rudolf reflect understandings of what ailed the emperor in terms no-one in the Renaissance would have understood. In his own time and place, however, it was clear to contemporaries that Rudolf was neither anal nor paranoid, and not a manic depressive, but a *melancholic*.

According to the Hippocratic system of the four humors, *melancholia* was a type of constitution and temperament thought to be produced by an excess of black bile in the body. Some believed demonic possession might be the cause, although Robert Burton in his magnum opus *The Anatomy of Melancholy* (1621) explained the condition in purely physical terms. Rather than a mere term of opprobrium, *melancholy* was a noble malady associated with some of the highest aspirations of Renaissance culture. Melancholics were typically aristocrats of an artistic bent who dwelled in the gray area between poetic inspiration and madness, as suggested by the mournful figure featured in Dürer's engraving *Melencolia I* (1514), who leans her head on her hand in tortured frustration—the melancholic's classic pose.

The melancholic proved irresistible to the Elizabethan imagination. Shakespeare cast both Hamlet and Prospero in this mold, as did Christopher Marlowe the figure of Faust. Marlowe's 1592 tragedy *Doctor Faustus* recounted the tale of a scholar who loses his soul in pursuit of knowledge and power. Faustus isn't just a melancholic, he's a collector: a scholar of "conjuring books" containing forbidden magical secrets. He realizes that "danger is in words" but cannot stop himself from conjuring up the demon Mephistopheles to get him books on astronomy, botany, and a volume "wherein I might behold all spells and incantations . . . [to] raise up spirits when I please." Faustus's life ends in misery: he ultimately pledges to burn those same books. But it's too late and his soul is damned to hell. The tragedy echoed down the centuries, above all in Mary Shelley's equally melancholic *Frankenstein* (1818), whose hero also collects magical books, which he uses to create a living being from dead body parts, only to wish in the end that he himself had never been born.[4]

Rudolf was neither a self-destructive Faustian recluse nor a Freudian repressive. His collections were neither symptom nor cause of his melancholy. In fact, Renaissance thinkers led by Robert Burton and the Siena physician Giulio Mancini argued that collecting could cure melancholy by lifting the spirits and diverting the mind. In reality, collecting was the opposite of an isolated pursuit, involving constant contact with other collectors through correspondence and the giving of gifts as part of diplomatic exchanges. The allegation that Rudolf's bewitchment, his collecting, and his madness were linked was, therefore, likely motivated by dissatisfaction with his religious and military stances among his fellow Catholics as much as anything else.

These realities did not, however, prevent the forging of a legend and an enduring image of the collector, destined only to deepen over time, as a gloomy gothic recluse who takes refuge from the real world in a private realm of things. This was a departure from earlier fears about collectors. Verres was terrifying because of his tyrannical passion and violence; the idolater was a laughable fool and miserable dupe. But Rudolf embodied the first stirrings of the modern idea that collectors are people who cannot face reality and prefer to lose themselves in a world of make-believe.

In the Renaissance, collectors were driven by renewed purpose. As Europe's economy rebounded owing to increased trade and colonization across the Atlantic Ocean and in Asia, and humanists began to recover lost ancient texts for modern readers, naturalists dreamed of surpassing ancient scientific authorities. As a result, the persona of the collector became a major preoccupation. In seventeenth-century Italy, for example, natural history collectors took to associating themselves with the iconography of the chameleon as well as the mythological figure of Narcissus, to reflect the view that collectors were dynamic and ever-changing, yet prone to vanity and self-absorption.

Such preoccupations were an early manifestation of collectors' self-conscious search for an identity, even if it meant looking backwards for models and exemplars. A more secular, Romantic, and idiosyncratic quest to define the identity of the collector would emerge in the nineteenth century. But in the Renaissance, the collector's quest was conventional: baroque, religious, and mystical—a sacred search for divine power epitomized by the patron saint of the Museum of Jurassic Technology, Athanasius Kircher.

Born in Thuringia in 1602, Kircher fled his native Germany during the Thirty Years' War to become an eminent member of the Jesuit order in Rome. At the Collegio Romano, the school founded by Ignatius of Loyola, he presided over a collection of specimens and curiosities sent to him by missionaries all around the world, from China to South America. Versed in occult learning like Rudolf, Kircher regarded the worlds of nature and technology as great esoteric puzzles. He was fascinated by magic lanterns that projected pictures and speaking trumpets that projected sound; the power of magnetism, with which he experimented; and even tried to translate the hieroglyphics on Rome's Egyptian obelisks. Lacking the Rosetta Stone as a guide, undiscovered until the nineteenth century, he failed. But his efforts were heroic.

In his writings, Kircher identified himself as a collector with both Christian and pagan forebears. His piety written into his name—*kircher* means churchman—Athanasius was inspired by St. Augustine and Loyola's confessional writings. His goal was to restore Catholic supremacy after the Reformation, while seeking spiritual self-knowledge in the process. Yet he also associated himself with countless forebears from classical mythology: Aeneas, Daedalus, Icarus, Osiris, Oedipus, and Hermes. In doing so, he cast himself as an ambitious exile, roaming encyclopedically across all branches of the world's knowledge, seeking out nature's truths wherever they might be.

Kircher was extraordinary. He has, however, often been remembered as a foil to the rise of modern science. This is why there is a shrine to him in the oddball canon of collecting's alternative heroes in the Museum of Jurassic Technology. Kircher is sometimes called the last man who knew everything but, modern writers insisted, used the wrong methods: those of the magus, not the scientist. "This kind of man thinks philosophy is a sort of book like the *Aeneid* or *Odyssey*," Galileo complained in a letter to Kepler in 1610, "and that truth is to be found out not in the world or nature but in the collection of texts." He was mocking savants like Kircher. Galileo, by contrast, was an experimenter who used instruments such as telescopes to calculate the motions of bodies with mathematical precision. By the seventeenth century, mathematics, not magic, was becoming the language of nature in the eyes of the learned. Decoding occult signs was not a dangerous Faustian bargain, just a fool's errand. "I wish I could spend a good long time laughing with you" about these fools, Galileo told Kepler.[5]

The Renaissance collector came in for stinging criticism, not merely in the sciences but also in the arts. In the premodern world, art and science were not considered separate domains. Another name for the cabinet of curiosities was the *Kunstkammer* because it contained works of art (*kunst*) as well as natural specimens. Art collectors were, however, beginning to emerge in their own right and as they became more prominent, and their collections more spectacular, they came under attack.

In fifteenth-century Florence, the Medici family used the enormous wealth it acquired through banking to achieve overwhelming influence in politics. Four Medicis became pope. Cosimo and Lorenzo patronized some of the greatest artists of the era, including Brunelleschi and Michelangelo, and amassed stunning collections of art and antiquities, including the ancient Etruscan sculpture called the Chimera of Arezzo and the Hellenistic Egyptian cameo known as the Farnese Cup. But their voraciousness drew fury from opponents who railed at them for corruption. In 1497, the Dominican friar Girolamo Savonarola, visionary preacher and sworn enemy of the Medici, organized a "bonfire of the vanities" in Florence's Piazza della Signoria. Savonarola and his allies burned tapestries, pictures, books, clothing, furniture, cosmetics, and musical instruments, denouncing those who hoarded luxuries as craven sinners. Not everyone sided with Savonarola, however. The scourge of the Medici was burned at the stake for his trouble the following year on the orders of the powerful Borgia pope Alexander VI.

Religious hostility to art collecting was intense in Protestant England. King Henry VIII dissolved England's Catholic Church in the 1530s, but a large Catholic population remained, and Catholics remained prominent in public life. When Charles I took the Catholic Henrietta Maria for his wife in 1625, his bride even organized her own Catholic court. As the Grand Tour became established as a way for British aristocrats to polish their knowledge and refine their manners on the continent, Charles employed several *virtuosos*—the term for *connoisseur* before the eighteenth century—to buy art for him around Europe. They included Thomas Howard, earl of Arundel, and one of the king's favorites, George Villiers, duke of Buckingham. With their help, Charles amassed a brilliant collection, and displayed pictures by Veronese, Titian, Raphael, and Leonardo da Vinci in Whitehall.

Lingering religious tensions, however, led many to look askance at Charles's collecting. To Protestants, the king's love of sensuous Italian art smacked of Catholic sensuality, moral corruption, even idolatry. Critics grew alarmed at the formal ritualism and fine altarpieces adopted by the Church of England under the leadership of his archbishop, William Laud. Some became convinced of the need to reform the Reformation. But how? The sight of Madonnas by Titian and Raphael in the halls of government inflamed the Puritan lawyer William Prynne, who insisted in his 1633 book *Historio-mastix* that "the making of any image or picture of God" was "sinful, idolatrous, and abominable." As punishment, Prynne was tried and had his ears lopped off while imprisoned in the stocks. But he survived to see a Puritan republic established in 1649 when Oliver Cromwell defeated Charles in the English Civil Wars. Prynne's revenge was doubly sweet. Not only did he see Charles executed, he personally organized the prosecution of Archbishop Laud, who met the same fate as his king.[6]

A century later, the novelist Horace Walpole would lament Charles's execution as the tragic loss of a martyr to the cause of art in Britain, brutally dispatched by savage philistines. But there was no Puritan bonfire of royal vanities of the kind Savonarola had carried out in Florence. Unlike William Prynne, the Puritan lord protector, Oliver Cromwell, didn't regard paintings as idolatrous, even keeping a few of Charles's tapestries for public spaces and the *Triumphs of Caesar*, a series of nine large paintings by Andrea Mantegna. Above all, the Puritan government needed money, so its newly minted Committee for the Destruction of Monuments of Superstition and Idolatry ignored works of art. While monuments, altars, and images in churches were to be "cleansed," paintings were to be sold. In one of the first instances of a royal collection being bought up by commoners, the Puritans auctioned off Charles's pictures. Despite this act of economic pragmatism, the notion that Charles was an idolater-tyrant who needed to be erased from history took hold anyway. In an outburst of Reformation-style iconoclasm, busts and statues of the monarch were desecrated in 1650. The following phrase was written over the head of one of these statues in

London's Royal Exchange: "Exit Tyrannus Regum Ultimus" (Exit the last tyrant king).[7]

As Charles became a focal point for animosity toward art collectors as sensuous and corrupt, a new kind of collector promised a possible solution to this problem. This collector possessed all the virtues lovers of oils lacked and was everything Puritans dreamed of: pious, humble, and devoted to God's creation. This collector's goal was not aesthetic pleasure, however, but scientific knowledge.

The figure of the devout specimen collector was central to science in the early modern era and lasted down to the publication of Charles Darwin's *Origin of Species* in 1859. Darwin's account of evolution by natural selection undermined belief in the literal truth of the creation story in the book of Genesis. Before that point, however, science and religion existed largely in harmony, so much so that Genesis furnished the very archetype of the natural history collector in the Christian imagination: Adam. In the beginning, Adam knew the names of all the plants and all the animals God had made. But when Adam and Eve tasted the forbidden fruit in the Garden of Eden, they fell from grace, were cast out of Eden, and Adam lost his knowledge of the natural world in the process. To early modern Christians, therefore, the act of collecting specimens, planting gardens, and naming species all became crucial ways to atone for original sin, which they believed they inherited from Adam as a result of the Fall.

Many scientific collectors compared themselves to biblical figures. Kircher featured Noah's Ark in his writings—another patriarch whom collectors often invoked. The London gardener John Tradescant called his collection of plants and curiosities Tradescant's Ark (it later became part of Oxford's Ashmolean Museum). The great Enlightenment naturalist Carolus Linnaeus revolutionized taxonomy in the eighteenth century with his system of binomial nomenclature. It was the beginning of modern scientific classification, but Linnaeus was also the son of a Lutheran minister. Devout if not entirely modest, he regarded himself as a new Adam as he set about naming all God's species.

Although natural history collectors sought knowledge, not pleasure, this by no means inoculated them from criticism. The early scientific virtuoso—the same term was used for scientific as well as art collectors—

was typically a courtier and, as such, expected to flatter the tastes of princely collectors by discussing their collections and acknowledging how impressive they were. But, like the magus, the virtuoso was often imagined as melancholy and gloomy. Robert Walker's 1656 portrait of John Evelyn renders him in the quintessential melancholic posture. Head bowed, Evelyn holds a skull as a *memento mori* to remind himself (and the viewer) of his mortality. Another seventeenth-century image, of an anatomy theater at Leiden, reinforced the point by populating it with skeletons, including a pair in the foreground depicted as Adam and Eve. The message? Christians should use their collections to ponder their souls and the afterlife. To leave viewers in no doubt of its meaning, the anatomy theater engraving was styled "a macabre antithesis of paradise." In a 1651 poem, Sir William Davenant referred to it as a "cabinet of death."[8]

But the virtuoso's most immediate concern was money. His esoteric learning seemed especially pointless in an era of burgeoning get-rich-quick schemes. Northern Europe was experiencing tumultuous waves of financial speculation that many saw as a form of madness. In the Netherlands, the "Tulipmania" of the mid-1630s witnessed the overvaluation of tulips as luxury goods, with pamphleteers portraying Tulipmaniacs as passengers on the allegorical "ship of fools." The cultural alarm bells that rang resounded with a fear of corruption that haunted the Dutch Protestant mind. It was no coincidence, therefore, that as the Dutch amassed luxury goods, art, and curiosities, they painted ever increasing numbers of still-life pictures featuring melancholy skulls to remind themselves that all earthly finery ultimately came to naught.

The lure of speculative wealth proved irresistible, however. A new age of buying and selling shares, and soon enough art, began to emerge. Auction houses were pioneered in the Netherlands in the seventeenth century and soon appeared in London. Auctions featured art and sculpture, but also natural history specimens, often prized as though they, too, were works of art. Although scientific virtuosos strived to be learned gentlemen, in other words, they had to contend with new commercial currents. Naturalists continued to invoke God as their guide, styling themselves new Adams and new Noahs. But the surviving correspondence of scientific organizations, above all London's Royal Society, shows how collecting became driven by the search for lucrative new drugs and the desire to manufacture costly imports like porcelain, to offset the trade imbalance that was draining European coffers to pay for Asian luxuries.

This new stress on economic profitability subjected the erudite natural history collector to withering scorn. Thomas Shadwell's 1676 play *The Virtuoso* mocked the learned fop Sir Nicholas Gimcrack, whose very name displayed his penchant for shoddy and useless baubles. Shadwell made Gimcrack a clownish latter-day magus who hunts after nature's secrets and sees himself as an adept, like an alchemist. But he is no tragic Faustian hero, just a pedant. He can tell minute differences between specimens, but does this knowledge possess any practical value? "I seldom bring anything to use," Gimcrack confesses, "'tis not my way."[9]

Such pedants were idiots, agreed Judith Drake, a seventeenth-century advocate of sexual egalitarianism. They would sell "an estate in land to purchase one in scallop, conch [and] muscle," she observed in 1696, and abandon "the acquaintance and society of men for that of insects." All the pedant craved was pretty, useless things. If you were a female collector, however, madness was often the charge rather than folly. Eleanor Glanville (née Goodricke) was a wealthy Somerset widow who collected insects, corresponded with prominent naturalists, and exchanged rare butterflies with them. After Glanville died in 1709, her family members contested her will. They cited her lepidopterism as proof of insanity.[10]

Such allegations exploited the ambiguity that surrounded female naturalists. Women who collected were often praised as the epitome of feminine virtue and modesty. Class and wealth often made a difference. Ladies of rank might collect specimens or art, while many women assisted their husbands as scientific collectors. But those who collected specimens and sought to take authorial credit for writing about them in print, notably Maria Sibylla Merian, who published illustrated books on the insects and plants of Surinam, were rare. Eve's corruption of Adam was never far from the Christian mind. Female curiosity was suspicious, questionable, even dangerous.

Enter Sir Hans Sloane: the man who sought to solve the problem of the scientific collector by making collecting about money, not magic, and one of the first collectors who undertook to diagnose what was *wrong* with all those who came before him.

Born an Ulster Protestant in 1660, Sloane moved to London and, after working as a plantation doctor in Jamaica, became one of the wealthiest physicians in the world's fastest-growing city. He used his fortune, and his connections, with single-minded purpose. Becoming president of both the Royal Society and the Royal College of Physicians, he bought up specimens and curiosities from travelers in North America and the Caribbean to South and East Asia. Sloane then persuaded Parliament to buy the collection—one of the largest natural history collections ever assembled—and the British Museum was created to house it in 1759.

Sloane's rise as a collector was meteoric, yet rocky. When he published an essay on some Chinese surgical implements, for example, some questioned just what he really knew about them. Anticipating Jonathan Swift's parody of the Royal Society as the Academy of Lagado in *Gulliver's Travels* (1726), the satirist William King mocked Sloane as a pedant who made vapid pronouncements about worthless trifles. Among the implements Sloane described was a set of ear-pickers. "But pray," King could not resist needling him, "of what use are the China ear-pickers, in the way of knowledge?" To critics, Sloane was all money and no learning, a fool who bought any and every exotic frippery he could lay his hands on. There was no point in Parliament paying for "sharks with one ear" and "spiders as big as geese," complained Horace Walpole, who acted as one of Sloane's executors. "Those who think money the most valuable of all curiosities," he told a friend, "will not be purchasers."[11]

But King and Walpole underestimated Sloane. Sloane got his public museum, although skepticism about the ultimate value of what he collected endured. To some, he was just another ignorant arriviste and a pretentious parvenu: a modern-day Trimalchio. "Doctor Slyboots," William King dubbed him—a wily character who used money to buy status through collections.

Unlike the Renaissance collectors before him, Sloane was no melancholic. He was far too bustling for that and far too interested in the connection between collecting and money, despite what his critics said. When he published a scientific account of the Jamaican cacao plant, for example, he stressed that the reason cacao mattered was the commercial market for chocolate as a food and a medicine. This, Sloane insisted, was the real purpose of natural history collecting: to figure out what species were good for, what they cost, and how to make money off them. The true scientific collector thought like the merchant, not the magus, as Sloane revealed in a highly significant letter he wrote late in life, where he explained his philosophy of collecting.

Writing in 1740 to the Abbé Bignon, librarian to King Louis XIV of France, Sloane explained that he was in the habit of acquiring manuscripts by alchemists and astrologers who employed magic to hunt for treasure, not because he considered them intellectually interesting, but in order to document the utter folly of their credulity. These included the writings of John Dee and Edward Kelley, both of whom Rudolf had invited to his court in Prague in the 1600s. Doctor Sloane came to bury them, not to praise them. He regaled Bignon with tales of incantations, conjurations, and "fumigations" performed with risible solemnity in countless absurd ventures for finding gold. The problem ran rather deeper than mere folly, however, as the good doctor saw it. Sloane diagnosed these estimable magi as suffering from severe "disorders of the mind," mental derangements that could only be cured by significant courses of blood-letting—Sloane's therapeutic stock in trade.[12]

The new British Museum thus began both as a temple of learning to exhibit Sloane's vision of enlightened commercial collecting and a tomb where he aimed to bury the magus for good—by displaying magical curiosities from John Dee's mystical scrying stone to the many Islamic talismans he owned bearing charms to ward off disease and evil spirits. Nature had no mystical code to crack, Sloane averred; Rudolf and Kircher were rank fools who damned themselves not to hell like Faustus, but to the ridicule of learned laughter. Nature was a machine to be taken in hand by manful empiricists, not cowed and prayed to by visionary fops.

And that is why David Wilson made the Museum of Jurassic Technology's spiritual godfather Athanasius Kircher and not Sir Hans Sloane. For a temple of the weird dedicated to the flights of intellectual fancy that were eclipsed by the triumph of modern science, it had to be Kircher, not Sloane, who came back to life in Culver City to embody the romantically lost world of magic as the ultimate countercultural scientific collector—the magician, the mystic, and the Catholic rather than the commercial and empirical Protestant.

But the twist in the tale of Sloane's triumph is that soon after his death, Sloane himself became reviled as a crank and a crackpot. Within just a few decades of the founding of the British Museum, its curators cremated his animal specimens as rotten examples of how not to preserve things. Then, in the nineteenth century, as a variety of new professional scientific disciplines developed, the ideal of an encyclopedic natural history collection became overtaken by a run of astonishing archaeological discoveries: the Rosetta Stone, the Parthenon Marbles, and sculptures from Assyria. Sloane's original collections were scattered across new departments and institutions as a result, including London's Natural History Museum and the British Library, which now house his specimens and manuscripts respectively—and to some extent forgotten.

By the twentieth century, the sober empiricist Sloane began to seem like just the kind of prankster he despised during his lifetime. In the 1970s, one historian referred to him as the "flamboyant eccentric" responsible for the British Museum's "confused beginnings." One of the most striking objects to survive from his collection is the branch of an oak tree bisected by the vertebra of an ox. Sloane was not the only collector to own such a piece, but museum labels from the last century sniffed that his payment of 10 shillings for the specimen was "surprising," calling it the whim of a "fanatical" collector. And when one of Sloane's pharmacopoeia drawers was rescued from a garbage pile back in 1935, the *Daily Mail* ran the headline: "'Magic' Chest [Found] Among Rubbish." Sloane had come full circle: *he* was now the magician and the dupe, the curiosity and the dunce. Sooner or later, it seems, most collectors face the ridicule of posterity and the unforgiving question: *Why on earth did they collect that?* Enlightenment, Sloane's story shows, often lies in the eye of the beholder.[13]

Sloane's commercial vision of scientific utility was not the only one to push the bounds of eighteenth-century collecting. In fact, the founder of the British Museum had no idea that on the other side of the Enlightenment lurked a completely different kind of revolutionary collector. Enter the libertine: someone who dreamed not of scientific order or profit but the freedom to pursue unbridled beauty and pleasure through things, only to plunge back down like a latter-day Faust into the eternal fires of hell and damnation.

CHAPTER FIVE

LIBERTINES AND
TRINKET QUEENS

I do not know where to turn, tempted here, robbed there,
moaning and desperate to buy at one moment and then
when I've bought something—! It is the most intoxicating,
feverish sensation you can think of.

—WILLIAM BECKFORD (UNDATED)

The British collector William Beckford hides in plain sight in among the townhouses and the palaces of Manhattan's Upper East Side. Situated behind the main staircase inside the Metropolitan Museum of Art on Fifth Avenue, Room 542—a hushed shrine to European Decorative Arts—is home to a sparkling rock crystal ewer raised to chest height on a pedestal. The jug has a gold and diamond base and, for its handle, an emerald green dragon with a looping tail and snarling face. This wicked little visage keeps guard over the ewer's contents, with a tongue sticking out as if it's lapping them all for itself. The ewer was made by the Italian craftsman Ferdinand Miseroni around 1680, but the dragon was added more than a century later in the 1800s. There's no mention of Beckford in Room 542, but he bought the piece in 1819, and it's entirely suggestive of his taste and personality: intricate, flashy, pointed, and, it must be said, a little wicked itself.

More Beckford treasures lurk nearby in Room 524. They include a pair of oak writing desks known as secrétaires and fine examples of Japanese lacquer-

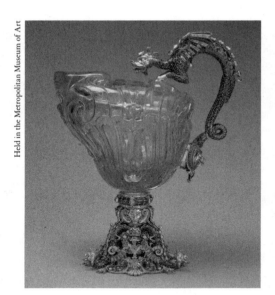

Held in the Metropolitan Museum of Art

*Dragon ewer (seventeenth and nineteenth centuries)
owned by William Beckford: The aristocratic British
libertine, Orientalist scholar, and Gothic fantasist
Beckford (1760–1844) adored intricate mannerist art
in the Rudolfine tradition like this crystal, emerald,
and gold ewer, attributed to Ferdinand Eusebio
Miseroni, crafted in the seventeenth century and
embellished in the nineteenth.*

ware done in gilt and ebony, made in Paris by Jean-Henri Riesner in 1783 for
Queen Marie Antoinette. By contrast with Beckford's grinning green dragon,
the secrétaires are tastefully understated, containing many different compart-
ments, some secret, where the doomed queen hid her correspondence.

The secrétaires are also clues to a personal connection or, rather, the
desire for one. During the French Revolution, Beckford made a pilgrimage
to Paris—"Lucifer's own metropolis," he called it. He stayed through the
Terror of 1793, which witnessed the guillotining of countless aristocrats,
until the rise of Napoleon Bonaparte. Himself a would-be aristocrat, Beckford was heir to his father's Jamaican sugar fortune, so he had money to
spend on collecting, and spend he did. His greatest delight was *objets de
vertu*: bejeweled items of the most astonishing craftsmanship he could find,
like the green dragon ewer. He loved rococo style, the lavishly ornamental

fashion of the ancien régime and was determined, if at all possible, to meet the living embodiment of its captivating excess: Marie Antoinette.[1]

At first, Beckford welcomed the revolution for its sheer fervor, but not for long. He was an aristocrat, not a republican. Shuddering at its violence, he likened the Place de la Révolution (now the Place de la Concorde), site of many executions, to the Temple of Vitzliputzli in Mexico: a place of frightful human sacrifice. Beckford viewed himself, however, as an aesthete and an intellectual above the fray. "What care I for Aristocrates or Democrates," he wrote in 1790, "I am an—Autocrate—determined to make the most of every situation."[2]

According to one account, Beckford managed to tour Marie Antoinette's apartments in 1792, although the queen had already abandoned them. She was executed on October 16, 1793, so Beckford's longed-for audience never happened. There was, however, consolation. The French Revolution combined the Reformation's icon-smashing with the more pragmatic auctioneering of the cash-strapped Puritans. Beckford was, therefore, able to purchase art and furniture owned by the French nobility and cart it off to his English country house, including specimens of the famed Sèvres porcelain that Marie Antoinette collected, as well as the queen's secrétaires, which now reside in the Met.

Beckford yearned to meet the queen and taste the presence of magnificence itself. But rather more links Marie Antoinette and her admirer than polished porcelains and fine fabrics. Both were incarnations of that hero of the Enlightenment, by turns idolized and demonized, who sought pleasure freed from the shackles of traditional morality and religion: the libertine.

The idea of the libertine first emerged during the Reformation. First used by Calvin and others in the sixteenth century against the Catholic Church, the word *libertin* derived from *liberté*. It heaped praise on those who sought liberation from religious dogmatism, superstition, and false belief. By the seventeenth century, the term became increasingly political and was used to refer more broadly to freedom of thought and action. By the time of the French Revolution, the libertine collector became a villainous figure in the tradition of Verres and Charles I: a murderous tyrant driven by hedonistic extravagance. Now, however, the most extravagant tyrant and the cruelest collector appeared in the guise of a woman: Marie Antoinette.

Marie Antoinette was not, however, the first libertine queen. The young woman who became Queen Christina of Sweden defied almost all conventions and expectations from early on in life. Born in 1626 with malformed shoulders, young Christina singularly and to observers' great chagrin adopted the manners of a man, swearing and wearing men's clothes, and refused to marry because she regarded sex with men as degrading and beneath her dignity. She was crowned queen in 1650 but abdicated soon after in 1654, and converted from Protestantism to Catholicism. Five years later, she exiled herself in rather glorious fashion to Rome, making the eternal city her home the rest of her days.

Christina provoked a stream of perturbation for rejecting virtually everything she was born into: her crown, her faith, and not least her body. In 1654, the statesman and spy John Thurloe reported "strange stories of the Swedish queen, with her Amazonian behaviour," gossiping that "nature was mistaken in her, and that she was intended for a man." The obsession with her body proved so enduring that her remains were exhumed as late as 1965 in order to satisfy the long-standing and rather invasive curiosity about what she was. The exhumation, however, resolved little or nothing about the complexity of the remarkable woman who would not be queen.[3]

But there was one inheritance Christina did not renounce: her love of collections. While still in Sweden in 1649, Christina's forces ransacked Catholic Prague and looted many of Rudolf II's mannerist treasures and Italian masters, hauling them back to Stockholm for her pleasure. Like Rudolf, Christina was keenly interested in alchemy, magic, and mysticism and patronized leading natural philosophers including René Descartes. She even took some of her collections to Rome, where she set herself up in Palazzo Riario, now Palazzo Corsini in Trastevere, across the Tiber from the center of the city, surrounding herself with a veritable forest of ancient sculptures.

Some scholars have sought to read Christina's art collection as a series of clues to her true identity. One suggests that she placed her throne in the Palazzo Riario at the spot where a statue of the muse of tragedy Melpomene had been, in order to identify herself with Melpomene's manly attributes. Others argue that Christina aspired to transcend notions of sex and gender altogether, associating herself with the emblem of the phoenix, a potent symbol of androgyny. Christina was neither a lesbian nor a woman who longed to be a man, despite her deep admiration for Alexander the Great, among others, a bronze of whose likeness she owned and whose writings inspired her in her own life. On this view, Christina wanted to be seen not as any kind of *type*, but as an irreducibly idiosyncratic individual—only and endlessly herself.

Christina's contemporaries placed her firmly in the libertine camp. Not only did the erstwhile queen "enjoy almost all advantages of both sexes," one observer commented, she also "loved pleasure and paid attention to neither moderation nor propriety" and was "known to take liberties with many people of different sexes." A French source from the 1660s linked her taste in art to freethinking currents in European culture, including criticism of Catholic clerics and the emergence of philosophically driven forms of pornographic writing, which acted as an incubation chamber for radical new social ideas. Palazzo Riario contained many female nudes Christina reportedly enjoyed using to cock a snoot at visiting prelates. On passing some particularly voluptuous Veroneses and Coreggios with an accompanying cardinal one day, Christina allegedly asked him: "When you see these paintings, Father, don't they make you envious to take part in their pleasures?"[4]

Christina's conversion to Catholicism might seem to indicate that she yearned to embrace conservatism and tradition. But there was nothing conservative about her temper. Indeed, owing to her abdication and personal defiance of custom and expectation, she was to many a quasi-revolutionary figure. Some idolized her as a true freethinking libertine heroine. A century later, however, with discontent about inequality between social classes rising across Europe, celebration turned to repeated accusations of "extravagance." This became a key term of attack on libertine leaders who pursued their own pleasure at the expense of their subjects. Christina's eighteenth-century biographer Jacques Lacombe, for example, denounced the "immense sums" she spent on curiosities and books for her library and "the great disorder in her finances for the gratification of this bibliomania."[5]

In the Enlightenment, the libertine most commonly appeared in the guise of a man or a woman in search of sexual freedom. The notion that sexual propriety is an artificial repression of natural drives found especially powerful expression in the writings of Jean-Jacques Rousseau, who railed against the corruptions of civilization. But it took many forms, including philosophical pornography: the infusion of sexually explicit stories with radical social and political ideas. The anonymous and highly graphic *Thérèse Philosophe* (1748) was inspired by Julien Offray de La Mettrie's scandalous *Man a Machine* (1748), which argued that it was natural for human beings to gratify their lust according to the dictates of nature. Such writers rejected sexual virtue as mere moral vanity and a sure path to personal misery in classic libertine novels, including Choderlos de Laclos's *Les Liaisons Dangereuses* (1782) and the philosophical pornography of the Marquis de Sade at century's end.

One of the most notorious Enlightenment libertines was also, in his way, a collector. The character of Don Juan dates to Tirso de Molina's 1616 play *The Trickster of Seville*. But it was the opera *Don Giovanni*, composed by Wolfgang Amadeus Mozart with a libretto by Lorenzo Da Ponte, first performed in 1787, that immortalized the sexual seducer as a compulsive collector. The story is based on the legendary amorous exploits of the Venetian adventurer Giacomo Casanova, who may have assisted Da Ponte in writing his libretto. One of its most famous sequences is the Catalog aria, where Don Giovanni's servant Leporello pays homage to his master's conquests by singing from the log-book where he tallies them with special brio:

Madamina, il catalogo è questo	Little Madame, this is the catalog
Delle belle che amò il padron mio	Of the beauties my patron has loved
Un catalogo egli è che ho fatt'io	A catalog which I made myself
Osservate, leggete con me	Observe and read with me
In Italia, seicentoquaranta	In Italy, 640
In Alemagna, duecento e trentuna	In Germany, 231
Cento in Francia, in Turchia novantuno	100 in France, in Turkey, 91
Ma in Ispagna, son già mille e tre	But in Spain, already 1,003

Don Giovanni is a true Enlightenment universalist, a libertine collector bent on seducing "women of every rank, of every shape, of every age"—from city girls to countesses, blonde and brunette, fat and thin, tall and short. Casanova was, in actuality, a sensitive lover who cared deeply for the many women whose company he enjoyed. Don Giovanni, by contrast, is indifferent to his conquests and his sexual appetite ultimately rather ambiguous. Is he driven by the ecstasies of passion in fact or the decidedly more bureaucratic satisfaction of cataloging his many paramours? "He conquers the old ones," Leporello suggests, merely "for the pleasure of adding them to the list."[6]

Don Giovanni is the Faust of sex. He must be punished for his transgressions of moral law and in the end is pulled down to hell and eternal damnation by the ghost of the *Commendatore*, the outraged father of one of his lovers, whom he dispatched in a duel. His victims rejoice, insisting this is the fate of all who do evil. But Don Giovanni is also charming and endlessly fascinating. Aesthetically, he is beautiful: Mozart and Da Ponte infuse him with poetry and exquisite music. He is a nobleman who tempts fate by pressing his aristocratic power beyond the limits of all reasonable prerogative on the eve of the revolution that sweeps it so violently away. But this collector of conquests is nonetheless a true Enlightenment hero who dies for defying superstition as much as morality. He perishes when he takes the hand of the *Commendatore*, whom he has already murdered, insisting that ghosts cannot be not real.

In real life, the libertine collector most reviled as a self-absorbed seeker of pleasure materialized in the guise of Marie Antoinette. Since ancient times, male commentators had insisted that women were naturally more covetous of beautiful things than men. Roman debates about sumptuary laws, for example, turned on the idea that female consumers would sap the economy with their love of luxury and vitiate Rome's martial virility. It was a bad omen, Seneca observed, when women began wearing Chinese silks. In China itself, under the Ming, "superfluous" things had worryingly become all the rage. In *The Plum in the Golden Vase*, the feckless Ximen Qing symbolized the effeminate pleasure-seeking of the merchant class as a precursor of the libertine, presaging the fall of the Ming.

In pious form, female curiosity and collecting were deemed eminently becoming impulses among the fairer sex. European women who collected specimens for natural history were seen as godly and devout, women of true faith and suitable modesty. The privileges of rank could also shield ladies from criticisms leveled at other collectors as pedants and cranks. Margaret Bentinck, duchess of Portland, was widely lauded for assembling one of the largest natural history and decorative arts collections in eighteenth-century Britain. And yet, despite such achievements and embodiments of chaste female diligence in the pursuit of natural knowledge, the figure of Eve continued to bedevil the image of the female collector with her aura of carnal seductiveness and lusting after forbidden fruit.

Enter Marie Antoinette—an avid collector and amasser of innumerable outfits, jewels, snuffboxes, Sèvres porcelain, fine furniture, finely bound books, and more besides. It's believed the queen owned a collection of some 348,000 earrings, for example. Marie Antoinette was not merely a consumer of fashion, however, but its greatest imaginable trendsetter. French husbands chafed bitterly at their struggles to pay for the latest royal hairstyles demanded by their wives and daughters alike, inspired by the queen and her train. As a result, much to her eventual chagrin, Marie Antoinette came to epitomize frivolity, greed, and indifference to the suffering of the French people in the eyes of her enemies, who painted her as a colossal burden on the lives of her subjects.

To critics, Marie Antoinette was the "trinket queen" who began each and every day by consulting with her dressmaker Mademoiselle Bertin, her "minister for trinkets." While the French people were laboring under growing hardship and strain, she amused herself by playing cards and redecorating the royal apartments. She even performed in little plays, as though she were acting out one of Jean-Honoré Fragonard's playfully frilly paintings—a bucolic frolic of gardens, swings, and make-believe.[7]

Most historians agree that Marie Antoinette naïvely misjudged the mood of her subjects and failed to grasp how her image was being manipulated by savvy antagonists. The so-called Diamond Necklace Affair made it look as though the queen had demanded an expensive necklace while refusing to pay for it. Her costly refurbishment of the Château de Saint-Cloud added to her reputation for selfishness and corruption. And she failed to realize that by promoting the latest fashions, and in effect the notion that all French women should dress like her, she was undermining the sacred character of the monarchy by making her royal person something for the common people to emulate as though queen and commoners occupied the same station in society. She didn't understand how foppishly outrageous hairdos could foster real political hatred.

But the queen was also framed by circumstance. It did not help that she was a foreigner, originally born in Austria, or that she inherited a pre-existing hostility to extravagant spending by women of status, including Queen Christina, not to mention the former king Louis XV's official mistresses, Madame de Pompadour and Madame du Barry. Well before Marie Antoinette became queen, they were also known for their love of porcelain, snuffboxes, and furniture. In a further twist, because her own husband Louis XVI took no mistress of his own, Marie Antoinette somehow became both queen *and* mistress in the increasingly antagonistic popular mind.

Republican propagandists represented the queen as a demonic incarnation of forces that had to be eradicated to save the French people. Depicting her in a series of pamphlets as a monstrous hybrid of animal and devil, they used the tradition of philosophical pornography to portray her as a whore with many lovers, though ultimately only in love with her own pleasure. Such images democratized the queen in brutal fashion, stripping her of both her clothing and her status, showing her engaged in acts of incest, lesbianism, bestiality, and in orgies. Symbols of her love of luxury were carefully included. She was referred to as one of those "beasts who wear tiaras," and several illustrations featured the ornate furniture she loved to collect, with salacious intimations regarding "sofas soiled by [the] criminal acts [of] tyrants."[8]

Marie Antoinette thus became the most notorious libertine collector of all. But it was the queen's demise that ironically forged her enduring appeal. After her execution, the queen's clothes were donated anonymously to a hospital for ordinary people. The new sartorial democracy dictated they should be worn by commoners who would never even know who owned them. While ascending the gallows, however, the queen had tripped, and one of her shoes came off. That shoe was not thrown away, nor was it donated. Instead, someone got hold of it and kept it. It can now be seen in a museum in the French city of Caen. Every wave of iconoclasm produces its own relics. Executing the queen not only made her immortal. It made everything she touched sacred all over again.

Marie Antoinette's "extravagance" cast a long shadow over the female collectors who came after her, especially the more powerful ones, notably Catherine the Great, empress of Russia. Catherine was a devoted Francophile who collected Sèvres porcelain with a passion via connections to

Madame de Pompadour, even setting up her own porcelain manufactory at Pavlovsk. Catherine acquired the libraries of the philosophes Voltaire and Diderot, whom she patronized and supported, and amassed great numbers of Old Masters, including Titians and Rembrandts. These formed the core collection of the Hermitage Museum in St. Petersburg, which she founded in 1764, part of a grand design to elevate Russian society by civilizing its tastes according to European styles.

Catherine was far more ruthless as a monarch than her French counterpart. She subjected and partitioned Poland and all but suppressed domestic criticism of her reign. She was also a true libertine. Her husband Peter III died when she was young, freeing her to take as many lovers as she pleased. As with Marie Antoinette, however, opponents began casting Catherine's sexual freedom and love of fine objects as signs of corruption. Some suggested that the empress owned her own personal collection of erotica, including graphic furniture carved with phalluses and depictions of fellatio. Others implied she had enjoyed carnal relations with a horse. Politically hostile British cartoons portrayed her as a despot who bedded her own soldiers and accused her of having murdered her husband Peter III—a charge repeated by Horace Walpole, who bitterly resented Catherine for buying up his father's beloved art collection at Houghton Hall in 1779.

After she died in 1796, Catherine's memory became even more fought over. Some depicted her as a heroic virago, others a shameful transvestite. Like Marie Antoinette, she lost control of her image, which became associated with the same tyrannical extravagance that had damned the French queen. After the democratic shockwaves of the French Revolution, the new bourgeoisie frowned upon Catherine's reputed love of pleasure. Posthumously, the empress of Russia became yet another libertine whose avid amorousness offended the rising middle-class's sense of moral propriety. Critics associated her with the Ottoman Turks, renowned for their alleged sensuality, and denounced her for her love of "Asiatic luxury" and "capricious and insatiable licentiousness," as one historian of Russia wrote in 1815.[9]

The legend of Marie Antoinette the libertine collector stretched to Turkey itself. In Istanbul in the early nineteenth century, Hadice the Younger, the sister of Sultan Selim III, became a collector and lover of porcelain. Hadice was also involved in redecorating the palaces along the Bosphorus according to liberalizing new French styles, but was criticized for doing so by conservative forces in Turkish society, who sought to use her as a scapegoat for the economic problems of the Ottoman Empire. They denounced her as an extravagant sensualist. Almost inevitably, at least one modern historian has called her as the Marie Antoinette of Turkey.

The most notorious modern echo of Marie Antoinette, however, is Imelda Marcos. Imelda was the wife of Philippines president Ferdinand Marcos, who held office for more than twenty years until 1986, when he was finally deposed. Marcos was notorious for his financial corruption, plundering the Philippines for his personal profit, and his brutal suppression of dissent. He was among the most mendacious and ruthless political figures of the late twentieth century, a classic kleptocrat who ruled to steal and stole to rule.

But it was Imelda's shoe collection that became the enduring symbol of the Marcos kleptocracy. Reported to number somewhere between 1,000 and 7,500 pairs, the collection led opponents of the regime to rechristen

Shoe collection of Imelda Marcos by Joel Nito (1986): Marcos's (1929–) collection of thousands of shoes, accumulated during her husband Ferdinand's presidency of the Philippines, inspired comparisons with Marie Antoinette, another shoe collector. In both cases, a love of fine objects symbolized feminine cruelty and aristocratic indifference to the suffering of ordinary people.

Imelda "Marie Antoinette, with shoes." Many survive to this day in the Marikina Shoe Museum, just east of Manila. Imelda's shoes are not the only remnants of the Philippines' most infamous old regime. Although her husband is long dead, the Marcos family returned to the center of Philippines politics in 2022, when her son Ferdinand "Bongbong" Romualdez Marcos Jr. attained the presidency.[10]

Don Giovanni was damned. Marie Antoinette guillotined. Catherine reviled. The Enlightenment was in eclipse and the libertine on the run. But what happened to William Beckford, the man who dreamed of meeting the French queen? What became of the libertine after the revolution?

To understand Beckford's life as a collector, we have to go back to before the French Revolution and before he started collecting. In 1781, Beckford threw a spectacular party for his twenty-first birthday at the family estate in Wiltshire named Fonthill Splendens. Here, Beckford hosted an opulent three-day event that indulged his mischievous love of pantomime in the form of an Oriental extravaganza staged by the London set designer Philippe de Loutherbourg. Loutherbourg filled Fonthill with optical projectors and lighting effects, as well as a chorus of castrati and "cabalistic mirrors" said to reveal the future. An Egyptian Hall was set up, as well as a Turkish Room in the style of a seraglio. The affair was a labor of love and a paean to the magical lure of the Far East, which Beckford had read about voraciously in Barthélemy d'Herbelot's *Bibliothèque Orientale* (1697) and the grand fables of the *Arabian Nights*.

Beckford was inspired to invent his own Orientalist fancy in the form of a Gothic novella called *Vathek*, one of the first works of fiction centered on a collector. Beckford wrote it in 1782, in French like a true libertine, before it was published in English as *An Arabian Tale* in 1786. Where real Eastern collectors (Hadice the Younger, for example) were modernizers who collected Western objects and emulated Western styles, thus appearing aligned with the democratic currents unleashed by the French Revolution, Beckford made his Orient medieval and magical. In *Vathek*, he reimagined the life of al-Wathiq Billah (812–47), Caliph of the Abbasid Empire in ninth-century Baghdad, adding details from the life of al-Wathiq's father, Harun al-Rashid, noted for his collections and the gifts he exchanged with the Holy Roman emperor Charlemagne. Beckford identified with his protagonist personally. He sometimes signed his letters *Le Caliphe*; his friend the poet Lord Byron addressed him *as* Vathek.

In Beckford's breathless telling, Vathek is a libertine who engages in "constant consumption." He adores food and women and possesses a palace dedicated to each of the senses. He hosts a feast called "the eternal or unsatiating banquet" and owns a treasury of rarities he calls "the delight of the eyes," with booty from "every corner of the earth . . . in such profusion as to dazzle and confound." They include pictures and objects inspired by the collections of Harun al-Rashid, such as magic lanterns.[11]

Vathek is also an enlightened rationalist. He rejects Islamic moralism and dogma, battling "zealots" in the name of reason (the real al-Wathiq was a devotee of the sciences and a follower of the rationalist Muslim group known as the Mu'tazilites). But Vathek's Enlightenment is double-edged. He carries on like a despot, imprisoning those who defy him and persecuting those who venerate the Qur'an with excessive zeal. His "insolent curiosity" is impious, driving him to seek "the secrets of heaven" for his own gratification. Like Faust, he is *too* curious, wishing to "know every thing, even sciences that did not exist."[12]

Vathek is seduced into pursuing forbidden knowledge by a mysterious Indian merchant named Giaour. Physically hideous and perversely sadistic, Giaour—whose name derives from the Turkish word for *infidel*—bewitches Vathek with a host of magical objects reminiscent of the *Arabian Nights*: slippers that walk by themselves, knives that cut by themselves, and enigmatic gem-encrusted sabers with runic inscriptions, which the caliph becomes determined to decipher. Vathek becomes obsessed with the sabers, as somehow the characters on the swords appear different every day. "The Caliph is out of his senses!" an onlooker cries in dismay. Fearing Giaour has beguiled him, Vathek orders his men to kill the merchant, only for Giaour to morph into a ball that proves impervious to their attacks.[13]

Giaour makes Vathek an offer he cannot refuse. In return for disavowing the prophet Muhammad and giving him the blood of fifty children to drink, Giaour promises Vathek all manner of terrifying powers. These include vast mineral riches from the bowels of the earth; possession of "the

talismans that control the world"; and the crown of Gian Ben Gian, legendary king of the jinn (or genies). Driven on by his remarkably wicked
mother Carathis (the name is based on that of Qaratis, one of al-Wathiq's
concubines), Vathek agrees and, fatefully, abjures Muhammad.[14]

A grotesque slouch toward hell itself ensues. Egged on by Carathis, who
uses a collection of serpents, skeletons, and rhino horns to ward off evil
demons, she and Vathek journey to the depths of the earth with Giaour.
The odyssey climaxes with obscene sublimity in scenes of extraordinary
excess. At first, the travelers witness paradisical visions of plenty: vases
"filled with excellent sherbet" and "a profusion of viands," saffron soups
and lamb *à la crème*, as well as a harem for the caliph's pleasure. Finally,
however, they find themselves in hell, where they encounter the fallen angel
Eblis. Carathis seizes the sacred talismans, only to have her head "corru-
gated with agony" as punishment. Her very heart turns into "a receptacle of
eternal fire." She and Vathek despair at the loss of heaven and are "doomed
to wander in an eternity of unabating anguish." Such, Beckford's narrator
reflects, are the wages of "blind curiosity."[15]

Scholars have naturally read *Vathek* in every imaginable way. To some,
it's tawdry Orientalism, pure and simple, a frightful sublimation of angst
about colonialism and slavery. Others attribute the sense of angst to sexual frustration, and not without reason: another version of the text makes
mention of illicit same-sex love. In its day, however, *Vathek* was regarded
as bravura scholarship, albeit in fictional form, because it was loaded with
scholarly notes. However we read it now, it was an act of genuine adoration
on the author's part for the magical Arabian legends on which he was raised.

And that's the best way to understand *Vathek*. The story of the first epic
collector in literature is not an autobiography, nor a mirror. It's like one of
the magic lanterns at Beckford's birthday party, projecting him into the
person of the caliph so that he could live out his fantasies and fears about
where his curiosity and hedonism might take him. It's not a story about a
real individual with a real interior life, of the kind that dominated Western literature from the nineteenth century onwards, but mythological and
Gothic. Nor is it a confession where the collector reveals his true self, but a
pantomime where the collector dresses up and conceals it.

Vathek renewed the idea there was something fatally wrong with the impulse to collect and that the quest for treasures was the path of obsession and damnation. If Sir Hans Sloane and the savants of the Enlightenment had buried magic as a way of knowing the world scientifically, they had not banished its hold over the imagination. In some ways, they intensified it. The magus was not dead after all, but resurrected as a Gothic antihero, destined to achieve a paradoxical immortality in the age of modern science, as its counterpoint.

Beckford was only twenty-two when he wrote *Vathek*, however. So what happened to the real-life libertine? Beckford was heir to a great West Indian fortune and, for all his aristocratic airs, a nouveau riche. He used much of his fortune to assemble a grand collection in decorative arts, buying from all around the world: exquisite *tazzas*, Chinese porcelains, cabinetry and furniture, Japanese lacquerware, and innumerable specimens of virtuosic craftsmanship, including the dragon ewer now in the Met. Like Rudolf reincarnate, he adored mannerist art: the more intricate, the better.

Beckford was a Protestant who flirted with Catholicism. But, libertine that he was, what appealed to him about religion was its trappings, not its doctrines. In this respect, he was like the Abbé Suger, turned inside out and secularized. He visited Saint Denis in Paris and marveled at the splendor Suger had wrought in his church. But unlike Suger, he felt no need to justify his adoration of jewels and stained glass. To Beckford, beauty was its own divinity.

Beckford married and had children. But in 1784, his reputation was ruined when his relationship with an eighteen-year-old named Christopher "Kitty" Courtenay became public. The affair ended Beckford's ambitions for a peerage and high office (and lends credence to the idea that sexual angst underlies *Vathek*'s sense of dread). The scandal induced him to retreat, like a latter-day Rudolf, into his palatial estate at Fonthill. He even built a wall, reportedly sixteen feet tall and miles long, to encompass the grounds, while adding a medieval tower so monumental, it eventually collapsed. But Beckford was undeterred. When he later moved to Lansdown Crescent in Bath in 1822, he built another tower, and this one still stands, overlooking the Bristol Channel.

Beckford was not pulled down to hell like Don Giovanni or Vathek, nor guillotined like Marie Antoinette. He was more like Queen Christina, seeking to live out his days on his own terms in exile. His early pantomime fantasies faded as he withdrew from society, though he did once entertain Admiral Lord Nelson and William and Lady Emma Hamilton, Nelson's lover. Did Beckford bury himself in his collections behind his high wall? The Swiss writer and theologian Jacques-Henri Meister described the master of Fonthill as a "gloomy and fantastical" hypochondriac, whose "air of melancholy and regret obscures the splendours" of his estate. Yet other visitors encountered a keen gardener and buzzing hedonist still given to gaiety, happy to host tours of his collections.[16]

Employing a host of brokers and agents, Beckford kept collecting over the years. For the caliph of Wiltshire, the act of acquisition was both ecstasy and torment. "I do not know where to turn," he once wrote, "tempted here, robbed there, moaning and desperate to buy at one moment and then when I've bought something—! It is the most intoxicating, feverish sensation you can think of." He bought with abandon. While in Switzerland in 1796–97, he purchased the historian Edward Gibbon's entire personal library just "to have something to read when I passed through Lausanne." He acquired a bust of Caligula owned by Horace Walpole and joined the architect and collector Sir John Soane for candlelit soirées in Soane's museum of antiquities and curiosities at Lincoln's Inn Fields, London. Collecting was in Beckford's blood, a fever he never shook. In his autobiographical fancy *L'Esplendente*, he recorded how "rages" and "furies" moved him to collect many different kinds of object, one leading to the next. As each "passion wore itself out, a violent admiration" for some new novelty invariably ensued.[17]

Beckford was wealthy, but no collector's resources are infinite. He bought at auction, but also sold at auction, eventually running out of money and selling off much of his collection. After selling Fonthill itself, he lived out his final years by tending to what remained of them in Bath. He did not end up like Vathek, but he *felt* like Vathek, tormented by his own desires, yearning for liberation from his passion. He was "retreat[ing]," he wrote to an associate, "like a spider into the midst of his web." Only death would release him from collecting, "this fatal, expensive, ruinous, treacherous, cursèd [*sic*] activity." He died in 1844, after catching cold while out riding one day as he was waiting to peruse yet another auction catalog. Libertine to the end, he refused any last rites.[18]

By the time Beckford died, the world had changed. Three years after his death, the cultural profile of the collector was transformed in Honoré de Balzac's novel *Cousin Pons*. Gone was the Gothic fantasy, replaced by a brutal worldly realism. Damnation and religion were off the table, replaced by struggles over money and fights for middle-class respectability, as aristocratic dreams of Oriental palaces dissolved into the cramped rooms of bourgeois society. As the French Revolution established a new democratic ethos and the Industrial Revolution spawned unprecedented material progress, a profound sense of rupture recast pre-nineteenth-century society as an utterly remote epoch to which the world would never return. As a result, the collector who now sought to preserve that past—hoping to save society's soul in the process—became a doomed Romantic trying to do the impossible in the face of progress, money, and the march of time. Collecting became increasingly democratized. But as large numbers of the bourgeoisie joined in the quest to collect, the ironic fruit of democratization was the beginning of the modern idea that *all* collectors are slightly insane.

CHAPTER SIX

BIBLIOMANIA AND THE ROMANTIC COLLECTOR

When I want a book, it is as a tiger wants a sheep.

—BOOK COLLECTOR QUOTED BY HOLBROOK JACKSON,
ANATOMY OF BIBLIOMANIA (1930)

As bibliophiles will tell you, there's so much more to books than reading them. Owning them; holding them; caressing them even. And yet
some look askance at those who deign to amass libraries without ever crack-
ing a spine. Already by the Renaissance, the *book fool*, as he became known,
was a figure of fun. Sebastian Brant's 1494 satire *Ship of Fools* features one
particularly well-known woodcut by Albrecht Dürer of a goggle-eyed bibliophile who adores his volumes, but never quite gets around to reading
them. At the other end of the spectrum, meanwhile, are those who read too
much. In the picaresque epic *Don Quixote* (1605–15), Miguel de Cervant-
es's eponymous hero is a different kind of book fool: a nobleman who sells
his land and his farms to buy books on his true passion—chivalry. Often
reading when he should be sleeping, Don Quixote devotes his life to reviving the chivalric ideal, convincing his contemporaries as a result that he is
quite mad.

Don Quixote was one of the first great book fools in literature. But by
the eighteenth century, when print became cheaper and books of all kinds
began to be published in unprecedented numbers, the worrying condition

known as *bibliomania* spread just as far and wide. "Don't you have some-thing better to do than . . . to pick up scarce books," the statesman Lord Chesterfield warned his son in 1750. "Take care not to understand editions and title pages too well," he went on, "it always smells of pedantry, and not always of learning." Chesterfield was bent on grooming his son to be a gen-tleman and man of the world, not a useless virtuoso like Sir Nicholas Gim-crack. Pity the fool who loves the outsides of books, he urged, more than their insides. "Beware," he cautioned, "of the *Bibliomanie*."[1]

The notion that book love is an illness caught on. *La bibliomanie* became ubiquitous among the learned in France, but the great modern outbreak of bibliomania erupted in nineteenth-century Britain. The ban-ning of the Jesuit order in 1778 and the French Revolution broke up vast private libraries in France, tossing floods of books onto the open market, where they found many willing buyers across the Channel. Among them were nouveaux riches including William Beckford—an intense bibliophile who, for all his auctions, never sold off his books—but many were landed aristocrats who delighted in rescuing as many orphaned tomes as possible from their defenestrated continental counterparts. They saw themselves as heroes, rescuing fugitive Greek and Roman editions and rare Shakespeare folios for posterity, valiantly preserving Europe's intellectual heritage from oblivion. Others saw them as ignoramuses, paying massive sums for Guten-berg Bibles or rare editions of Boccaccio's *Decameron*, inflating the price for books like the hedge-funders who buy contemporary art today.

The preeminent chronicler of this frenzy was not a nobleman but a com-moner who kept noble company. Born in Calcutta, Thomas Frognall Dib-din was the son of an East India Company mariner. He came to England, got an Oxford education, and hoped to become a lawyer but instead became a deacon in the Anglican Church and a prolific bibliographer, publishing widely on book collecting, libraries, and antiquities. His destiny, however, was to diagnose the foibles of his aristocratic employers. Working for Lord Spencer of Althorp, Dibdin aided and abetted his lordship's book hunting, helping to establish the Roxburgh Club for bibliophiles—the offshoot of a heated 1812 auction that propelled the cost, passion, and profile of the bib-liomaniac life into the stratosphere.

Dibdin first published *Bibliomania, or Book-Madness* in 1809. It recounted the history, the symptoms, and more optimistically, prescribed the "cure" of that terrible affliction. Immensely popular, *Bibliomania* ran to several expanded editions down through the century, each groaning with more satirical footnotes than the last. Taking Robert Burton's *The Anatomy of Melancholy* as his model, Dibdin launched the first full-scale diagnosis of collecting as a disease in Western cultural history, catching up to the Chinese some three centuries after Ming cognoscenti began diagnosing *pĭ*. *Bibliomania* sounded like a joke, read like a joke, and indeed *was* a joke—but it was a historically significant joke. Dibdin was engaged in no less a venture than launching the whimsical modern wheeze that *all* collectors, and not just bibliophiles, are mildly mad, if not somewhat cracked.[2]

But how to define the dreaded bibliomania? The situation was grave, and Dibdin lost little time in proffering his history with diagnoses and prescriptions. Bibliomania actually dated back to ancient Rome, he informed his readers, had flared again in the Renaissance (Dibdin reprinted the image of Dürer's book fool) and was now raging, rife among the nobs of Regency Britain. Book love was a species of monomania, which Dibdin defined as "an excessive attachment to any particular pursuit"—horses, dogs, snuffboxes, suits of armor, or books. Dibdin diagnosed the dead with especial abandon. History's illustrious sufferers included Richard de Bury, tutor to Edward III; Henry VII, whom Dibdin claimed had perished from the affliction; while those great humanists Sir Thomas More and Erasmus he counted "downright bibliomaniacs." The malady had "almost uniformly confined its attacks to the male sex"—with conspicuous exceptions such as Elizabeth I and the heiress Frances Currer—and the "higher and middling classes," spreading rapidly from palace to palace, but leaving laborers and peasants unscathed.[3]

Dibdin looked on with pitying dismay as bibliomania ravaged his contemporaries. The collector Richard Heber's house was "choked" and "suffocated" by heaving tomes. Dibdin's portrait of the bookseller John Bagford was positively haunting, because Bagford could not resist a single volume he came across. His "eyes and his mouth seem to have been always open to express his astonishment at, sometimes, even the most common and contemptible productions." Bagford owned a vast array of title pages and was addicted to immaculate copies above all. As a result, however, his brain had become a tabula rasa, wiped clean by obsession. "His whole mind," Dibdin observed, appalled, "was devoted to book-hunting."[4]

The symptoms of the condition were distressing. Chief among them was a peculiar kind of idolatry, involving the ogling of beautiful spines, spurred on by a "passion for possessing books, not so much to be instructed by them, as to gratify the eye by looking on them." Other telltale signs included the singular proofs of *not* reading: the love of uncut copies, not to mention the additional insanity of leaving books deliberately uncut "merely to please [one's] friends." Then there were the obsessions with illustrated copies and unique copies; the hunger for copies printed on vellum (animal skin); the deepening obsession with first editions; the quest for error-free "true editions"; and the greatest *idée fixe* of the era—the desire for editions printed in Gothic script.[5]

In the end, Dibdin enjoyed describing the malaise far too much to say anything very detailed about how to cure it. It came down to this: try *reading* your books. As Chesterfield told his son: "buy good books, and read them." But that was easier said than done.[6]

What kind of cultural phenomenon *was* bibliomania? It was harmless, of course, a romp of a malady: *pī* as infinite jest, a dignified Ming obsession turned into downright British silliness, little more than wordplay and nomenclatural babble involving the addictive attachment of the prefix *biblio* wherever it might amuse, rolling off the tongue—an endless riff in which book love floated, unmoored, in its own jolly loops of language.

In the process, Dibdin the commoner got his own back on his employers. They had the money to do what he could only dream of: collect. Bibliomania was his lament, dressed up as mock diagnosis, but in reality it was a bibliographer's revenge against his deep-pocketed patrons. It was, however, dainty not derisive, envious not eviscerating. Nor was book love the foible of fops alone. Seemingly anyone could now embrace the bookish way of being, as bibliomania became highly fashionable. In fact, bibliomania became dandyish, associated with the *man-about-town*, that gentleman of fancy in Regency Britain who was epitomized by the London commoner turned aristocratic flaneur Beau Brummell—himself, naturally, an avid collector of fabrics, snuffboxes, and books.

Dibdin delighted in pinning the bibliomaniac label mockingly on his betters. But, like those who suffered from *pĭ* and *pyŏk* before them, writers in the Romantic movement of the early nineteenth century wore the badge of obsession with pride. These Romantics yearned to live, and love, through books. The essayist Charles Lamb kissed his volumes. The critic and poet Leigh Hunt was "wedded" to his. Books, they were convinced, created their own world, and collecting them was what made life worth living. Buying them when you were wealthy was all very well, Lamb wrote, but the rich would never taste the singular ecstasies of buying what you *couldn't* afford. *That* was true collecting. Hunt insisted the book collector was no mere drudge but could rise to the level of genius—at least sometimes. He lionized the Renaissance poet Petrarch, who also rescued rare Latin manuscripts from oblivion, as a "god of the bibliomaniacs." Hunt praised him, in a signal phrase, as "a collector *and* a man of genius, which is a union that does not often happen."[7]

Bibliomania proved as enduring as it was endearing. In 1930, the Liverpool-born journalist and renowned bibliophile Holbrook Jackson published the even more Burtonian *Anatomy of Bibliomania*. Jackson caught a full-blown case of Victorian book love and went word crazy. In more than 500 pages of glorious indulgence, he ranged from discussions of "bibliophily" (the physical love of books, especially their smell) to "bibliotaphs" (those who like to hoard and even bury them). He was convinced that "bibliolatry" was a universal human urge and recounted stories about infants imploring their parents with the request "book please" even before they could read, as though they were Oliver Twist asking for *more*.[8]

Jackson by no means took the "bibliosanity" of his subjects for granted. "How often have I watched a customer turning over the leaves of a Dickens volume," he quoted one bookseller, "as though hypnotized." Some suffered from such grievous "book hunger," they'd do almost anything to gratify their urges, like the "book-ghouls" who mutilated their most treasured editions by making insertions in them. Luckily, however, bibliomania was a "sweet madness," not a ravaging one, a "soothing affliction." Like *pĭ*, this malady was something of an elixir. Jackson waxed lyrical like a Ming poet. What *was* collecting? His answer was one of the most memorable of any era: "Collecting is but writing in water." It is the noble attempt of human beings to grasp the infinity of existence whose futility teaches humility in the face of the absolute.[9]

Jackson had to admit that beneath an often placid exterior, barbaric passions stirred the bibliomaniac soul. Covetousness drove collecting, turning some into unscrupulous "biblioklepts," savage beasts stalking defenseless prey. "When I want a book," one confessed, "it is as a tiger wants a sheep." Never satisfied, they were always on the prowl for their next tome. And there was *always* a next tome.[10]

Gustave Flaubert, who would achieve immortality with the publication of *Madame Bovary* in 1856, had already begun to conjure up this improbably demonic bookish animality when he was only fifteen in a story called "Bibliomania." Published in 1836, the story was apparently based on a real case involving a man named Don Vincente in Aragon, Spain, who stopped at nothing to get the volumes he wanted. Flaubert's telling recounts the life of one Giacomo, the owner of a bookshop in Barcelona. Giacomo is a rather peculiar bookseller: he loves his books so much that he cannot bear to part with them. He gives his soul to them and likes nothing more than to lose himself in his shop. Sometimes he even sleeps on his books. Giacomo, Flaubert suggests, is perhaps more sorcerer than bibliophile.

One day, a young nobleman from Salamanca comes into Giacomo's shop, asking to buy a manuscript called *The Chronicle of Turkey*. A tantalizing battle of wills ensues. The Salamancan says he is studying to become a doctor and a bishop and simply must have the manuscript to complete his studies, hinting he may even become pope if he succeeds. At first Giacomo resists the man's insistent overtures, but he ultimately relents, selling the Salamancan *The Chronicle of Turkey*. In return, the Salamancan sends Giacomo to another bookseller where, to compensate for his loss, he tells him he will find a rare manuscript called *The Mystery of Saint Michael*. When Giacomo finds out that *The Mystery of Saint Michael* has already been sold, however, he is dismayed. He has been tricked.

Subsequently, Giacomo decides he must capture the first book ever printed in Spain—a Latin version of the Christian Bible—and is thrilled when its owner suddenly dies. But he fears that another nemesis, a rival bookseller named Baptisto, will beat him to it, as Baptisto always outbids him. Sure enough, it happens again: Baptisto acquires the Bible. Sometime later, Baptisto's house catches fire. Seizing his chance, Giacomo runs into the burning building and grabs Baptisto's Bible.

Giacomo is then arrested for a series of murders, including Baptisto's, with the motive of stealing his Bible. The twist comes when Giacomo's lawyer produces another copy of the Bible in order to exonerate him in court—Baptisto's was not the only copy, so there was no overwhelming motive to take it. But instead of being delighted at this turn of events, the depth of Giacomo's insanity is revealed. Devastated at the thought that his own copy of the Bible is not unique, Giacomo destroys the lawyer's copy. "I told you truly that [mine] was the only copy in Spain!" Giacomo exclaims. He confesses to various crimes and is sentenced to be executed. For some collectors, it seems, there are indeed fates worse than death – such as having people think you collect mere copies.[11]

If Flaubert imagined the bibliomaniac as a monster, Sir Thomas Phillipps was the real thing. In 1973, the American oil magnate and art collector J. Paul Getty achieved a unique infamy when he refused to pay the ransom demanded by kidnappers who had seized his grandson in Rome. Getty became a proverbial collector-"monster": someone who loved objects (and money) more than people, including his own relatives. Sir Thomas Phillipps, however, was arguably the original collecting monster who sacrificed the happiness of his family, and even the integrity of his collections, because of the sheer ferocity of his urge to accumulate.

Born in 1792 in Manchester, the epicenter of the Industrial Revolution, Phillipps inherited a substantial fortune from his textile manufacturer father, even though he was technically an illegitimate son. Like Sloane and Beckford before him, Phillipps was a nouveau riche (only later did he acquire the rank of baronet) and started collecting and cataloging rare manuscripts while still in his teens during his time at Rugby School. It was only the beginning of what turned out to be the most titanically bibliomaniac career in history. By the end of his life, Phillipps had acquired an astounding 60,000 manuscripts and some 40,000 books, at a cost of roughly £200,000 to £250,000, consuming his father's legacy and racking up mammoth debts in the process. He once wrote in rather alarming capitals: "I WISH TO OWN ONE COPY OF EVERY BOOK IN THE WORLD!!!" Spanning fields such as genealogy, typology, and literature of many kinds, his collections included a host of spectacular items ranging from the earliest known account of the quest for the Holy Grail to writings by Petrarch and an original Babylonian cylinder.[12]

© National Portrait Gallery, London

Sir Thomas Phillipps by Alexander George Tod (ca. 1860s–70s): a man of irascible temper who fought bitterly with his own family over his collections, Phillipps (1792–1872) was heir to an industrial fortune and became the most accomplished yet also most obsessive of Victorian manuscript and book collectors, frequently outbidding the British Museum and other major rivals at auction.

This would have been an extraordinary achievement for any collector, but Phillipps's ambition was propelled by an equally extraordinary animus toward his fellow collectors. Phillipps called his bibliomania his "ardour" and regarded it as his solace, but he collected with a venomous spitefulness that constituted one of his ardor's principal wellsprings. He diagnosed himself a maniac—"a perfect vello-maniac," as he once said, referring to his fondness for manuscripts made of animal hide. He became especially determined to rescue illuminated medieval manuscripts from "villainous" mercenaries who sought to strip their precious metallic contents for profit.[13]

Phillipps was quite notorious in his day. He terrorized Sir Frederic Madden, director of the British Museum, by single-handedly outbidding that august institution at auction (at the time, the museum housed the books and manuscripts that would later compose the British Library). Phillipps's appearance at these auctions signaled a depressing futility for all rivals in attendance, because he was always more than willing to outspend his rivals, no matter what the cost, often inflating prices by bidding exaggeratedly high. The invidious Madden could only observe of his imperious and implacable foe that Phillipps often acquired manuscripts "merely to gratify a selfish and silly feeling," even when he didn't want or need them, "[like] a dog in a manger."[14]

In the end, Madden resigned himself to Phillipps's rivalry, and the two men even became friends of a sort. When Madden visited Phillipps's house, however, and saw for himself how books were strewn everywhere in malodorous disarray, he recoiled at the "sickening" atmosphere that confronted him. Madden finally drew the line on the bitter occasion when Phillipps neglected to commiserate with him on the death of his son. "Has this man no heart?" he asked.[15]

Had Phillipps indeed no heart? That was precisely the question. Phillipps's own family had cause to wonder. After he became estranged from his mother, Phillipps systematically crossed the words *mother* and *son* out of their correspondence. Phillipps did have children of his own but never trusted them with his collections, so he cut them out of his will. They saw him as increasingly deranged. "He is going rather cracked," his daughter observed. When Phillipps's wife had the temerity to criticize his life's work as a collector, he batted her away, replying stubbornly, "I am going on with the old mania of book-buying." Self-aware yet unrelenting, he once signed a letter, "bibliomaniacally and sincerely yours."[16]

So defiant was Phillipps that in the end his collections went neither to his family nor to the general public. Initially, Phillipps tried to reach terms to bequeath his books and manuscripts to the British Museum, but despite the encouragement and support of Benjamin Disraeli, then chancellor of the Exchequer, the effort failed. After Phillipps died in 1872, his will was contested, with the Court of Chancery ruling that his collections were too important to remain locked up and that they should be auctioned off.

The auctions of Phillippsiana that ensued are remarkable for two reasons. Like the great manic collector he was, Phillipps bought such large bundles of material that he himself lost track of their contents, so when they came up for auction, buyers didn't always know what they were bidding for—though, given Phillipps's reputation, they assumed it must be good. In addition, the legal complications surrounding Phillipps's estate meant that these auctions happened not over years but decades and even centuries, and in many different countries including Holland, Belgium, Germany, and the United States. Illustrious buyers included the New York financier J. P. Morgan and the California railway magnate Henry E. Huntington. There were major auctions in 1929, 1946, and 1977, with one of the most recent in 2006. In some strange way, it's almost as though Phillipps never died, or carried on collecting after he died, because he's continued to surprise and astound the world with the range of his treasures.

The doyen of Phillipps studies, Alan Noel Latimer Munby, did not spare his subject with his assessment of the great collector's humanity, or lack thereof, declaring him "vain, selfish, dogmatic, obstinate, litigious and bigoted." Phillipps was not just any old monster, however, but a peculiarly Victorian one, in that he violated some of the ideals his Dickensian era held most sacrosanct: familial relations, sentimental fellow-feeling, and domestic harmony. Instead of keeping his family and collections together under one happy roof, he blew them up with a savagely self-destructive bitterness. His bibliomania was not fond but furious. As such, Phillipps embodied the new ideal then emerging in the nineteenth century of a Romantic collecting self, taken to the extreme of the truly obsessive individual. Phillipps was so determined to make and preserve his collection without help even from his nearest and dearest that, in the end, it fragmented across the globe. More than a Giacomo, Phillipps was the Ahab of collecting: a true monomaniac destined to disappear into the heart of his obsession. His towering will made his collection, then smashed it to smithereens.[17]

Bibliomaniacs could be fond like Dibdin or ferocious like Phillipps. But whatever the passions that drove their collecting, from the cuddly to the cruel, they were all part of the nineteenth century's cult of Romanticism. After the American, French, and Haitian Revolutions declared that governments should be founded on the universal natural rights of the citizen, a new way of looking at human beings emerged: as equal individuals. There was a powerful new idea under the sun: that every member of society possessed a unique, essential, and irreducible selfhood, irrespective of social rank, class, or caste. This was a self, Romantic philosophers insisted, that yearned to explore and express itself, and define its own destiny by thinking *about* itself, its feelings and what those feelings meant. Collecting was to prove one of the most important means of expressing those feelings—and who you *really* were.

Artists and philosophers in Germany, such as Caspar David Friedrich and Johann Wolfgang von Goethe, as well as the British poets Lord Byron, John Keats, and Percy Bysshe Shelley, led this bold new journey of individual self-discovery. They painted stirring pictures of travelers dwarfed by mountains and wrote verse after verse about how nature and history expressed their true feelings. Collectors became Romantics, too. They embraced the idea of a Romantic collecting self: namely, that *all* collectors are in fact Romantics whose collections are expressions of an essential inner identity, rather than mere fashion or convention. Together, over time, Romantic collectors resurrected and deepened the idea, first articulated in Ming China and Chosŏn Korea, that when we see someone's collection, we are looking not just at their things but at the manifestation of a complex and otherwise hidden individual self.

To see how this idea emerged—how the essence of collecting shifted from convention to compulsion—let's return to the case of Sir Hans Sloane. Thousands of guests toured Sloane's collection of curiosities in his London home during the eighteenth century. But none came away with the idea they had glimpsed Sloane's true self because they'd seen his collections. They marveled at his curiosity, his piety, his wealth, and his reach—but none would have thought to say they knew him as an individual or in any intimate or profound way as a result of seeing his objects. This is because Enlightenment collections—and indeed most if not all collections prior to the Romantic era—were assumed to be impersonal: they showed you something about the Creator, and about nature, and quite possibly about someone's taste, but they were not presumed to tell any kind of tale about the collector as an irreducibly singular individual. The link between collecting and personal identity, in all its idiosyncratic glory, had not yet been invented.

Romanticism changed all this by shifting the meaning of collecting from convention to compulsion. In his 1816 novel *The Antiquary*, for example, Sir Walter Scott introduced a character through a description of that character's collection. Early on in the story, we enter the den of the passionately hobbihorsical amateur antiquarian Jonathan Oldbuck in his house Monkbarns on the northeast coast of Scotland. This den, Scott tells the reader, is crammed with "a chaos of maps, engravings, scraps of parchment, bundles of papers, [and] pieces of old armour." Oldbuck's leather seat is ancient and worn, and he possesses many poisonous "volumes of dust" on overcrowded bookshelves—possibly one of the first literary evocations of the proverbial dusty library. A "grim old tapestry" lines the walls, as do portraits of old Scottish heroes. An oak table groans under "a profusion of papers" and "nondescript trinkets and gewgaws." The floor is awash in "miscellaneous trumpery." Don't sit in my chair, Oldbuck warns a friend—it has spurs on it he recently dug up from a bog.[18]

Before we even meet the man himself, Scott is telling us, Oldbuck *is* his collection: a fond mess of relics and papers, a daydream of antiquarian reverie, unmarried and unharried, trammeled by a sublime whimsy of disarray. In theory, Oldbuck's deeply cherished curiosities are genuine artifacts of Scots history and folklore, important specimens of the very fabric of the Scottish past, but are they of any real value beyond their personal meaning as favorites of Oldbuck's, a man who seems to prefer fable to fact? Perhaps not, Scott suggests, given their ramshackle condition. But that made his hero Oldbuck all the more Romantically endearing. It's why readers rather like Oldbuck, too, and why Scott did—in addition to the fact that Oldbuck was a thinly veiled self-portrait of the author. Because, besides becoming one of the most successful, popular, and enduring novelists of all time, Sir Walter Scott was himself a highly serious collector, dedicated to the documentation of almost every aspect of the history and culture of his native land.

Scott lived at a time of tremendous upheaval, when the French and Industrial Revolutions were creating an unprecedented sense of rupture from previous eras. The present was no longer a mere continuation of the past but now stood in sharp contrast to it. The promise of democratic political rights; the impact of new industrial machinery and the factory system

on human labor and natural landscapes; the notion of progress from barbarous violent conflict to a polite and commercial civilization—all these
things fostered a profound sense that the past was alien and *over*, an irrecov-
erable land of yore. This was certainly the case in Scotland, where leading
thinkers in Edinburgh—the "Athens of the North"—penned histories of
civilization that celebrated Scotland's happy evolution from the savage and
rebellious culture of the Highlands to a state of urbane Enlightenment and
modern political economy, spearheaded by Adam Smith's confident vision
of the benefits of free trade in *The Wealth of Nations* (1776).

Scott reacted to these momentous developments by conjuring up a deeply
and alluringly Romantic vision of the past as a never-never land to act as the
ideal counterpoint to the brutally serious business of modernity. His vehicle
was not the historical novel, but the *romance*, infused with legend and lore.
Scott's *Waverley* novels breathed pulsating life into Scottish history through
tales of figures including the outlaw Rob Roy and the chivalrous knight Ivan-
hoe, becoming wildly popular bestsellers as a result. This was why Scott collected historical curiosities, too, many of which remain on display today at
Abbotsford, his house on the banks of the River Tweed in the Scottish Borders: he was documenting the past both as history and as lore. These include
treasures such as Rob Roy's purse, Napoleon's blotter, and a cockade worn by
a French soldier from the battlefield at Waterloo, which Scott took the time
to visit and collect personally. Scott's collecting, in other words, went hand
in hand with his writing as an attempt to memorialize an essential national
identity—some say he invented the very idea of Scotland, while others blast
him for reducing it to Tartan—by dreaming up an irresistibly Romantic past
as an antidote to the march of bourgeois civilization. Realizing that modernity now lent suits of armor the potent charm of fantasy, Scott collected and
curated a nation in his own home with the genius of a true mythologizer.

Oldbuck, then, might appear a fool, muddling his history much of the
time, but he's really a hero. He resists the passage of time and progress
through his bumbling adoration of everything antique. Just as important,
he resists the pull of the profit motive. He's not the sort of bibliomaniac who
amasses books "by force of money," like so many of his contemporaries, but
collects as a labor of love, as when he haggles joyfully for a "bundle of [old]
ballads." Scott makes the same point as Dibdin: big spenders are the real

Photograph by the author, 2023

Entrance Hall of Abbotsford, the home of Sir Walter Scott (1771–1832) in Melrose in the Scottish Borders: Despite his reputation for romanticizing the past though his novels, Scott's home (now a public museum) is crammed with objects relating to Scotland, reflecting his devotion to the collection of objects pertaining to the history and folklore of his native land.

fools. The joy Oldbuck takes in reading from the old broadsides he collects about ghosts (a subject that Scott collected in real life) is pure, not calculating. "On these the antiquary dilated with transport," Scott wrote glowingly. The true collector is never motivated by material gain but by the desire to save a lost world that would otherwise perish.[19]

The most striking collector in Scotland, however, was not Scott but his friend and associate Charles Kirkpatrick Sharpe. Sharpe, or Fitzpatrick Smart as he was also sometimes known, assisted Scott in collecting old Scottish poems and ballads for a multivolume early-nineteenth-century work called *Minstrelsy of the Scottish Border.* Like Scott, Sharpe collected curiosities and books of all kinds. But what stands out about Sharpe is not *what* he collected but what people thought his collections said about him as an individual. In a series of biographical recollections of him published after his death in 1851, Sharpe emerges as one of the greatest embodiments of the Romantic collecting self: someone for whom the meaning of collecting was utterly personal and inescapably idiosyncratic.

Sharpe enjoyed a peculiar kind of notoriety. Descended from a storied family in Dumfriesshire, he became an Oxford-educated society man who associated during his time in London with Queen Caroline (wife of King George IV), Lord Byron, and the French novelist Madame de Staël. He was something of a gossip, a teller of "queer and witty stories"—"Conversation Sharpe," they called him. Not only was he "charmingly antiquated in his manners" but also possessed of a peculiar walk and expressed himself in a "manner and voice [that were] effeminate and odd." He owned two green silk umbrellas one of which, presumably rather large, he called Noah's Ark. Tall and ruddy, he looked like an "old beau clinging to the fashions of his youth," sporting a large overcoat and a billowing neckerchief.[20]

A talented artist who produced books of etchings, Sharpe was a dilettante and a scholar who, like Scott, wrote about witchcraft and demonology as part of Scottish folklore. His work was not popular, commentators observed, because he was unable to "follow the prevailing taste" in art or perhaps simply unwilling to. He was far too self-satisfiedly aristocratic and his style too "fanciful and facetious," all of which made him "a sealed book" to the "vulgar." He didn't want to be popular, he wanted to be himself.[21]

Sharpe was also an antiquarian and the owner of a collection of curiosities at his house in Princes Street opposite Edinburgh Castle. He was a keen buyer, snapping up items from Horace Walpole's Strawberry Hill, for example, which he called his "Strawberries." The collection was maintained by a housekeeper and a maid Sharpe wittily called "Dirt and Destruction." His museum appears to have contained portraits; manuscripts and miniatures; vases and chinaware; a library; suits of armor (by then de rigueur); enamels and statues; chairs and silverware; and the mummy of a mermaid. He talked about them all to his visitors, his tone ranging from "grave to gay, from lively to severe."[22]

Like Scott's collection at Abbotsford, Sharpe's was a treasury of relics of the Scottish past. But there was something new in the way contemporaries described his collection. According to one observer, Sharpe's collections were "all amassed after no particular principle of method of arrangement." Instead, "each article had an atmosphere of association about it which it was pleasant to breath[e], and its story was often more interesting than its intrinsic merit or value," making it "difficult, nay, impossible" to classify the collection "in a word or phrase." When you entered Sharpe's museum, in other words, you entered the very labyrinth of his person in all its singularity.[23]

What united the collection? The sheer fact that it was Sharpe who assembled it and the personal relationship he had with each object. Why did he love this particular item of "unutterably" ugly clothing? Because of some "particular association it had to his wayward fancy." Sharpe operated according to "a principle of selection peculiar and separate from all others, as was his own individuality from other men's. You could not classify his library." Or his walk for that matter: "There was no way [of] defining his peculiar walk save by his own name." Rejecting the latest metropolitan fashions epitomized by Beau Brummell in London, Sharpe was like Old-buck in *The Antiquary*: a dandy out of time who made up his own style and taste—eccentric, even bizarre, but that of a singular human being who was always wholly himself. Here was the new Romantic collecting self on parade: a person who expressed himself against the prevailing winds of progress, fashion, democracy, money, and modernity.[24]

It was the beginning of the modern cult of the *true collector*—the veneration of a new kind of cultural hero who sets aside all motive of gain to collect as a form of authentic self-expression. And the first person to immortalize this ideal in fiction was Honoré de Balzac in *Cousin Pons* (1847), the first realist novel about a collector ever published. Anticipating some of Freud's key ideas about collectors by half a century, Balzac's Pons is the prototype of the collector in the modern imagination: a bourgeois loser who cannot deal with real life, yet a noble martyr to love, beauty, and the integrity of his own soul.

Balzac was born in 1799, in the throes of revolution, war, and French imperial ambition under Napoleon. His father was an artisan and his mother a haberdasher. His own life was a drama of social mobility set against the turbulent backdrop of successive republics and restorations, as the French aristocracy vied with the bourgeoisie for social and political supremacy during the nineteenth century. In his prolific writings, Balzac became a vivid chronicler of French mores through the cycle of stories he called *la comédie humaine*, depicting the passions and foibles of his contemporaries with a piquant vibrancy.

Balzac used the income from his successful career as a writer to become a collector. He was not alone. In the early decades of the new century,

Held in the Metropolitan Museum of Art

Honoré de Balzac's head sculpted in clay by Auguste Rodin (1891): the prodigious Balzac (1799–1850) was himself a spendthrift collector who authored the first great fictional portrait of a collector in Cousin Pons *(1847), anticipating several Freudian themes in his story of a passionate art connoisseur who is a romantic and professional failure but lives through his collection of paintings.*

unprecedented numbers of middle-class people became collectors in France and Britain, acquiring art, antiques, and fine furniture to decorate their houses in the name of respectability and tasteful self-expression. Balzac's own tastes ran to the expensive, including fine art and antiques. A tempestuous personality, possessed of manic ambition and driven by insatiable appetites, he yearned to enter the ranks of the nobility and attempted suicide more than once. He spent lavishly, especially after marrying the Polish aristocrat Ewelina Hańska. Developing a monomania for collecting he struggled mightily to control, he often erred and bought forgeries and sometimes had to sell off acquisitions to raise money, getting Ewelina to bankroll his purchases. "I shall win your confidence sooner or later, in bric-à-brac," he told her in 1846. "Set your mind at rest," he reassured her, "I never yield to any spontaneous fancy." He wasn't quite telling the truth. "Never become a collector," he wrote more honestly elsewhere, echoing William Beckford, or you will be ruled by a "jealous demon."[25]

Sylvain Pons, Balzac's hero in *Cousin Pons*, is a collector, yet bears little resemblance to his creator. A musician by profession, Pons is unlucky in both love and work, so instead finds joy in friendship and his raison d'être in collecting. He lives with his faithful companion Schmucke and pours his soul into acquiring almost 2,000 Old Masters. With the brilliance of a connoisseur, he buys masterpieces for small sums, doing so for love, not gain, refusing ever to sell his collection. It is his "beautiful mistress," Pons explains, his great "compensation" for the romantic and professional disappointments of his life, "a poultice to the soul."[26]

Pons is the poor cousin of a family of nouveau riche industrialists named the Camusots de Marville who are wealthy but have no appreciation for art. They represent the rise of the new bourgeois civilization: keenly acquisitive, yet rather philistine. Pons likes to dine with the Camusots and shares their love of fine food. But when his suggestion of a suitable match for their daughter goes awry, they cut off all relations with him. After this unfortunate social blunder, Pons is taken ill. His condition gets steadily worse over time. Seemingly everyone he knows begins to circle him like vultures, wondering just what will happen to his remarkable art collection should he happen to pass away. The most vulturous of all his acquaintances is his landlady, Madame Cibot, who feigns deep concern for her tenant while cannily plotting with a Jewish art dealer named Elias Magus to take control of Pons's collection.

Pons entrusts his collection to his friend Schmucke, instructing him to bequeath it to a great public museum such as the Louvre. But after Pons finally expires, Schmucke proves a naïve and ineffective legatee, losing control of Pons's legacy through the chicanery and manipulations of others. After Schmucke himself dies, Pons's will is then contested. In the end, his cousins the Camusots de Marville succeed in acquiring his paintings for themselves. They still know nothing about art but, in light of their stunning inheritance, forget their former grievances and remember their poor cousin with new fondness, thrilled to take possession of such valuable paintings.

In Pons, Balzac created the first fully realized modern portrait of a collector, one destined to echo down through Freud and beyond. Pons is not an emperor or a warrior, a magus or a caliph, but a bourgeois. He is not violent or raving or possessed—quite the opposite. Like Oldbuck and Sharpe before him, he is a man out of time: an "archaeological specimen" from the Napoleonic era and an aging dandy whose fashions are out of date. Physically unprepossessing, he suffers from "excessive melancholy." Like his rival Elias Magus and like *all* modern collectors, Balzac suggests, Pons's collecting is a substitute for sex and love, not an extension of them. Balzac describes both men as sexless, yet also "the most impassioned men on the face of the earth." Beneath the collector's placid surface rage formidably repressed passions. Balzac emphasizes this even more with Magus, whose name is a nod to the magical tradition in collecting, but in reality, he's a "Don Juan of the picture-gallery" who lives in a "harem of paintings" and whose otherwise "cold heart" is touched by masterpieces the way "a libertine is roused by the sight of a lovely girl."[27]

Where Beckford made Vathek a pantomime victim of fabulistic torments, Balzac makes us suffer every pang of frustration and disappointment with Pons, as he evolves from lovable loser to sentimental martyr. Above all, Pons is a Romantic everyman who lives, feels, and suffers through his collection and the risk of its potential loss. In a way, it's the threat of that loss that kills him. But, though Pons dies, his collection lives and he through it, as what Balzac calls the true "heroine" of the story outlives him. The paradox—familiar from Pu Songling's tale of the fisherman and the rock and other tales—is that in serving their collections, collectors endure dread, despair, even destruction. What *is* collecting? An act of folly perhaps or just possibly a Christ-like act of self-sacrifice.[28]

Such was the predicament of bourgeois bibliomaniacs and art lovers in the new Romantic era. From Sir Thomas Phillipps to Sylvain Pons, collectors now distinguished themselves as charismatic individuals through a lifetime of passionate acquisition. But the Romantic collecting self was vulnerable. If collecting defined you, and building a collection now meant building your self, could you keep that collection and that self together in a world of social climbing and money grubbing? The Sword of Damocles hanging over the collector was no longer the damnation Verres or Don Giovanni or Vathek faced—it was now the auction hammer. Nobody actually kills Pons. But his death feels like a murder, because control of his collection is so cruelly taken away by a world of schemers who'd do almost anything to seize his treasures.

In the nineteenth century, however, the most charismatic incarnation of the Romantic collecting self was the explorer. As European empires expanded, and technology and travel entered the industrial era, collectors encircled the globe in order to build vast specimen collections for new natural history museums. Explorers journeyed to hazardous places at great personal risk, thrilling readers with the extravagant tales of adventure they published, all in the name of scientific knowledge and civilizational progress. Their dream could not have been more Romantic: seeing nature as a vast unified organism, they collected specimens to assemble a gargantuan catalog of all its contents. But, as what one writer called "the wonderful century" wore on, the naturalist's dream of total cataloging eventually disintegrated, and the collector gradually slipped from religious, imperial, and scientific confidence into doubt, horror, and madness.

CHAPTER SEVEN

☙❀☙

THE GLORY OF
THE NATURALIST

All science is either physics or stamp collecting.

—ATTRIBUTED TO NUCLEAR PHYSICIST
ERNEST RUTHERFORD (1930s)

In South Kensington, West London, the twin spires of the Natural History Museum pierce the sky like those of an Anglican cathedral. That is no coincidence. Designed by the architect Alfred Waterhouse, the museum opened in 1881, a testament to the forces of professionalization and institutionalization in Victorian Britain, yet also a monument to science as a deeply pious pursuit.

Inside stands the statue of one of the world's great scientists. Cast in bronze by Anthony Smith and erected in 2013, it features a man wearing boots and a wide-brimmed hat, with a bag or box hanging off his hip. He sports a cheerfully bushy beard and is adjusting his hat—or maybe hanging on to it. In his right hand he holds a pole, from the end of which dangles a net.

The plaque that accompanies the statue reveals that the explorer in question is a "man of action" and "dressed in his collecting clothes." "Follow his gaze," it invites us, "what has caught his eye?" Nothing less than an Indonesian golden birdwing butterfly: *Ornithoptera croesus*. This is scientific collecting as a mythical act of discovery, virtuous and virginal, featuring the

Anthony Smith, statue of Alfred Russel Wallace (2013), Natural History Museum, London: Wallace (1823–1913) contributed thousands of specimens to the museum and is often overlooked as the co-founder of evolution by natural selection with Charles Darwin, in part because representations like this statue emphasize his work as a field collector rather than a theoretician.

collector as a divine hunter destined to redeem Adam's fall from grace: one who comes in peace for knowledge's sake alone. This is the moment the collector gets just a little closer to God. Perhaps even too close. The Victorian naturalist Charles Kingsley sensed this and worried about it. Collecting was "morally dangerous," Kingsley thought, because it "brings with it the temptation to look on the thing found as your own possession, all but your own creation . . . as if God had not known it for ages since."[1]

But there are no such worries at the Natural History Museum. The plaque explains that the collector featured in the statue was an expert in biogeography—the science of the global distribution of species—and that the museum possesses thousands of the specimens he gathered. Not only this, he pioneered the theory of evolution by natural selection and published a crucial paper on it, "chang[ing] the way we understand the natural world."

The man with the net is not Charles Darwin, however, but his rival and friend Alfred Russel Wallace. Wallace discovered the theory of evolution by natural selection independently of Darwin; his key paper on the subject was presented at a scientific conference in 1858 along with Darwin's work, one year before Darwin shook the foundations of science and religion alike with his authoritative account of evolution in *On the Origin of Species*.

Wallace was a brilliant theorist *and* a great field collector. This is what makes his statue so interesting. Given that he was both theorist and collector, why emphasize the former over the latter? By the same token, Darwin wasn't only a theorist but also collected specimens from an early age, a practice that very much informed his theories. But from portraits like the one that hangs in Christ's College, Cambridge (where he studied), to his own statue inside the Natural History Museum, Darwin is represented time and again as a brain with a beard—a theorist, not a collector.

In reality, many scientists work as both collectors and theorists, who gather data and also interpret it, but we often imagine these two kinds of scientific labor through seemingly irreconcilable personas. Scientists are either great minds (Darwin) or toiling laborers (Wallace), not both. This division of labor tends to assume there's something inferior about *mere* collectors. "All science is either physics or stamp collecting," the nuclear physicist Ernest Rutherford is said to have quipped in the 1930s. *Real* science means paradigm-busting intellectual breakthroughs; everything else is data-filing, pen-pushing, and paper-chasing—busywork for dullards. Collecting is presumed to be the opposite of genius no matter what the field. Recall, for example, the Romantic critic Leigh Hunt's praise for Petrarch as "a collector *and* a man of genius, which is a union that does not often happen." Wallace's career shows that this dichotomy between collecting and genius is false. How, then, did it become so proverbial?[2]

The roots of the puzzle lie deep in early modern science. At the start of the seventeenth century, England's lord chancellor Sir Francis Bacon urged his countrymen to send ships beyond Europe to discover new knowledge and new resources to contend with the growing power of the Spanish and Portuguese Empires. To drive his point home, Bacon penned a fable called the *New Atlantis* (1626), in which he mapped out an ideal division of labor to realize these ambitions. Travelers and "merchants of light" would bring back information and specimens of all kinds, he wrote, for an elite cadre he called the "interpreters of nature," who would explain and exploit the natural world for England's benefit. Collectors, in other words, should be the foot soldiers of science and empire.[3]

Sir Hans Sloane illustrates Bacon's vision well. When Sloane became president of the Royal Society, succeeding Sir Isaac Newton in 1727, some among its Fellows scoffed at the presidency passing from a genius to a pedant, as they saw it. Newton himself, one of them observed, always insisted that attaining the honor of the presidency should require "something more than knowing the name, the shape and obvious qualities of an insect, a pebble, a plant, or a shell." Ironically, the reputation of the scientific collector actually suffered because of the declining belief in magic. Rudolf II and Athanasius Kircher saw themselves as magi versed in nature's arcana. Critics assailed them, but they possessed undeniable grandeur. Empirical collectors, for all their philosophical modesty—or because of it—could more easily be dismissed as mere pedants. Not that Sloane lacked prestige—far from it. When Colonel William Byrd of Virginia asked him to send over some minerals for comparison with American specimens in 1708, Sloane replied that Byrd should rather send *his* minerals from Virginia to London, where Sloane would do the comparing.[4]

In the grand schemes of empire, scientific collectors were seen as second-order laborers. This image of the scientific collector changed dramatically at the turn of the eighteenth to the nineteenth century, however, with the Latin American voyage of Alexander von Humboldt: a modern scientific traveler who was both a heroic collector and a theorist of cosmic proportions.

Humboldt was a hybrid. A Prussian mining engineer by training, he became an expert in the new precision instruments produced at the turn of the century. In an era sometimes called the Second Scientific Revolution, scientists sought to reduce human error by developing improved tools to substitute numerical measurements for verbal accounts of natural phenomena. So when he embarked on a dramatic expedition during 1799–1804 to Venezuela, Cuba, Colombia, Ecuador, Peru, and Mexico, Humboldt brought with him a wide range of devices to gather as much data as possible: thermometers, barometers, electrometers, eudiometers, inclinometers, telescopes, and more.

Humboldt was friends with the polymaths Johann Wolfgang von Goethe and Friedrich Schiller and steeped in Romantic thought and the German scientific tradition known as *naturphilosophie*. These modes of thought emphasized that nature was a vast, complex yet unified organism. To Humboldt, measurement was not a tool to reduce the world to number alone, therefore, but a means of grasping the forces that made the cosmos both coherent and sublime. He possessed not only an eye for detail but also a feeling for the aesthetic beauty of the world. His goal was to use measurement to grasp that beauty, not erase it.

Humboldt's highly popular *Personal Narrative of a Journey to the Equinoctial Regions of the New Continent* (1814–25) was a travelogue filled with lavish descriptions of wild landscape and both his ecstasy and humility on confronting the sublimity of the American continent. Humboldt cast himself as the quintessential Romantic explorer. He described his fatigue and illnesses—later attributing his rheumatism to nights camped out on wet American ground—and astonishing scenes like the time a team of Native Americans in Cumaná, Venezuela, employed stampeding horses to capture dangerous electric eels for him to study. He became *the* Romantic scientist, recording nature's power firsthand through personal experience. To Humboldt, science was akin to poetry—rapturous, majestic, compelling—and he was its poet, regaling his reader with dramatic evocations of the monumental lushness of South American nature that stirred the soul.

There are many portraits of Humboldt. Some render him as an explorer in the wilderness, while others cast him as a library-bound sage after his return to Europe, processing and synthesizing the astonishing quantity of information he collected. Still others portray him as both. Henry Leutemann's drawing dresses Humboldt in a fine jacket and places a book in his hand, while surrounding him with scientific instruments, dead animals, and Native Americans. He's a philosopher in the jungle—an idea that still made sense before the advent of the professional specialized scientist during the middle of the nineteenth century when Darwin and Wallace worked. A natural philosopher who straddled many scientific fields, Humboldt was

Henry Leutemann, "Alexander von Humboldt and Aimé Bonpland in a Jungle Hut by the Orinoco" (1870): This depiction of the Prussian polymath von Humboldt (1769–1859) presents him as a philosopher in the jungle, a rare fusion of the collector and the theoretician in the same persona, before Victorian thinkers recast collecting and theorizing as fundamentally different kinds of scientific activity.

heralded as a universal genius. He epitomized the Romantic collecting self as a man of heroic action yet complex sensibility.

His crowning achievement was *Cosmos*, the multivolume masterpiece he published between 1845 and 1862, and *the* signature statement of Romantic natural philosophy. In it, Humboldt sought to explain how vegetable, animal, and human life varied across the globe, by measuring the local physical conditions that gave rise to different species in different places. Poly-disciplinarity was one of *Cosmos*'s defining characteristics, driven by what Humboldt called his "irresistible impulse to the acquisition of different kinds of knowledge." His, he insisted, was a higher purpose than that of the specialist: grasping "physical phaenomena in their widest mutual connection, and to comprehend nature as a whole." *Cosmos* was no "mere accumulation of unconnected observations of details," he observed. He was no mere collector but a master of the "generalization of ideas," who willed himself to overcome the prejudice that science was sterile and "chill[ed] the feelings." *Cosmos* was thus the apotheosis of Romantic science: a spectacular collection of data to enable one to *feel* the beauty of the ordered universe.[5]

In some ways, however, *Cosmos* marked the end of natural philosophy's

bpk Bildagentur/Art Resource, New York

ambitions to synthesize all of scientific knowledge into a unified statement of poetic truth. Humboldt virtually acknowledged as much when he
mocked himself for "the mad fancy [which] has seized me of representing in a single work the whole material world." His throwaway remark
was one of the first instances of likening the dream of scientific order to a
form of madness—a theme that resounded in the work of one of Humboldt's great admirers, Edgar Allan Poe. *Cosmos* inspired Poe to publish
Eureka, his own cosmological treatise about the origins of the universe, in
1848. He dedicated it to Humboldt and, echoing his hero, defined it as "a
poem" that reached beyond mere facts for "those who feel rather than those
who think."[6]

Eureka was never acclaimed by the scientific community, who saw folly
in its ambition rather than genius. Far more significant among Humboldt's
followers was the inspiration he provided young Charles Darwin. Born in
1809—the same year as Poe—Darwin started collecting specimens, shells,
and coins at the age of eight. This "passion for collecting," he later reflected,
was "clearly innate." Like his hero Humboldt, Darwin thought science
deeply poetic. "No poet ever felt more delight at seeing his first poem published," he wrote, than he did at first seeing "the magic words, 'captured by
C. Darwin, Esq.'" He soon developed a love of hunting, too. As an affluent
young gentleman, he read guides to shooting, learned taxidermy, and in a
single two-month period once killed 177 hares, pheasants, and partridges.
He subsequently rejected studying anatomical dissection at the University of Edinburgh, however, in part because he could not stand the sight of
blood, even though he still thought hunting "bliss."[7]

After abandoning a potential medical career, young Charles studied natural history at Cambridge, where he first learned about the new ideas that
were challenging the literal truth of the book of Genesis. By the later eighteenth century, naturalists led by the Comte de Buffon and Jean-Baptiste
Lamarck in France had begun to speculate about the effects of climate and
diet on the global variation of species through the inheritance of acquired
characteristics, as Lamarck put it. At the Muséum national d'Histoire
naturelle in Paris, the comparative anatomist Georges Cuvier presided over
an ever-expanding collection of animal specimens. According to the ancient
Aristotelian idea of the Chain of Being, the universe consisted of beings of

descending yet fixed complexity—from God to mollusks via man. But new disciplines like geology were beginning to regard nature as an entity that changed over time rather than remaining the same, though no one theory could account for such change. The geologist Sir Charles Lyell favored a gradualist explanation known as "uniformitarianism," while Cuvier preferred a theory of ruptures or "catastrophism," suggesting species could even disappear altogether.

Darwin began tackling the puzzle of explaining biological change over time by emulating Humboldt's voyage to South America, sailing on HMS *Beagle* as ship's naturalist in 1831. Carrying a copy of his hero's *Personal Narrative* with him, he marveled at its "rare union of poetry with science." He'd publish his own *Voyage of the Beagle* eight years later. In it, Darwin copied Humboldt's style of Romantic scientific adventure, describing how he once "crawl[ed] close along the ground" to kill a buck near Maldonado, Uruguay, as well as the "indescribable" odor it gave off "whilst [I was] skinning the specimen." But Darwin also used his specimen hunts as grist for theoretical speculation. He compared some armadillo-like remains he found in a Uruguayan river to some specimens in Argentina, seeing them as clues to the traits of South American animals in a former era. He later claimed the entire theory behind the book he published on coral reefs in 1842 had been thought out on South America's west coast, before he saw or collected a single coral branch.[8]

As the years passed, Darwin's views on killing animals for science shifted. After "consulting my sister," he wrote, "I concluded it was not right to kill insects for the sake of making a collection." Both socially and intellectually, he came to see the taking of animal life as beneath him. "The pleasure of observing and reasoning was a much higher one than that of skill and sport," he decided, poking fun at himself: "the primeval instincts of the barbarian slowly yielded to the acquired tastes of the civilized man." He found shooting got in the way of observing, so he paid servants to do it for him, elevating himself to the status of gentleman-naturalist, focusing on classification and taxonomy instead.[9]

Darwin's account of evolution by natural selection in the *Origin of Species* is one of the greatest theoretical achievements in the history of science. But this theory was still the achievement of a collector. Even after swapping the adventures of the Pacific Ocean for the calm of Down House in Kent, Darwin "[n]ever intermit[ted] collecting facts bearing on the origin of species." In part, he collected facts rather than specimens in later life because he was often ill, suffering headaches, palpitations, and insomnia. Collecting information allowed a debilitated Darwin to keep working and keep thinking. His models included Thomas Henry Buckle, whose works of history were based on a prodigious system of collecting facts, which relied on indexing the many books Buckle scoured. Darwin once asked Buckle just how he knew which facts would prove useful? One develops an instinct, Buckle replied. Following his example, based on "true Baconian principles," Darwin claimed to collect pure data "without any theory," delaying publication of his ideas for decades because he always craved more information to justify them.[10]

Ironically, however, Darwin became one of the first writers to reflect on the damage collecting can do to the self. Looking back in his posthumously published *Autobiography* (1887), Darwin credited himself with "industry in observing and collecting facts," combined with "common sense" and "invention." But sorting information had produced a "curious and lamentable loss of the higher aesthetic tastes," he believed. Into his thirties, he found "intense delight" in Milton, Byron, and Shakespeare, "but now for many years I cannot endure to read a line of poetry," he confessed. Shakespeare "nauseated" him and he'd "lost any taste for pictures or music"—popular novels became his only entertainment. "My mind," he concluded ruefully, "seems to have become a kind of machine for grinding general laws out of large collections of facts, but why this should have caused the atrophy of that part of the brain alone, on which the higher tastes depend, I cannot conceive."[11]

He went further in his lamentation. "The loss of these tastes is a loss of happiness, and may possibly be injurious to the intellect, and more probably to the moral character, by enfeebling the emotional part of our nature." Something had gone wrong with the finest scientific mind of the century. In the hour of Victorian science's most dramatic triumph, its greatest architect found he had destroyed Humboldt's dream of science as poetry, and his own sense of beauty, even morality. It was a key statement, destined to be repeated: the scientific collector is stunted in some way, intellectually and/or emotionally, by the grindingly repetitive work of voluminous fact gathering and analysis.[12]

As Darwin's theories wrought their momentous impact, his work as a collector tended to become obscured. The cultural logic of Victorian science dictated that, by definition, a genius could not be a mere compiler. The collector became *the* proverbial drudge. Later works recounting the great cultural debates of the day, notably Edmund Gosse's memoir *Father and Son* (1907), underscored the point. In it, Gosse recounted his conflict over Darwinian evolution with his father, Philip Henry Gosse, a well-respected naturalist who took young Edmund collecting in the picturesque tidal pools of the Devonshire coast in southeast England, wading into the water to gather specimens. Philip produced many pictures of aquatic specimens in particular and became a leading promoter of the domestic Victorian craze for the aquarium, which became the fixture of many a sitting room.

As an evangelical Christian, however, Philip could not bring himself to accept Darwin's theories. Edmund considered his father "a humble slave of revelation" and guilty of a "failure in theorizing." He marveled that his was "a mind so acute and at the same time so narrow." It was all to do with collecting. As "a collector of facts and marshaller of observations, he had not a rival in that age," indeed, "his very absence of imagination aided him in this work." Unlike Humboldt or Darwin, however, Philip was utterly incapable "of forming broad generalizations and of escaping in a vast survey from the troublesome pettiness of detail." A great collector he might be, attentive to the minutest detail of God's creation. But as such he would never grasp the larger truths of nature, Edmund concluded, owing to the "pettiness" of his mind and soul—the pettiness of a collector.[13]

Darwin's collecting helped transform Victorian science. But ironically, his theoretical achievements had the effect of splitting the Romantic scientist in two, by destroying his own sense of nature's beauty. In the cultural imagination, scientific collectors were becoming far worse than pedants. Humboldt may have joked that his Faustian ambition to see nature whole as a natural philosopher was a "mad fancy," but scientific specialization and professionalization—along with religious dogma—now made collectors seem impervious to change and blind to truth.

The theme of unity struck such a deep chord in the Romantic imagination because of the many perceived threats to it. To Romantics, it seemed, some wholeness or essence was in danger of being tragically lost at almost every turn. The menace Humboldt and Poe believed professional specialization posed to the unity of scientific truth was only one instance of this dilemma.

Artistic and archaeological looting provoked outraged laments that nations who were deprived of their cultural patrimony by foreign powers were no longer whole and would not be whole again until that patrimony was restored to them. In 1796, a veritable era of loot and loss was inaugurated when Napoleon Bonaparte's forces invaded Italy, plundered its art and antiquities, and carted them back to France. The French rejoiced at their dramatic seizures as an epoch-making coup for Europe's rising power. "Rome is no longer in Rome," the French are said to have sung, "it is all in Paris," imagining their city as the new cultural capital of the world. To the critic Quatremère de Quincy, however, Napoleon was little more than a latter-day Verres, whose "Verrine lust" for art he decried as a crime against knowledge because he removed works of art from their original context. Scattering Italian masterpieces across different countries would make it impossible to comprehend them properly, Quatremère insisted. What he called the "genius of tyranny" had wrought a brutal "dismemberment" that made it impossible to appreciate art when seen out of place.[14]

The most notorious act of dismemberment took place in 1801, when the Scottish diplomat and collector Thomas Bruce, Lord Elgin, removed marble sculptures from the frieze adorning the Parthenon in Athens. Elgin brought the marbles back to England, then sold them to the British Museum. The marbles came to be praised by the artist Benjamin Haydon as "the finest things on earth" and they soon became heralded as the pinnacle of aesthetic achievement in all of classical civilization.[15]

Elgin, by contrast, achieved a unique infamy. His most outspoken critic was neither Greek nor Turkish but the Romantic poet Lord Byron. It was no coincidence that Byron was a great admirer of Humboldt's and shared his anti-imperialist politics. He excoriated Elgin's actions as a moral outrage. Righteous judgment flowed through his pen like lava from a volcano. "Barren" of mind and "hard" of heart, Byron wrote in his Romantic narrative poem *Childe Harold's Pilgrimage*, Elgin had "rive[n] what Goth, and Turk, and Time hath spared." Like Quatremère's condemnation of Napoleon, he emphasized the sin of separation: Elgin had put asunder that which was destined to be together, violating the Romantic credo of wholeness, essence, and natural belonging. By so doing, he claimed, Elgin had in fact cursed himself, which the facts of the Scotsman's life strangely seemed to bear out. On returning to England from Greece, Elgin's wife left him, he was plagued by financial problems—forcing him to sell the marbles—and his nose became disfigured by disease. "Noseless himself," Byron mocked him, "he brings home noseless blocks, / To show what time has done and what the pox."[16]

The lore of the collector's curse was to deepen during the course of the nineteenth century as Europeans came to wield power over many parts of the world and place their treasures in their museums. But what about the naturalists who scoured the globe for exotic plants and animals in the age of universal survey collecting for natural history museums: Were they regarded as looters of the biodiversity of the Americas, Africa, and Asia?

For most of the Victorian era, Western naturalists appeared highly confident of their right to collect specimens anywhere in the world. Reared on spiritual primers, notably Anglican clergyman William Paley's *Natural Theology* (1802), they were driven by the conviction that the scientific study of nature was a form of religious devotion, which more than justified its collection, possession, and display. On the domestic front, the burgeoning middle classes of the industrial era delighted in gardening, keeping live plants in terrariums and fish in aquariums. Natural history tourism included coastal holidays featuring specimen hunting and taxidermy. Dioramas of birds under glass became a symbol of domestic Victorian scientific bliss. The family that stuffed together prayed together and stayed together.

But even some of the greatest collectors harbored intimations of disquiet at their activities. While traveling in Chile, Darwin witnessed an argument over his right to make collections of local specimens. In the *Voyage of the Beagle*, he recorded an occasion where a German man asked an inhabitant of Chile what he "thought of the King of England sending out a collector to their country, to pick up lizards and beetles?" "I do not like it," the Chilean replied. "If one of us were to go and do such things in England, do you not think the King of England would very soon send us out of his country?" Darwin evidently recounted the story because he found it amusing, but it registered an awareness that some questioned his right to collect.[17]

There was in fact a long tradition of local skepticism at European natural history collecting. "I have been suspected for one that studys [*sic*] witchcraft [and] necromancy," the diplomat Jezreel Jones reported in 1701 when he sent plants from Cadiz back to the apothecary James Petiver (a friend of Sir Hans Sloane) in London. Jones claimed those who saw him chasing butterflies and picking plants "thought him a madman." On the Pacific island of Tahiti in 1792, where British mariners had collected specimens and objects since Captain Cook's first voyage in 1769, naval officer George Tobin recorded that the islanders "laughed at the avidity with which such collections were made." At the turn of the twentieth century, botanical explorers including the renowned Ernest Henry "Chinese" Wilson documented vast quantities of Chinese flora with the help of paid local laborers, whom Wilson praised as "faithful, intelligent, reliable, cheerful under adverse circumstances, and always willing to give their best." The Chinese authorities, however, threatened to punish those who assisted British collectors while laughing at those collectors' refusal to be carried in sedan chairs, out of a desire to experience the Chinese countryside as manfully as possible.[18]

Alfred Russel Wallace was particularly conscious of indigenous peoples' misgivings at the intrusion of European collectors. "Wherever I went dogs barked, children screamed, women ran and men stared with astonishment," he observed on his grand collecting voyage through Southeast Asia in 1854–62. Wallace was sure locals regarded him as "some strange and terrible cannibal monster." Such statements might appear to be simple chauvinism: *the natives think us magicians or maniacs because they do not understand our science.* After all, the nineteenth century saw an unprecedented hardening of scientific racism in light of Western industrial, financial, and imperial superiority. This meant most Europeans never questioned their right to collect exotic specimens in the name of religious devotion or—after Darwinian evolution eroded Christian faith—science and progress.[19]

Wallace, however, was more far more complex than this. His published travelogue *The Malay Archipelago* (1869) was a gripping adventure story that portrayed the act of collecting with visionary ecstasy as a sacred scientific quest. "I trembled with excitement as I saw it come majestically toward me," he wrote of the *Ornithoptera* butterfly in the Aru Islands near New Guinea. "[I] could hardly believe I had really obtained it till I had taken it out of my net and gazed upon its gorgeous wings of velvety black and brilliant green." On the occasion he laid eyes on the bird of paradise—once thought to be mythical—he was nearly overcome by emotion and practically swooned. "In about two months," he exulted, "I obtained no less than 700 species of beetles, a large proportion of which were quite new." The ecstatic sentiments Wallace expressed redeemed all the suffering he had to endure. Once, when he had dysentery and a fever, his mouth was so sore he couldn't eat solids for days. Sand flies, he wrote another time, "penetrat[ed] to every part of my body." Like Humboldt, he martyred himself for science and never despaired—at least not on the page.[20]

In total, Wallace is thought to have collected about 125,000 specimens. Unlike Darwin, who was a wealthy gentleman, he lacked financial independence, so he collected for money—a difference that further explains why Darwin appears in portraits as a brain with a beard and Wallace the man with a net. Wallace's collecting was part of international efforts to build up universal survey collections in natural history museums. Like all naturalists, he did not collect alone but relied on others. These included fellow travelers from Europe, but mostly Asian islanders, including a young Malay man who became known as "Ali Wallace" and who may have taken as many as 5,000 specimens for him. Wallace didn't question his right to collect but did acknowledge that locals objected. "My pursuits were of course utterly beyond their comprehension," he wrote of the inhabitants of Bouru Island, Indonesia. "They continually asked me what white people did with the birds and insects I took so much care to preserve" and why he valued "small ugly insects." According to Wallace, they concluded "there must be some medical or magical use for them which I kept a profound secret." An old man in the Aru Islands imagined Wallace's specimens all came back to life again after being collected. The collector as magus was back—this time as a plunderer of native habitats. "I was set down as a conjuror," Wallace wrote.[21]

Instead of ignoring such skepticism, Wallace began to see that collecting could in fact do harm. He became an anti-imperialist who noted that Western encroachment was eroding traditional ecological habitats. Realizing that birds of paradise and many other species were becoming harder to obtain, he understood why locals started concealing their locations. In time, Wallace became a socialist, antimilitarist, and opponent of the racial doctrines of eugenics, criticizing both domestic and imperial exploitation. "The wealth and knowledge and culture of the few do not constitute civilization," he concluded, "and do not of themselves advance us towards the 'perfect social state.' Our vast manufacturing system," he went on, "our gigantic commerce, our crowded towns and cities, support and continually renew a mass of human misery and crime absolutely greater than has ever existed before." In his book *The Wonderful Century* (1898), Wallace lamented the "plunder of the earth" by the world's great powers and judged that the Victorian era was one of both "progress and retrogression."[22]

Armies of specimen hunters drove the heroic age of survey collecting—an attempt to catalog nature on a worldwide scale. The American Museum of Natural History (AMNH), founded in New York in 1869, employed backwoodsmen for the purpose. American hunter-naturalists epitomized by John James Audubon were an ideal combination of "scientific accuracy" and "rude lore," judged the explorer Charles Wilkins Webber. They were rugged frontiersmen in the service of science, and there were many frontiers*women*, too. Defying Victorian truisms that sought to confine ladies to domestic pursuits, many took to the field. Fannie Chapman assisted her husband and AMNH ornithologist Frank Chapman on bird-collecting expeditions from Canada to Tierra del Fuego. The Hawaiian sugar heiress Annie Alexander collected birds and fossils before founding the Museum of Vertebrate Zoology at the University of California. And the Prussian naturalist Emilie Snethlage led expeditions in Amazonia from 1905 to 1917, collecting 10,000 birds and mammals for Brazil's National Museum in Rio de Janeiro, once stoically amputating her own finger after she was attacked by piranhas.

For some, collecting, like hunting, offered a deeper promise of spiritual renewal. Big-game hunters had long insisted that confronting wild animals revealed one's character and proved one's mettle. This ethos shaped collecting and display, too, for example in Carl Akeley's diorama of stuffed African gorillas that stare directly out at the viewer in the AMNH's Hall of African Mammals—a magnificent re-creation of the mythical moment in which hunter and prey lock eyes.

To others, however, commercialized collecting for museums perverted the spiritual nobility of the hunt. "This miserable collecting," Frank Chapman complained in 1890, "it is the curse of all higher feeling." Specimen hunting for museums wasn't about skill or sport, the hunter's knowledge or communion with his prey, but just a business, where what counted were numbers. "Unless you have tried it," Chapman rued, "you cannot imagine what a difference there is between collecting for a museum or yourself. There is just exactly the difference between market shooting or shooting for pleasure. Notes on habits has [sic] no value at all in dollars and cents." A British taxonomist concurred two years later: "The glory of the field naturalist has departed."[23]

The early twentieth century signaled the beginning of the end for both the hunter and the survey collector. The days of Victorian administrators amassing animal heads and skins as trophies of imperial dominion, and the many thousands of specimens captured by commercial specimen hunters, were numbered. Anti-vivisectionist campaigners argued with increasing force that cruelty to animals was morally wrong, while the new movement known as conservationism responded to the depletion of animal populations by pushing to restrict both hunting and collecting. Zoology shifted from an emphasis on killing large numbers of animals for museums to preserving living creatures for observation. Like Wallace, even the Gosses of the world began to realize that the Victorian craze for such innocent-seeming pastimes as storming tidal pools had led an "army of collectors" to ravage "the fairy paradise" of nature.[24]

The result was a paradox of environmental progress. The collector morphed from nature's plunderer into its steward, often depriving common people and indigenous hunters of access to their traditional prey—all in the name of conservationism. Some elite figures including U.S. president Teddy Roosevelt still combined the virtues of the hunter and the collector. A keen naturalist and collector, Roosevelt continued to hunt as a pastime, but only because he enjoyed the moral authority of being a leading conservationist who helped create America's national parks. Because entire species including the bison and passenger pigeon had recently gone extinct, scientists would now kill only selectively to document species. By the middle of the twentieth century, therefore, naturalists were shooting animals with cameras more than guns and declaring that the age of subsistence hunting was over. Many were colonials, for example the British administrators who insisted they must preserve African wildlife from the people of the African continent, in order to defend nature itself.

As attitudes changed at the turn of the twentieth century, the image of natural history began to darken from a sacred hunt to one of disturbing slaughter. Dead animals could symbolize salvation, innocence, even redemption. In Gustave Flaubert's deeply affecting story "A Simple Heart" (1876), a devout woman named Félicité finds solace in a parrot named Loulou. Worn down by her unhappy existence, Félicité is sustained by Loulou's companionship, even *after* the bird dies. She has him stuffed and preserved by a local chemist and he becomes a sacred figure: the center of the shrine that is her room, filled with rosaries and other religious objects, where she prays to him. She places a picture of the dove representing the Holy Spirit next to Loulou and is amazed by the resemblance. By the time Félicité catches pneumonia and nears her own end, Loulou is rotting away, eaten by maggots. But in Félicité's eyes, he remains beautiful and glorious—her redeemer. She dies imagining a giant parrot welcoming her into heaven.

Science's stuffed animals, however, began to symbolize damnation more than redemption. In 1881, the French magazine *Le Gaulois* published a short story called "At the Natural History Museum" by Flaubert's protégé Guy de Maupassant. Maupassant is best known for his cutting stories of Parisian high society, especially *Bel Ami*, but he was far more than a denizen of the *beau monde*. Starting in the 1870s, he attended Jean-Marie Charcot's lectures on hypnosis at La Salpêtrière Hospital, which featured demonstrations of "hysterical" female patients, as would Sigmund Freud a decade later. Maupassant became fascinated by psychiatry, wrote about mesmerism, experimented with hallucinogenic drugs, and wrote about his hallucinations. He also traveled to Algeria and became a critic of French colonial policy in North Africa. He died after spending time in an insane asylum.

His highly curious and obscure tale "At the Natural History Museum" features an imaginary tour of the great Paris science museum with the real Georges Pouchet, Cuvier's successor as professor of comparative anatomy, whom Maupassant knew. In the story, Maupassant's narrator hasn't been back to the museum since he was a child, and Pouchet shows him around in an encounter that proves rich in "revelations about the unknown underside of being."[25]

Pouchet shows his guest all manner of specimens, from monkeys and antelopes to elephants and rhinoceroses. They all look rather jolly to the visitor, if also a tad monstrous. The sight of pelicans, however, calls to mind an episode of sheer terror, he says. He recounts a story involving a man and a woman who happened to fall asleep in an aquarium at Le Havre. When they woke up, the couple found every creature before them dreadfully magnified by the "hellish glow" of a full moon and soon found themselves under attack from a ferocious pelican, who pecked at them like the devil himself, almost killing them in the process.

Pouchet and Maupassant's narrator make their way into the laboratory of comparative zoology, where Pouchet shows him a huge cabinet of bones, carcasses, and the remains of different animals. All is bloody and there is a foul stench of macerated flesh. Pouchet seems increasingly perverse and macabre in the pleasure he takes from the gore, "rubbing his hands like monomaniac collectors when they open their bibelot cupboards," showing his guest a series of monstrous whale fetuses.

The two men then enter a sinister building resembling a morgue, where a rotten and decomposed head looks out at them from under water. This is where dead animals are skinned. There is also a building of "leftovers": miscellaneous bones as if they'd been gathered up from a battlefield. This, Pouchet proudly states, is where provincial savants come for spare parts to complete their collections. Finally, the two men visit a cellar filled with grimacing creatures trapped in a sort of "animal purgatory." Among the remains is a mastodon who "waits for his day of deliverance."

Scientists, Maupassant's narrator concludes, will always pursue the unknown. But in doing so, they are not constructing a temple of knowledge, as the twin spires of London's Natural History Museum might suggest. Instead, they are building "the strange and sinister museum of a butcher who is both a collector and a madman." How Maupassant came to see natural history collecting as a scene of murderous horror is not entirely clear, though his interest in psychology, use of drugs, anticolonial politics, and personal troubles may all have played some role. One thing, however, is certain. His rejection of science's claims to reason and progress was but one manifestation of a deepening current of antimodernist thinking that would soon find expression in a range of major cultural movements, from psychoanalysis to surrealism.

As this revolution in sensibilities unfolded, the heroic stoicism of explorers from Humboldt to Wallace began to drift into doubt, insanity, and horror. The Romantic collecting self was disintegrating, sometimes literally. In 1872, the German naturalist, anthropologist, and South American traveler Carl Appun—endorsed by Humboldt himself—died suddenly when he spilled sulfuric acid on his face from the bottle that he kept at his bedside to repel attacks from Indians. The collector was now entering the heart of darkness, as Joseph Conrad called his 1899 novella. In an early scene in that story, Conrad—whose favorite bedside book was Wallace's *Malay Archipelago*—sends his narrator Marlow to a doctor who measures his head as a polite phrenological formality before he departs for the Belgian Congo. When Marlow asks whether the doctor plans to measure him again on returning, the doctor replies there is no point: "The changes take place inside, you know." Collectors were becoming psychologically interesting and increasingly troubled, none more so than the seemingly civilized dandies of the fin de siècle who, for all their learning and sophistication, were teetering on the brink of madness and murder.[26]

CHAPTER EIGHT

DECADENTS AND DEADLY DANDIES

*There's something horrible ... in snatching this and that
away from its real home and hanging it on a wall of
priceless damask made for somewhere else, above furniture
higgledipiggled from other places, strewn with objets d'art
ravished from still other realms ... that seem as if they were
bleeding to death in those dreary super-museums.*

—MARY BERENSON AFTER VISITING
ISABELLA STEWART GARDNER (1920)

Imagine a collector who simply adores Oriental rugs. Now, imagine one of these rugs, lovingly woven from yellow and plum-colored wool, is his particular favorite. This collector is an obsessive and he becomes fixated with the idea that he needs to bring out the rug's colors more, because they look dull for some reason. Being a great eccentric, he owns a pet tortoise. One day, the collector sets his pet down on the rug, thinking the dullness of its shell will do the trick and bring the rug to life. But the creature's muted carapace only seems to dull the carpet further.

Suddenly, the collector changes his mind. The carpet is not too dull, it's too garish. He's possessed of a rather unusual brainwave. He sends his tortoise out to a local lapidary to have its shell covered in gold. When the creature is returned, however, the collector realizes he hasn't gone far enough. So he sends the tortoise out again to have its shell studded with fine gemstones. A true connoisseur, the collector selects a Japanese drawing of a bouquet of flowers as the basis for patterning the stones and picks the very rarest he can: chrysoberyls, peridots and olivines, cymophanes and sapphirines. The edge of the animal's shell is lined with hyacinth of Compostela, aquamarine, and the pinkest of rubies.

The collector salutes the triumph of his own taste by drinking toasts from eggshell China. His pleasure? A medley of liqueurs he samples as though he were playing symphonies to himself. Every flavor corresponds to a different instrument: Curaçao is the clarinet, kirsch a trumpet, marc-brandy the tuba.

But the collector's carefully constructed bliss implodes without warning. The scent of one of the liqueurs unexpectedly calls to mind a particularly hellish dental encounter he endured, when one of his teeth was extracted amid gushes of blood and spit. Rousing himself from the trauma of the memory, he realizes his gem-studded tortoise is lying dead on the rug before him. The luckless animal has expired under the weight of "the dazzling luxury imposed upon it."[1]

The tale of the doomed bejeweled tortoise, acidly comic and decidedly grotesque, is told in Joris-Karl Huysmans's epoch-making fin de siècle novel of 1884, *A Rebours*. Sometimes translated as *Against the Grain*, sometimes *Against Nature*, it's the story of the most perverse collector ever imagined: the aging French aristocrat Jean Des Esseintes, duke of Floressas. Des Esseintes is the king of queasy, hyper-refined and self-absorbed almost to the point of distraction. He seems a shell of a person: passive, withdrawn, defeated. But his passivity is deceptive. An amoral aesthete and a deadly dandy, Des Esseintes marked a distinctly modern return to the idea that the collector is a danger not merely to themselves but to others.

The fin de siècle term for Huysmans's descent into ornamental grossness was *decadence*, and the avatar of decadence was Charles Baudelaire. Baudelaire was the quintessential flaneur, a writer who hailed Parisian life in all its urban degradation and fiercely opposed attempts to modernize it. He embodied the artist as a visionary who pursued beauty at the expense of self, health, "good taste," and morality. "One should always be drunk," Baudelaire quipped, "with wine, with poetry, or with virtue, as you please.

But get drunk." He considered modern Paris akin to ancient Rome reincarnate. With civilization collapsing, the decadent stood heir to the libertine, albeit with one crucial difference. The decadent aristocrat didn't fear his social class was doomed, he *knew* it was. Unlike his libertine forebears, therefore, he embraced the agony and the ecstasy of ineluctable civilizational disintegration, living it to the full, consoled by the belief that such decadence was glorious because only decadence could produce truly great art.[2]

Baudelaire's volume of poetry *Les Fleurs du Mal*, published in 1857, can be translated as the *Flowers of Evil* and just as aptly as *the Flowers of Illness*. It became the decadent manifesto. Its verses deal graphically with sex and death in a sensuous and erotic style. "Close, swarming, like a million writhing worms," Baudelaire told his readers, "a demon nation riots in our brains." In "most repugnant objects," he wrote, "we find charms." "I am the wound and the blade," he declared, "the victim and the executioner." Prosecuted for offending good taste and scandalizing public morality, he was widely reviled.[3]

But he catalyzed an entire movement. Above all, decadence was about style. The critic Théophile Gautier likened Baudelaire's to gangrene. This was not criticism, but praise. The Irish writer George Moore compared decadent style to the smell of dead roses. Baudelaire and others were drawn to the Gothic short stories of Poe, who believed the greatest subject in art was the death of a beautiful young woman. Baudelaire himself wrote about the worms who "kissed" female corpses. Decadent style was *sick*, but found vitality, poignancy, and beauty in that sickness. This was unquestionably true of Huysmans as well. "Everything that revolted his senses," the poet Paul Valéry wrote of the author of *A Rebours*, "excited his genius."[4]

Historians ignore collectors, wrote the art critic and collector Edmond Bonnaffé in 1878, philosophers shrug their shoulders at them, artists scorn them as mere money grubbers. "Only the doctor and the physician will tip their hat to you," Bonnaffé went on in the spirit of Dibdin's *Bibliomania*, addressing an imaginary collector, "in hopes of soon making you one of their patients." He was not wrong. For the Hungarian-born Jewish physician Max Nordau, the sickness of the decadent was no metaphor, but a biological fact, one in which collectors were directly implicated. Nordau defined the entire fin de siècle as an epidemic of what he called *Degeneration*, the title

of his 1892 magnum opus. Seeing symptoms of cultural pathology everywhere, like his contemporaries the psychologists Paul Moreau and Richard
Krafft-Ebing, Nordau diagnosed the degenerate individual as neurasthenic
and hysterical. Modern industrial society itself was on the verge of a nervous
breakdown. And so too, Nordau reckoned, was the collector.[5]

There were many period terms for collecting, most connoting triviality,
vanity, and a preposterous faddishness, especially in France: *la collectiono-
manie, bric-à-brac, bibelot*. In his 1881 novel *Bouvard and Pécuchet*, Gustave
Flaubert mocked his eponymous heroes as a pair of boobish pedants who
jump from one fad to another, including archaeological collecting, tiring of
each pursuit without ever really understanding any of them. The philosopher Friedrich Nietzsche heaped scorn on the impulses of such "walking
encyclopedias" as contemptuously vapid. They embodied the age's "blind
rage for collecting, a restless raking together of everything that has ever
existed," he wrote, sad proof that the human quest for truth had shriveled
to "an insatiable thirst for novelty, or rather for antiquity." Antiquarianism
for its own fashionable sake he judged a symptom of cultural degeneracy,
intellectual emptiness, and spiritual bankruptcy.[6]

Nordau was likewise convinced that the craze for collecting betokened
the death of any truly vibrant civilization. Its most glaring symbol was the
overstuffed domestic Victorian interior, crammed with furniture, rugs, pictures, antiques, and bibelots of every conceivable kind. More and more, you
were what you owned, and you made sure you showed others. The Harvard
psychologist William James codified this idea in the first volume of his 1890
work *Principles of Psychology*. An "instinctive impulse drives us to collect
property," James wrote, so much so that collections "may become . . . parts
of our empirical selves." To be was to own and to own was to be. In Gilded
Age America, James thought that anyone who lost their fortune faced the
existential "annihilation" of their "material self." What if you owned too
much, however? The pressure to possess as many beautiful things as possible was becoming overwhelming, an arms race of taste and fashion, which
the sociologist Thorstein Veblen coined the term "conspicuous consumption" to describe.[7]

The "house beautiful"—a phrase associated with a flurry of magazines
and theories of interior decorating—became one of the great dreams of the

era. Everyone who was anyone bought a mansion and packed it with an almost infinite variety of art and bibelots: the Boston heiress and art collector Isabella Stewart Gardner; the journalist, novelist, and aesthete Gabriele D'Annunzio at the Vittoriale degli Italiani, his home on Lake Garda in Northern Italy; the newspaper magnate William Randolph Hearst at Hearst Castle in San Simeon, California, later the inspiration for Orson Welles's 1941 film *Citizen Kane*. And many more.

To Nordau, eclectic accumulation was especially pathological. "Everything in these houses aims at exciting the nerves and dazzling the senses," he wrote, but it was all "disconnected" and "bewildering." It was merely "aimless bric-à-brac," neither useful nor beautiful, a "discrepant, indiscriminate jumble" he considered hyperfeminine, compulsive, and neurotic. "The purchases of these persons," Nordau concluded, "are due to their delusion as to their own greatness."[8]

The art historian Mary Berenson rather agreed. Married to Bernard Berenson, the renowned connoisseur who made his reputation advising wealthy collectors including Gardner, Mary was damning after a visit to the "Cleopatra of the Charles," as she called her. "There's something horrible . . . in snatching this and that away from its real home and hanging it on a wall of priceless damask made for somewhere else," she wrote, "above furniture higgledipiggled from other places, strewn with objets d'art ravished from still other realms, Chinese, Japanese, Persian, Indian objects, that seem as if they were bleeding to death in those dreary super-museums." Penned in 1920, Berenson's tirade might seem like a diatribe against American collecting as rapacious plunder and as money masquerading as taste to conceal a new cultural imperialism. Berenson's real animus, however, was rather more personal than this, driven as it was in part by envy and resentment that Gardner (and her fortune) took credit and attention away from her husband and his talent, as well as harming his reputation through some ill-advised acquisitions. The colorful Mary was herself an avid collector who once defaced a picture of the Madonna she had bought by cleaning it with excessive zeal.[9]

Berenson blasted the people who were shaking the art world to its foundations with their money—the robber barons of America's Gilded Age who gathered in communities like Newport, Rhode Island, whom she called "squillionaires." Around the turn of the century, American industrialists, financiers, and countless heiresses used vast new fortunes to collect art from China to the Middle East but set their sights on Europe in particular. It became known as the great art drain, the Americans as picture pirates. America pillaged and Europe wept. "As a painting you must have heard a lot about me, / For I lived here for many happy years," went Cole Porter's lyrics about the railway magnate Henry Huntington buying Thomas Gainsborough's *The Blue Boy* in 1921, "Never dreaming that you could ever do without me, / Till you sold me in spite of all of my tears . . . / We've got those Blue Boy blues." The picture pirates transformed the American museum landscape in the process. According to one count, the total number of U.S. museums ballooned from 50 to 2,500 from 1850 to 1914.[10]

There were many such pirates. "Almost everyone," observed Archer Huntington, Henry's son and founder of the Hispanic Society of America, "is a collector of something" and wants "a little museum of his own." J. P. Morgan became the most famous and the most reviled of all such figures, epitomizing the titanic potencies of new American money. Morgan was a New York banker who dominated Wall Street finance more ruthlessly than any other individual. He became a great collector of art and books, creating the Morgan Library as a private collection, while acting as president of the Metropolitan Museum (founded in 1870) and helping to establish it as America's premiere art gallery. To many, he was a civic hero, but to others a villain. One cartoon shows Morgan seizing the Colosseum itself in Rome. Another has him sizing up European paintings like cadaverous courtesans. In "The Magnet" (1911) by Joseph Keppler Jr., he uses a giant dollar-sign-shaped magnet to hoover up art from across the Atlantic.[11]

Like all budding collectors, Morgan necessarily depended on the expertise of art advisers. He went motoring around Italy with the English critic Roger Fry, on whose counsel he often relied to collect Old Masters, just as Gardner relied on Berenson. Collectors had the money but not the knowledge. To some, this made them weak, not powerful at all. Joseph Duveen, the most influential art dealer of the era, goaded Henry Huntington by assuring him that he, Duveen, had the best eye in the world for English art. "Your name will live forever," Duveen promised him, but only if Huntington followed his advice. Duveen brokered Huntington's purchase of *The Blue Boy* not merely for the glory of the collector, but in no small part to

Joseph Keppler, Jr., The Magnet, *printed in* Puck *magazine (1911): Keppler depicts the New York financier J. P. Morgan (1837–1913) with a giant magnet hoovering up fine art from Europe and beyond, echoing the warning in Henry James's novels that American robber barons were soulless commercial plunderers of the world's great civilizations.*

serve his own turn by gaining introductions to bigger beasts, notably Hearst and John D. Rockefeller of Standard Oil. To Duveen, the collector was no titan, but the dealer's plaything, a pawn in a giant transatlantic chess game.[12]

The idea of the American collector's monstrous moneyed power proved too good to give up on, however. The expatriate American novelist Henry James, younger brother of William James, is renowned for the psychological complexity of the characters in his stories, but when it came to collecting, the message of "The Master" (as James was known) was remarkably clear and consistent: robber barons were destroying civilization itself by commodifying and collecting everything and everyone. James knew wealthy collectors on both sides of the Atlantic, from the Boston of his youth to London (he lived not far from the capital at Lamb House in Rye, East Sussex, from 1897 to 1914). He likened Isabella Stewart Gardener to the "barbarians of the Roman Empire," while lamenting that in New York, "there was money in the air, ever so much money." The problem extended to Europe. James likened the collections of Baron Ferdinand de Rothschild at Waddesdon Manor, Buckinghamshire, to the fruits of "murder and rapine." He himself never achieved financial security and was always worried about money, yet lived surrounded by a transatlantic elite whose impulses he came to regard as entertaining, if amoral and corrosive, not to say inescapable.[13]

The theme resounds throughout James's novels from the 1880s to the 1910s. In *The Portrait of a Lady*, the dandified American expatriate Gilbert Osmond seeks to make the Bostonian heiress Isabel Archer a "figure in his collection of choice objects." In *The Princess Casamassima*, the idealistic Hyacinth Robinson concludes that the artistic treasures of Venice, indeed the achievements of civilization, all rest on "the despotisms, the cruelties, the exclusions, the monopolies and the rapacities of the past." *The Golden Bowl*'s protagonist Adam Verver epitomizes the robber baron who collects objects and people alike. His twin passions are his desire to found a great museum and find a suitable husband for his daughter.[14]

The Spoils of Poynton reads like a manifesto against the cult of Victorian domesticity and the idolization of ownership as selfhood espoused by Henry's brother William. In the story, Mrs. Gereth is driven to despair by her doomed obsession with preserving her family home and its possessions, seeing them as "living things," even calling them her family's "religion." "They were *us*!" she exclaims at one point. Finally, in *The Outcry*, a satire on Yankees plundering Europe, James describes the American Breckenridge Bender as a collector who yearns to buy "an *ideally* expensive thing"—just because it was expensive. Money had become not merely the essential measure of value but the only measure.[15]

This was James's transatlantic warning. The American collector's ascendancy over decadent Europe might look like the triumph of democracy and the renewal of civilization, but the power of the dollar was far more destructive than the aristocratic values it was replacing. James's collectors were cold, colorless, and robotic. All calculation and no soul, their drive to accumulate reflected a mechanical will to power rather than any quest for selfhood, self-expression, or the realization of a personal vision. They represented everything Oldbuck and Pons feared about the direction of modern collecting: the replacement of individuality, authenticity, and passion by the sheer "force of money." The Romantic collecting self of the nineteenth century looked done for.

So much for the Americans. To Nordau, European collectors were no better and possibly even worse. *A Rebours* was "drivel," Nordau thundered, Des Esseintes just another "anaemic" Baudelairean pervert. But Nordau missed the point and failed to grasp Huysmans's wit. It's not just that Des Esseintes's perversity imbues him tremendous vitality, though that it surely does. Far more than Oldbuck or Pons, Huysmans's magnificently waspish creation marks a turning point in the long cultural history of the collector. This is because Des Esseintes is the first collector in literature to be represented as a semi-villainous antihero and a decidedly countercultural foil, set against modernity in the name of the rebellious individual, albeit in staunchly aristocratic guise.[16]

Huysmans was born in 1848, the year William Beckford died and Balzac published *Pons*. In some ways, he was the complete opposite of Des Esseintes, in others his alter ego. Unlike his irascible invention, Huysmans lived a quiet modern life as a bureaucrat who worked at the Ministry of the Interior in Paris—a model bureaucrat, too, by all accounts. He did, however, share his creation's melancholia, his hypochondria, his sexual despondency, and, most importantly, his deep disillusionment with the Roman Catholic faith in which he was raised and which he sought to replace with new sources of meaning.

Huysmans used his novels to explore ways of filling this religious void. In *A Rebours*, Des Esseintes uses collecting to do so; in *Là-Bas* (1891), the character Durtal investigates Satanism and the occult. Starting out as a disciple of the novelist Émile Zola, a realist in the tradition of Balzac, Huysmans was initially much taken with Zola's scientific approach to documenting social ills through fiction. But he turned against Zola and the explanatory power of science as boring, vapid, and spiritually lifeless. He wrote to a friend that the problem with the psychological trials on hysteria then being conducted by Jean-Marie Charcot at La Salpêtrière Hospital, which gained great notoriety in the 1880s, wasn't that they were suspect or melodramatic or unbelievable, but that they threatened all too scientifically to disenchant the mind and the world. Huysmans, by contrast, insisted that scientific materialism (not to mention literary naturalism) was fundamentally misguided. "I want to show Zola, Charcot, the spiritualists, and the rest," he wrote, "that nothing of the mysteries which surround us has been explained . . . the Devil [still] exists . . . [and] reigns supreme." This urgent personal quest for meaning eventually culminated in recommitting himself to Catholicism more deeply than ever.[17]

Huysmans wrote to provoke. While composing *A Rebours*, he told a friend that he was "immersed in the depths of a very strange novel, vaguely clerical, a bit homosexual, the story of the end of a family devoured by memories of religious childhood and nervous illness." His model was the foppish Parisian aesthete Count Robert de Montesquiou-Fézensac. One of the most colorful characters of the era, Montesquiou appears to have also provided inspiration for Oscar Wilde's Dorian Gray and for the Baron de

The Miriam and Ira D. Wallach Division of Art, Prints and Photographs: Print Collection, The New York Public Library

Count Robert de Montesquiou-Fézensac (undated): Montesquiou (1855–1921) was perhaps the most renowned and hyper-refined dandy in fin-de-siècle Paris, providing the model for both Des Esseintes in Huysmans's A Rebours *and the Baron de Charlus in Proust's* Remembrance of Things Past.

Charlus in Marcel Proust's *Remembrance of Things Past*. The quintessential dandy, Montesquiou was naturally a collector as well, the proud owner of one of Beau Brummell's canes and a tortoise that Montesquiou had covered in gemstones, whose existence evidently intrigued Huysmans.[18]

Huysmans never met Montesquiou. Instead, he used the writer Stéphane Mallarmé as a spy to observe him in his natural or rather artificial habitat. Inspired by the example of Ludwig II, Germany's "fairy tale king" who built medieval-style castles in nineteenth-century Bavaria, Montesquiou decked out his extravagant apartments in a manner that recalled the eclecticism and Orientalism of Beckford's Fonthill Splendens. Some rooms were Japanese, others Arabian, and he stuffed them all with bibelots. Montesquiou had high decadent form, excessive yet sublime. One visitor called his home "queer, disturbing, baroque, yet individual and even beautiful."[19]

In *A Rebours*, Huysmans's kaleidoscopic reimagining of Montesquiou and his world, Des Esseintes is an aristocrat who has quit Paris for the country. His life is behind him; the stories he tells are largely memories. He has retreated from society into his lavish collections, which replace the religious faith he has forsworn. He owns a triptych that features not Christ, for example, but three pieces of writing by his idol Baudelaire.

Like the Rudolf of legend, Des Esseintes lives through his collections. He spends hours rearranging his collection of Goya's unsettling portraits of the foibles of contemporary society, the *Caprichos*. He fondles his books, but he's not a classic bibliomaniac because he actually reads with purpose. Making his way through his collection of ancient Roman literature, he seeks to understand the relationship between decadence and culture. Rejecting the virtuous oratory of Cicero, he concludes that periods of vice and decay produced the best Latin prose, not republican virtue. He agrees with Baudelaire: decay is compelling, beautiful, and noble. He adores the darkly symbolist paintings of Odilon Redon and Gustave Moreau and Poe's sinister stories, judging them masterpieces of malaise.

More than a collector, Des Esseintes fashions his entire home as an elaborate work of art, a veritable temple to artificiality. "Nature, he used to say, has had her day." Just look at the "revolting uniformity of her landscapes and skyscapes." Having learned to love mechanical trickery from his Jesuit schoolmasters, he revels in all kinds of contrivances, such as the real flowers he owns that *look* fake—a reversal of the famous glass flowers blown by the Blaschka family—and the astonishing aquarium he constructs with colored water, "red like glowing embers." He delights in seeing its mechanical fish getting tangled up in fake seaweed.[20]

Des Esseintes's pleasures, however, leave him melancholic, hypochondriac, and neurasthenic. They never satisfy for long, only creating more yearning. As such, Des Esseintes embodies a hollowed-out version of the Romantic collecting self. The dream of expressing his individuality through collecting leads him to lose himself in his funhouse of fancies. He appears the opposite of Henry James's American collectors—all caprice and no plan—yet shares their predicament: he is bereft of any genuine sense of self.

Prone to neuralgia, nausea, insomnia, spitting blood, vomiting, blackouts, and impotence, Des Esseintes's hypersensitive frame is withering away. His various dubious capers to jolt himself back to some semblance of interest in life come to naught. His improbable hopes for a relationship with a physically dominating American circus performer called Miss Urania fizzle out, as does his attempt to get a sixteen-year-old named Langlois addicted to the pleasures of brothel-going (initially, he pays for Langlois's dalliances, then cuts him off to see if the boy will turn to crime to keep them going). And he proves a lethal companion to his innocent tortoise. Des Esseintes's delusions of grandeur end not with a bang, but a whimper.

Although Des Esseintes seeks a life of pleasure, he defines himself as much by his hatreds. Like Henry James, he loathes the vulgarity of commercial civilization, only with greater venom. He detests the "jovial bourgeois"— the middle-brow booster whose grubby mercenary values are devouring the degenerate scions of the "decayed nobility." With its mass culture, immigration, and racial mixing, America spells doom for Europe. "Commercialism had invaded the cloisters," Des Esseintes writes, resulting in "the suppression of all intelligence, the negation of all honesty, the destruction of all art." The aristocracy, battered since the French Revolution, was now facing its final extinction, and Des Esseintes would be the last of his line. The awesome power of money, rising and rising from Scott and Balzac to James as the scourge of the *true* collector—the visionary, the enthusiast, the seer—had grown irresistible. Resistance was indeed futile. In any case, to fight would be vulgar. The decadent thing to do was perish in a supernova of sophisticated spite.[21]

But something was changing in the cultural profile of the collector. Des Esseintes was no fond fool like Oldbuck and no Ponsian martyr. His collections were a proxy for life and sex, a substitute for a paradise of pleasures lost. Impotent Des Esseintes may have been, but he was also vicious and vibrant. Stagnant yet hedonistic, passive yet aggressive, the decadent dandy may have lived in his head, but was driven by increasingly violent passions. The figure of the collector was no longer a dupe or a fool but becoming edgy and dangerous again—withered, to be sure, yet unnerving and menacing.

A Rebours, one reviewer wrote, was "an unhealthy book." But it was a highly influential one. Five years later, a rather different incarnation of the decadent collector materialized south of the Alps in the Italian novel *Pleasure* (*Il Piacere*) by Gabriele D'Annunzio. No waspish neurasthenic, D'Annunzio's imaginary collector was an ardent sensualist, for whom physical objects were charged with sublime erotic force. Where Huysmans's collector lived in his mind, D'Annunzio's lived in his body, and with increasing volatility.[22]

D'Annunzio is a singularly queasy figure in Italian history. There are two main reasons for this. One is political, because D'Annunzio was a progenitor of fascism. A militarist and ethnic nationalist unhappy with Italy's treatment at the end of the First World War, in 1919 he led a renegade occupation of the city of Fiume (now Rijeka in Croatia), which had a large Italian population. He set up a sovereign government with a corporatist constitution, declared himself Duce, and only relented when the Italian Navy bombarded him. D'Annunzio influenced Benito Mussolini but had a tense relationship with him, fiercely opposing his alliance with Adolf Hitler and the Nazis. A keen aviator, D'Annunzio embraced futurism and the power of modern technology. Part of his nationalism, it was a way to propel Italy into modernity.

Reactions to D'Annunzio also turn on the melodramatic style of his prose and his life. Born to a wealthy provincial family in Pescara on the Adriatic Coast, he gravitated toward Rome and Milan, working in journalism and politics, and becoming a noted poet. His literary style dripped with erotic self-indulgence to the point of self-parody. In an era when it was fashionable to be *sick*, like Huysmans he wrote to provoke. He once wrote that "the three wonders of the terrestrial world are lobster, the pubic hair of a blonde woman, and the 'clean, clean, clean' flavor of oranges." At twenty, he published an especially scandalous poem about fellatio, which one reviewer called "the product of an illness." The Marxist philosopher Antonio Gramsci agreed, calling D'Annunzio's overwrought rhetoric the symptom of "a disease." A latter-day libertine who conducted numerous affairs into his dotage, not to mention cocaine-fueled orgies sequestered in his villa, D'Annunzio believed life was style and style was life, and neither should be dull.[23]

D'Annunzio also followed the rage for collecting, interior decorating, and the idea of creating a home as a temple to oneself. In 1921, he retreated to the Vittoriale, a stunning hillside villa overlooking Lake Garda, where he spent the last two decades of his life. He stuffed it with "divans, precious fabrics, Persian carpets, Japanese plates, bronzes, ivories, trinkets, all those useless and beautiful things for which I have a deep and ruinous passion." Now open to the public, the villa boasts lacquered walls, blue and gold ceilings, the copy of a horse's head from the Parthenon that D'Annunzio aged himself by using tea and—in a nod to his inspiration—a dead tortoise adorned with bronze. The scholar Mario Praz saw the Vittoriale's eclectic reveries as proof of D'Annunzio's "homicidal lust for things." Praz crammed his own houses in Rome full of collections, so perhaps he spoke from experience.[24]

Written by D'Annunzio at the age of twenty-six, *Pleasure* is an erotomaniac's lament. Like Huysmans the bureaucrat, D'Annunzio the journalist was a bourgeois who imagined the psychic twilight of the aristocracy as a form of hyper-refined madness. Only, in this case, the madness was carnal.

Pleasure's plot is simple enough. Andrea Sperelli is a hedonistic dandy who lives above the Spanish Steps in Rome. He falls in love with the aristocratic Elena Muti, but their affair ends and she marries another man. Refusing to accept his loss, Sperelli fights a duel over Elena, is injured and obliged to endure a long convalescence. He then starts an affair with another woman called Maria Ferres, but he cannot free himself from his obsession with Elena and strives to regain her affections. Will he succeed in regaining the woman he craves or lose his mind in the attempt? Ultimately, he winds up alone, his desires tormenting him and driving him to the brink of insanity.

Art and beauty dominate Sperelli's quest for pleasure. Like Des

Esseintes, he considers himself the last of "an intellectual race" whose lineage he traces back to the Bourbon dynasty in the fifteenth century, now facing extinction from the "gray democratic flood" of modernity. Collecting, therefore, a "mania [that] spread like a contagion" among the Roman upper classes, offers Sperelli a means of creating his own private world, defying the times and imagining he lives in another era. He furnishes his home in the style of a Renaissance palace, buying majolica, tapestries, furniture, books, and ivories at auction. To him, Elena herself is a work of art. Her hands and arms are like "an ancient vase," and she reminds him of Correggio's painting of *Danäe*, mother of Perseus.[25]

To Sperelli, the most charismatic objects are erotically charged ones. He wants to touch every auction lot that has been caressed by Elena's hands and carries a "particle of [her] amorous charm," conveying "truly a magnetic sensation of pleasure." Collecting is also a means to seduction. "She will love my house," Sperelli tells himself, and "she will love the things that I love." Objects reinforce the mystical union he imagines between them. *Pleasure*'s pages groan with decadent epithets: *diaphanous, palpitation, scintillate*. Sperelli would "have liked to surround [Elena]," D'Annunzio wrote, "draw her inside himself, suck her, drink her, possess her in some superhuman way." The problem is that the souvenirs Sperelli keeps of his moments shared with Elena produce only more masochistic yearning. The subtitle of *Pleasure* could be *Pain*.[26]

Objects also act as fetishes in scenes of characteristically dubious decadent taste. At the May Fair, a charity event organized by Elena, men pay five *luigi* to eat fruit that has been bitten into by the Marchioness of Atleta and drink "champagne from Elena's cupped hands." For one *luigi*, they can buy a cigarette "much moistened" by the ladies or smoke a Havana cigar that has been playfully seasoned in one of their armpits. One man offers 500 lire if Elena will oblige him by consenting to dry her hands on his beard. The event, Sperelli comments, has a "courtesan-like air" that encourages "impure fantasies."[27]

But Roman life isn't all fun and games. Convalescing after his duel, Sperelli comes to resemble Des Esseintes: an invalid who falls into a deep melancholia frustrated by his inability to realize his deepest desires. Collecting beautiful objects promises distraction and relief, so Sperelli becomes obsessed (almost inevitably) with the languorous paintings of Laurence Alma-Tadema, the Dutch artist who depicted ancient and Oriental decadence with an overwhelmingly torpid dream-like brush.

As with Des Esseintes, however, collecting fails to satisfy the decadent's yearnings, and Sperelli's story culminates in crisis. In one particularly vampiric sequence, he and Maria drink tea from each other's mouths. "You are taking my very life," she tells him. His desire for her is so overpowering, he fears it is he who may soon swoon and expire, although D'Annunzio counters it is Maria who is in real danger. While close to her, Sperelli becomes as "agitated as a murderer," *Pleasure*'s narrator observes, and Maria recoils as if "from the arms of Death." Will the aesthete's drive for beauty, pleasure, and possession turn him into a murderer?[28]

In the end, D'Annunzio pulls back from the brink. Sperelli doesn't kill. *Pleasure* ends instead with two images that put the collector's madness back in the box. The first is of Elena's elderly husband Lord Heathfield, Marquis of Mount Edgcumbe. The man she married for money instead of Sperelli is a semiparalyzed collector of erotica, an aged libertine who delights in rococo classics including Laclos's *Liaisons Dangereuses* and the Marquis de Sade. It's a foreshadowing of the Freudian image of the collector not as a vampiric Verrine rapist, but as a faded sexless male. *Pleasure*'s final scene suggests Sperelli's fate may not be entirely dissimilar. After all his rutting and raving, we witness D'Annunzio's protagonist retreating into his home, traipsing after an armoire crammed with bibelots bought at auction. The consolation of things awaits the disappointed lover.

Des Esseintes shrivels spitefully away in his enmities. Sperelli lurches lasciviously toward the brink of madness, yet in the end retreats. But in Oscar Wilde's supernatural thriller *The Picture of Dorian Gray* (1891), the decadent collector sold his soul for beauty and immortality, going all the way over the edge into murder.

Born in Dublin, Wilde was a prodigious writer of verse, plays, and stories who became the greatest wit of the age. An affluent member of the rentier class who toured the salons of Montesquiou, Théophile Gautier, and others while in Paris, Wilde was an avowed aesthete and ardent advocate for the house beautiful movement. "We must surround ourselves with beautiful objects," he urged, and furnished his own London home to fine effect, spending with abandon. But the dandy's dandy was plagued by scandal and suffering. He was prosecuted for homosexuality, then a medical term and a criminal offense, and served two years' hard labor in Reading Gaol during 1895–97.[29]

In *Dorian Gray*, Wilde fused the pursuit of beauty with a pervasive sense of crisis to produce a supernatural gothic melodrama about art, class, and murder. The young debutant Dorian charms his artist friend Basil Hallward so completely with his Adonis-like beauty that Basil feels compelled to capture it in a portrait. He does so to stunning effect. But it is Dorian who falls most in love with his own likeness, soon wishing that *he* might stay young while the portrait ages. He then comes under the influence of the hedonistic philosophy of Lord Henry, a charismatic and supercilious aesthete. Dorian becomes increasingly self-obsessed as a result. When a music-hall actress named Sibyl Vane falls in love with him, Dorian rejects her, and she tragically commits suicide. Dorian reacts with chilling indifference to her pitiful demise. He begins to notice a sadistic sneer developing in his portrait, one that was not there before.

Dorian then devotes himself to becoming a collector. His greatest inspiration is not Lord Henry, however, but none other than Des Esseintes: Lord Henry gives him a copy of *A Rebours* and its "curious jewelled style" beguiles him. Recognizing Huysmans's creation as the "prefiguring type" of himself, Dorian orders *nine* copies of the book and seeks to live out its dream of omnivorous aesthetic eclecticism and endless pleasures. He immerses himself in perfumes; collects musical instruments from around the world; jewels (including the same rare gems with which Des Esseintes encrusts his tortoise); tapestries and embroideries; and, in the rapturous list of a sensual cataloger reminiscent of Don Giovanni:

> *dainty Delhi muslins, finely wrought with gold-thread palmates, and stitched over with iridescent beetles' wings; the Dacca gauzes, that from their transparency are known in the East as "woven air," and "running water," and "evening dew"; strange figured cloths from Java; elaborate yellow Chinese hangings; books bound in tawny satins or fair blue silks, and wrought with fleurs de lys, birds, and images; veils of lacis worked in Hungary point; Sicilian brocades, and stiff Spanish velvets; Georgian*

work with its gilt coins, and Japanese Foukousas *with their green-toned*
golds and their marvellously-plumaged birds.[30]

For Dorian, such beauty is not mere indulgence or decadence but a
flight from his own depravity. He collects treasures as a "means of for-
getfulness, modes by which he could escape" his sense of foreboding and
assuage his guilt over Sybil Vane's death. Like Des Esseintes, Dorian spins
from one kind of collecting to another, finding neither peace nor gratification, each fleeting obsession giving way to indifference and the quest for
new sensations.[31]

Increasingly tormented by his sneering portrait, Dorian murders his
friend Basil in a fit of rage. He then covers up his crime by blackmailing
an old college acquaintance named Campbell, convincing him to dissolve
Basil's body in acid. But the mayhem only spreads. Campbell commits suicide, and Sibyl Vane's brother dies while trying to avenge her. No longer able
to endure the merciless cruelty of his portrait, Dorian decides to destroy it.
But when he plunges a knife into the canvas, it is Dorian himself who dies,
leaving the picture to return to its original image of virginal youth, while
he is at last disfigured by the evil he has wrought. It is only by examining
the rings on his fingers that his ravaged and dissipated body is identified.

Dorian Gray returns to familiar themes in the history of the collector,
Wilde piling on the allusions to collectors past, overloading the story with
resonance. With its supernatural theme, Dorian is a Faustian magus and
a dark sorcerer who commits sacrilege and is damned to hell. Wilde also
models Dorian as a reincarnation of classical forebears, comparing him to
Adonis, Greek god of beauty; Narcissus (Dorian kisses his own portrait at
one point); Hadrian's lover Antinoüs; Paris, whose elopement with Helen
helped trigger the Trojan War; a wicked satyr; and the Emperor Caligula.

The theme of reincarnation is neither accidental nor metaphorical;
the notion was in high vogue when Wilde wrote. Heinrich Schliemann's
archaeological discovery in 1870 that Troy was a real city, rather than a
mythical one, raised fundamental questions concerning the relationship
between modern and ancient peoples. Especially in the context of social
Darwinist notions of the "survival of the fittest" and growing perceptions
of the inevitability of a war between classes and races, many European

intellectuals became obsessed with tracing their ancestry to Greek civilization and brooded on questions of lineage and destiny. Because the outcome of this struggle seemed so uncertain, it produced a powerful desire to take flight into the past in search of a deeper identity. But reincarnationist impulses were literal, too. The thriving late-century spiritualist movement boasted many educated followers who sought ways of communicating with dead ancestors. Fed by such currents, *Dorian Gray* is as much a novel of the séance as the salon.

Dorian, for one, appears to believe in reincarnation. We're all "complex multiform creatures," he states, who "lead myriad lives." But as such, our "very flesh is tainted with the monstrous maladies of the dead." We are all cursed, he believes, prisoners of heredity, our destiny preordained, doomed in his case by "a ruined grace." This is the Darwinian fatalism of the fin de siècle: there's no escape from a predestined extinction. Like Des Esseintes and Sperelli, the real Dorian is never quite there, a phantom from many different pasts, searching for a true identity that always proves elusive. "There were times when it appeared to Dorian Gray that the whole of history was merely the record of his own life."[32]

Dorian Gray also dissects the class anxieties of the decadent. Wilde writes about a "curious race-instinct" that produces conflict between different classes and presents Dorian as someone who is plagued by his mixed-class background. He is the grandson of a lord, but his noblewoman mother married down by wedding an infantryman, leaving Dorian to lead a double life, gliding through the *beau monde* of artists and aristocrats while often slumming in the *demi-monde* of music halls and opium dens. Dorian is two men like Jekyll and Hyde—a story Wilde admired—an aesthete and a ruffian desperate to experience every sensation in the world.[33]

Dorian Gray is also a story about homosexuality. The initial *Lippincott's Monthly Magazine* version published in 1890 suggested more openly that Dorian and Basil are lovers. It was attacked and re-edited to make their relationship more idealized (this is the best-known version today). The remaining language, however, is still ardent. Basil "worships" Dorian, an idolatrous sin for which he prays for forgiveness and for which he pays the ultimate price. He protests that his passion for Dorian is "not that mere physical admiration of beauty that is born of the senses." Yet, in another

instance of Wilde's obsessive genealogizing, Basil declares his love a reincarnation of that spiritual affection evident in the art of Michelangelo, the
essays of Montaigne, the sonnets of Shakespeare, and the art criticism of
Johann Winckelmann. All these references suggest a genealogy of same-sex
love. There's a nod to William Beckford, too: at one point, Dorian is asked
whether he wants to buy a frame from Fonthill Splendens.[34]

Wilde doesn't insist that Dorian's collecting, let alone his killing, is
driven by "the love that dare not speak its name." Rather, Dorian collects
because he idolizes beauty, above all his own, and seeks pleasure in objects
to evade his guilt. He's a keeper of secrets and yet another Rudolf, retreating
into collections to fly from reality. He wants nothing more than to collect
himself. In the end, his narcissistic desire for status and pleasure explodes
in murderous violence. As such, *Dorian Gray* acted as a stepping-stone to
the image that was to dominate the figure of the collector in the twentieth
century: that of the "creepy" closet homosexual and sociopath. This was a
person who loved things yet hated people—and, for all his self-love, hated
himself, too—making him a menace to all who came into contact with
him. The collector was becoming a truly paradoxical figure: someone so
pathologically weak, he is dangerous.

A revolution was under way. As Huysmans, D'Annunzio, and Wilde
told their tales of collecting and mayhem, an obscure Vienna psychologist finally went inside the mind of the collector to declare once and for
all that the urge to collect was an expression of sexual repression, not class
aspiration. The new science he invented, psychoanalysis, was highly democratic, insisting that sexual neuroses could explain all of human psychology,
regardless of social class. But the upshot of this new democratic psychology
was to prove highly ironic. If we are all potentially collectors, then we are
all potentially repressed and all potentially dangerous. It was the beginning
of a hazardous cultural journey from the snooty connoisseur who accidentally did away with his pet tortoise to the wholesome boy next door who
stuffed birds, had a very strange relationship with his mother, and might
just kill *you.*

CHAPTER NINE

THE INNER FIRE

The box lid was not merely closed, it was slowly but deftly
pushed shut and the tension of the fingers showed that the
closing was of some inner significance.

—EDGAR ANDERSON DESCRIBING ALFRED KINSEY (1961)

In the middle of the twentieth century, Alfred Kinsey began collecting vast amounts of data about sex. He founded the Institute for Sex Research at Indiana University in 1947 and published two influential reports on sexual behavior in 1948 and 1953. Kinsey collected photographs and pornography, pioneered the sexological interview, and filmed people having sex and masturbating. He devised a numerical scale from 0 to 6 to measure homosexual tendencies (6 indicating full homosexuality) and had relationships with men himself, including one of his own students, even though he was married.

After visiting him in Bloomington once, Robert Morison of the Rockefeller Foundation wryly observed that Kinsey and his team had a "very vigorous drive to collect things without always knowing why." But Morison was not the first to hint that something other than science was behind Kinsey's collecting. When Kinsey was still working as an entomologist—his original career—his colleague the botanist Edgar Anderson observed his behavior with scientific attention to detail:

> *The urge to build up a significant collection is a special sort of inner drive. . . . In Kinsey the strength of this compelling inner fire showed*

*itself increasingly and in various ways, when he closed one of the tight-
fitting insect boxes and put it back on the shelf in the proper place, when
he inserted one of his coded sex-survey data cards and closed the steel
filing case, there was a physical reaction which I have noticed in other
scholars and collectors. The box lid was not merely closed, it was slowly
but deftly pushed shut and the tension of the fingers showed that the
closing was of some inner significance. When the drawer of the filing
cabinet was pushed shut the fingers lingered on the drawer until it slid
firmly into the closed position and there were meaningful tensions of the
arm and back muscles.[1]*

In the nineteenth century, the invention of the Romantic collecting self
redefined collecting as an activity that expressed the personal identity of
the individual collector. Then, in the fin de siècle, that self corroded into
decadence, money, and murder. The Romantic collector hollowed out into
a haunting specter, whose quest for meaning proved increasingly vicious
and dangerous.

But at the very end of the century, the Romantic collecting self returned
with a vengeance, transformed by Sigmund Freud. Freud's invention of psychoanalysis provided a way of looking at collectors that came to dominate
the twentieth century, and it permeates Anderson's description of Kinsey.
According to psychoanalysis, collecting was indeed an expressive activity,
but the meaning it expressed was otherwise hidden. As Anderson stressed,
for Kinsey, shutting a wasp in a box was no longer just shutting a wasp in a
box but possessed an "inner significance."

Collecting now became seen as a response to repressed neuroses stem-
ming from events early in the life of the individual. Consequently, for the
first time in history, collectors became people who had not just eccentricities
or problems but also stories to tell that might explain *why* they collected,
stories it was the psychoanalyst's task to unearth and decode. More than
just positing answers as to the meaning of collecting, which writers since
Balzac had done for decades, Freud and his followers invented the question
"Why do people collect?" and made it one of the cultural obsessions of the
twentieth century.

Born in 1856, Freud established himself as one of Vienna's leading psychologists by century's end. In the 1880s, like Guy de Maupassant and countless others, he attended Jean-Marie Charcot's dramatic trials on patients suffering from hysteria at La Salpêtrière Hospital. Charcot emphasized the role of unconscious neurological function in human behavior and experimented with hypnosis as a form of treatment. Freud learned from him the importance of carefully staged psychiatric interventions, even as he adapted Charcot's methods from the public hospital to his private clinic back in Vienna—and to the couch.

Most nineteenth-century psychologists aimed to diagnose pathologies by social group and type, including categories such as women, homosexuals, and criminals. Freud, however, made psychology the study of the individual human subject. Each of us, he argued, has our own personal unconscious, made up of urges rooted in infancy and family relationships. Repressed by our conscious ego, these urges are sexual in origin and remain in the unconscious (the id), while manifesting themselves as neuroses seeking resolution. The ills afflicting the modern bourgeois individual, who was formed by industrial civilization and mass consumer society, were now to be diagnosed and cured on a personal basis rather than explained by recourse to class, sex, or hereditary characteristics.

Fascinatingly, Freud saw psychoanalysis and collecting as related endeavors. He became a devoted antiquities collector in middle age, purchasing many small sculptures from ancient Greece, Rome, Egypt, Babylon, Mesopotamia, and China. As Freud acknowledged, he began collecting in 1896 as a "source of exceptional renewal and comfort" after the death of his father. In total, he amassed around 3,000 pieces, which he took pains to ship from Vienna to London when he fled the Nazis after they annexed Austria in 1938. He displayed them around his office in both cities, as visitors to the Freud Museum in Hampstead can see to this day.[2]

Freud intended these objects as prompts for his patients, so he placed them where they could see and react to them, rather than putting them in his private quarters. They intrigued several of his well-educated clients who were familiar with classical mythology. The poet H.D. (Hilda Doolittle) made such connections, for example, although she felt somewhat unsure about whether Freud meant for her to do so. She intuited that Freud's collection formed part of the "game" of psychoanalysis. But "did he want to

Sigmund Freud with his antiquities at his desk in Vienna, by Princess Eugenie of Greece (ca. 1937):
Freud (1856–1939) claimed to model psychoanalysis on the methods of archaeology as a science of
mental excavation, and was a devoted antiquities collector who displayed his pieces in his office,
which he took pains to ship to London when he fled the Nazi annexation of Vienna in 1938.

find out how I would react to certain ideas embodied in these little statues,"
she asked, "or did he mean simply to imply that he wanted to share his treasures with me?"[3]

Freud's methods as a psychoanalyst were those of a collector in several
respects. For example, he noted down fragments of his patients' speech and
their unintentional gestures as clues to their unconscious motivations. Freud
borrowed this strategy in part from art connoisseurs, especially Giovanni
Morelli. Morelli insisted it was possible to tell forgeries from authentic works
of art by studying the incidental details of pictures, such as ears in portraits.
Freud followed suit. He collected his patients' personal information into
case histories, including their memories and dreams, and made more general collections of slips of the tongue, jokes, and Jewish anecdotes. Thoughts
discovered in any obscure "stratum" of the mind, as H.D. observed, "were
things, to be collected, collated, analysed, shelved, or resolved" and pieced
together like the fragments of a bowl or vase.[4]

More than acting as a mere tool, collecting inspired Freud's very con-
ception of psychoanalysis. Freud was, he liked to say, an archaeologist of

the mind. He read the works of Arthur Evans, who had recently excavated the ruins of ancient Crete, as well as archaeological journals, and made an annual antiquarian pilgrimage to Rome. He followed new discoveries zealously, especially Heinrich Schliemann's excavation of Troy in 1870, and invoked archaeology as a model of scientific rigor for psychoanalysis to emulate. The mind had strata into which the analyst must descend to excavate buried truths. "Our psychic mechanism," Freud believed, "has come into being by a process of stratification," and these strata would speak to him as stones "spoke" to the archaeologist.[5]

Freud didn't analyze his patients' collections, let alone his own, and only rarely discusses collecting in his professional writings. When he does so, he emphasizes his view that collecting stands in for some form of personal anxiety. In *The Interpretation of Dreams* (1899), for example, he discusses a dream of his where he turns the pages of an illustrated book on botany, before coming across an actual dried plant. The dream makes Freud recall his youthful passion for collecting and owning books, although he interprets it as a "condensation" or combination of several different ideas: his authorship of a paper on the coca plant (the source of cocaine, which he sometimes took) and a memory of finding a worm in an herbarium at school. In the end, Freud interprets his dream as an attempt to justify not giving his wife flowers more often.

The "may-beetle dream" he records of an elderly female patient is more suggestive of deeper hidden meanings. A woman dreams that she must release two beetles from a box or they will suffocate. When she opens the box, one flies out of the window, but the other is crushed when she closes the window. Freud relates the dream to the woman's memories of her daughter's cruelty to insects and to the woman's fear that her husband is aging and becoming impotent. Freud associates the beetles with aphrodisiacs including Spanish fly, which is made of crushed beetles, rather than to entomology or collecting as such.

Fragments of his unpublished writings reveal, however, that Freud saw the urge to collect mainly as a substitute for sex. "When an old bachelor collects snuffboxes," he wrote to his colleague Wilhelm Fliess in 1895, it reflects his "need for a multitude of conquests. Every collector is a substitute for a Don Juan Tenerio." Like "old maids" who keep a dog for a companion rather than take a husband, the collector's objects constitute the "erotic equivalents" of human partners. Both men and women collect for this reason. Some women, Freud observed, are loyal to just one doctor, but those who keep changing doctors collect them like lovers. Freud called this "psychical displacement." The same applied when "a bachelor becomes an enthusiastic collector," transferring his affections to a series of inanimate love-objects.[6]

In Freud's view, both men and women turn to collecting when they repress their sexual desire or simply can no longer fulfill it. The collector is "one who directs his surplus libido onto the inanimate object" and commits to the "love of things." Objects were like women and cats: fundamentally narcissistic and interested only in themselves, but it was precisely such exquisite indifference that rendered them irresistibly attractive. Indeed, Freud once watched as a cat purringly inspected the antique figurines in his office without knocking over a single one of them. Charmed, he rewarded the cat with a saucer of milk.[7]

Freud was not the first to see collecting as the absence of sex and its substitution. Walter Scott and Balzac in particular had said as much decades earlier in their depictions of the lovable bachelor losers Oldbuck and Pons. The collector was someone who sought compensation for pleasures lost—a mollifying pact with one's most intimate disappointments. In the modern bourgeois imagination, collecting was the refuge of the impotent and the solace of the refined. But Freud triggered an intellectual revolution nonetheless. His insights, combined with the general idea that psychoanalysis offered a rigorously scientific method for decoding collections as expressions of repressed neuroses, paved the way for subjecting the collector's motives to unprecedented scrutiny. From now on, the act of collecting was always about something *else*, and never entirely about the thing collected. The question "Why collect?" became pressing in a way it had never been before, and more disquieting.

In his classic *Civilization and Its Discontents* (1929), Freud concluded that all human beings harbor a "savage beast" within, one that must be repressed to allow civilization to function. Seen this way, the collector embodied civilization's triumph through the sublimation of destructive animal drives into the pleasure of peacefully acquiring fine things. Were collectors, however, really all sad but safe? The Romantic collecting self was back, but could it maintain self-control? Perhaps because Freud thought of himself as the archetypal collector—a retiring middle-aged antiquarian—he underestimated how the collector might morph from a harmless neurotic into a psychopath.[8]

Freud suggested that we all begin life as collectors—of our own feces. In his 1908 essay "Character and Anal Erotism," he stressed how infants realize that they can exercise power over their parents by retaining their excrement, experiencing a highly gratifying autoerotic pleasure in the process. Most people outgrow this "anal" impulse, although sometimes it forges an "orderly, parsimonious and obstinate" character that lasts a lifetime. This argument scandalized Freud's early readers, but he himself thought it nothing new. There was a long tradition of associating waste with value and treasure dating back to the Babylonians, he observed, who held that gold is "the faeces of hell."[9]

Freud's disciples enthusiastically followed his lead. Writing also in 1908, Karl Abraham, whom Freud considered his finest student, pointed out that physical things figure prominently as a form of "object-love" among the young, as a substitute for fading parental affection. "Man transfers his libido not only to animate but also to inanimate objects," Abraham wrote, "and this relation originates in his sexuality." In fact, he thought, all our relations with things are sexual, inescapably pervaded by our libido, our attraction to them being "analogous to sexual attraction." "The human being," Abraham concluded, "sexualizes the universe."[10]

What we collect reflects this pattern. "The direction taken by our taste in the choice of objects," Abraham believed, "completely conforms to our sexual object." The collector "who shrinks from no sacrifice" is a "lover" whose passion for objects acts as a "surrogate" and "sublimation" of desire for other people. In the end, however, the act of collecting fails to satisfy and creates new problems. It is merely the symptom of a deep neurosis involving repression, perversion, and "abnormal sexual activities" it cannot resolve.[11]

Freud's associate Ernest Jones went further. "All collectors are anal-erotics," Jones wrote in 1918. "The objects collected are nearly always typical copro-symbols," meaning symbols of our relation to our own fecal matter and the infantile impulse to anal retention. For Jones, the meaning of collecting depended more specifically on *what* gets collected, though his list of copro-symbols tended to be rather broad to say the least: money, coins, stamps, eggs, butterflies, books, pins, newspapers, and more besides. Anyone who collects these kinds of things, Jones claimed, was really just replaying the infantile hoarding of feces.[12]

Such striking and indubitably imaginative ideas took on a vigorous life of their own. In part because Freudians were thoroughly well-educated devotees of high culture, they began to depict the act of collecting as one of momentous psychoanalytic significance in works of art. In 1921, for example, the Vienna psychoanalyst Alfred Winterstein, another of Freud's colleagues, reviewed a new novel by Victor Fleischer called *The Collector* (1920) in the pages of the recently founded journal *Imago*, which focused on psychoanalysis, art, and culture. Fleischer's novel is a wonderfully disturbing tale of a highly sophisticated yet deranged collector. It features as its protagonist an apparently respectable retired official named Baumgartner who devotes himself to the collection of sculptural reliefs. However, when Baumgartner encounters a devilishly handsome rival collector named Hübner—who bears an uncanny resemblance to Dorian Gray—he panics that his own collection will be judged inferior and that he will be exposed as a fool who has bought forgeries. In the novel's climactic scene, Baumgartner is possessed by a frenzied and almost unbearable paranoia. Convinced that Hübner is about to assault him, Baumgartner lashes out to defend himself against his enemy, only to realize he is in fact striking his own reflection in the mirror, injuring himself in the process.

Winterstein's analysis of the story in *Imago* was full-on Freudian. Baumgartner's collecting exhibits a pathetic substitute for human relationships, he judged, and is driven by anal-erotic compulsions, repressed homosexual desire, and classic narcissism. Attacking his own reflection in the mirror constitutes a symbolic suicide. Fleischer's novel brilliantly captures the darker side of the Freudian collector—not the harmless self-pleasurer or the retired lothario, but someone so tormented by desire that they pose a danger to themselves and possibly others, too. This is what is so unnerving about Baumgartner's apparently civilized self-repression. The collector forges a strong yet entirely false sense of security through his collection, so strong and false that when some external force threatens that security, the collector plunges into a paranoia so volatile he can no longer tell the difference between fantasy and reality. So much for repression as the bedrock of civilization; it threatened to explode and destroy it.

Freudians associated collectors with more abstract kinds of violence as well. Inspired by Scottish anthropologist Sir James Frazer's magisterially sprawling account of magic, science, and primitivism in *The Golden Bough* (1890), Freud began to look for ways to apply psychoanalysis to the anthropological study of non-Western cultures and societies. In 1912–13, he published *Totem and Taboo*, with the unforgettable subtitle *Resemblances Between the Mental Lives of Savages and Neurotics*. In it, he discussed such themes as incest in Pacific and African societies and the projection of magical influences onto the physical world. He wanted to explain how what he deemed primitive forces were in no way consigned to the dustbin of evolutionary history, but remained very much at work in the modern neurotic mind, while seeking to use psychoanalysis to show that "savages" were driven by similar kinds of neuroses as all other human beings, regardless of even radical cultural difference.

Many anthropologists derided *Totem and Taboo* as unscientific, and still do. Yet psychoanalysts embraced it, in part because it made Freudianism universally relevant to the human condition, expanding its claim to explain the workings of the mind irrespective of culture or epoch. Now, or so it seemed to Freud's followers, anyone anywhere could be psychoanalyzed as fair Freudian game. The book's stylistic charm and brilliance is undeniable, and its key concepts seduced even popular culture. The 1955 Marilyn Monroe comedy *The Seven Year Itch*, based on a stage-play by George Axelrod, is among other things a droll satire on *Totem and Taboo*, mining Freud's subtitle for all of its humor by exploring the "savage" instincts of modern Manhattan neurotics in their dalliances with psychoanalysis and each other. The film's opening sequence knowingly compares the inner struggles of contemporary New Yorkers to those of Manhattan's original Native American inhabitants, suggesting little has changed in the intervening centuries.

Freud did not discuss collecting in *Totem and Taboo*, but the fusion of anthropology and psychoanalysis reshaped discussions of collecting after him. For Karl Abraham, the figure of the cannibal became another key metaphor for understanding the collector. Harking back to the notion that collecting was rooted in infantile anal retention, Abraham reasoned that craving objects was "cannibalistic," driven by the collector's "instinctual aim . . . to incorporate the object in himself." Collecting thus marked a return to the "primitive stage of libidinal development." This is why some people suck their possessions and some even sit on them, Abraham explained, a behavior he observed in both children and dogs (he took great professional interest in what he described with requisite psychoanalytical sobriety as his own dog's "obsessional neuroses"). Echoing William James, Abraham used etymology to link the drive to acquire property with a deeper urge for physical incorporation. The Latin *possidere* and the German *besitzen* both signified property or possession and suggested associations with sitting. Modern collectors were neurotic cannibals, Abraham concluded, whose behavior restaged "the cannibalism of primitive people."[13]

If collectors were cannibals, then the idea of the collector as vampire could not be far behind. And so it proved, in second-generation Viennese analyst Otto Fenichel's richly inventive account of collecting as a form of supernatural trophyism. Like Abraham, Fenichel sought to understand the meaning of possession at its most fundamental level. He agreed with his predecessors that the love of things substituted for the loss of parental affection after infancy. The origins of the collecting mania, he concurred, lay in the infantile attitude toward feces. What *is* an object truly possessed? "That on which one sits." But the drive to possess is so powerful, it can lead us beyond our normal scruples to acts of transgression. Here is how Fenichel imagined the thinking of the obsessive collector who breaks the law in order to achieve the act of possession (by theft, for example): "I have acquired something by force or fraud that originally belonged to someone more powerful, but which is now a talisman for me, or which connects me magically with the previous possessor." The collector is driven by a mystical desire to channel the power of previous owners. He is a vampire and collecting a form of trophyism.[14]

Fenichel's view of collecting as trophyism is, in other words, a magical theory of pedigree. Collecting was a way of accumulating phallic power to ward off the threat of castration, and the collector not merely a Freudian figure but a mythological and morally ambiguous one not unlike Prometheus, who was punished for stealing fire from the gods. Like Freud, Fenichel compares the collector to Don Giovanni, whose sexual conquests he calls "collections of trophies." But, like Sperelli sipping wine from his lover's mouth in *Pleasure*, there is something cannibalistic and vampiric about Fenichel's collector, who seeks out "objects which have had some contact with his love object in order . . . to incorporate them." The collector is a ghoul who wants to absorb the power of the dead. Slowly but surely, Freudianism was turning in on itself. Instead of the lovable loser whose collections symbolized a retreat from life, Fenichel recast the collector as a sinister supernatural predator desperate to steal as much extra life as possible.[15]

Once sparked, the psychoanalytic romance with the collector proved irresistible. Freud provided not merely a set of ideas or an intellectual movement, but an entire way of understanding the self that pervaded Western culture through the twentieth century. As the poet W. H. Auden observed after Freud died, the inventor of psychoanalysis may sometimes have been "wrong," even "absurd," yet "to us he is no more a person / now but a whole climate of opinion / under whom we conduct our different lives."[16]

The notion that women were afflicted by a peculiar urge to accumulate possessions, and the question of what might explain this urge, became a distinct Freudian preoccupation. The theme was ancient, dating back to Roman fears of the corrupting effects of women's alleged predilection for luxury. By the nineteenth century, the idea had been lent a new scientific veneer. Victorian doctors codified women's passion for possessions as the criminal urge they called *kleptomania* and a pathological form of the collecting instinct, first defined by the French physician C. C. Marc in the 1840s, which they insisted was rooted in the uterus and linked to abnormal menstruation, hysteria, and sexual overexcitement. "We know from the psychoanalysis of kleptomania," Otto Fenichel stated with confidence in 1939, reinforcing the link between kleptomania and collecting more generally, "that its object is often the penis."[17]

Kleptomaniacs weren't always women. "The Mad Collector," one of several such notices in the late-century popular press, told an unsettling story of "monomania" in—where else?—Vienna. The case involved an affluent banker accused of stealing a handkerchief from a lady's pocket. Odd perhaps, but not all that unsettling until one understood the full extent of the man's "mania for collecting handkerchiefs." He initially paid five or six pounds for each one, until he was reduced to poverty and finally crime. On searching his apartment, the police found no less than 1,450 handkerchiefs, "all catalogued and classified" according to their scents. The magistrate committed the "unfortunate collector" to an asylum.[18]

Kleptomania was, however, overwhelmingly identified with female compulsion. In his 1883 novel *The Ladies' Paradise*, Émile Zola dramatized the new phenomenon of the department store, recounting the romance between a manager named Mouret and a humble shopgirl called Denise. But the book's real protagonist is the store itself, by turns paradisical and demonic in its power to seduce female shoppers with its wares. Zola describes women driven mad with desire by the store's opulent museum-like interiors, inebriated by the sensual pleasures of silk, lace, and fine carpets. The shop, Zola warned, was alive, and the ladies in its thrall.

Freudians were fascinated by kleptomaniac angst. Karl Abraham related the phenomenon to "the female castration complex," linking one female patient's history of thieving to penis envy and an unconscious desire to castrate her father. She stole phallic symbols from him, Abraham noted, including money, pens, and pencils. She also removed "an enema tube" from his room to use it "as a substitute for his male member—for anal–erotic purposes." These acts gave the woman an overwhelming sense of power and sexual satisfaction, Abraham believed. He imagined her subconscious reasoning thus: "I do possess that desired part of the body, and so I am equal to my father."[19]

Women's relationships with Freudianism were complex, especially when it came to collecting. The vast fortunes of the Gilded Age created a new class of wealthy American heiresses who sought to distinguish themselves as art collectors and museum patrons. They included figures such as the Chicago socialite and Standard Oil heir Edith Rockefeller McCormick—a leading advocate of Jungian psychoanalysis in America—and Catharine Lorillard Wolfe, heir to tobacco and real estate fortunes who gave heavily to the Metropolitan Museum in New York, where her paintings hang to this day.

In many ways, the most influential such collector was Gertrude Stein. Best known for her experimental modernist writing and her embodiment of the "new woman" of early feminist ideals, the California-raised Stein was heir to vast Western streetcar and real estate fortunes and made a point of collecting modern art rather than Old Masters. Moving to Florence and Paris early in the twentieth century, she became a mainstay of avant-garde art circles. Together with her brother Leo—a committed student of psychoanalysis who benefited from advice on art from Bernard Berenson, but also became his rival—the Steins started buying works by Picasso, Matisse, and others in the 1900s, when they were virtually unknown.

The profile of collecting was changing. It wasn't just driven by status or money, as Henry James insisted, or a symptom of decadence, as Max Nordau feared. Instead, collectors were returning to the Renaissance ideal that beautiful things might cure the soul, though in a modernist key as a means of psychological liberation and self-realization. Epitomized by Stein, the urge among upper-class women to find themselves through art and collecting thus had extraordinary appeal in these years, though not all who acted on it entirely believed it. Claribel and Etta Cone of Baltimore, sisters and textile mill heiresses, came to know Stein, Picasso, and other artists in Europe and became dedicated collectors of modern art. But Claribel, for one, expressed misgivings about the will to collect. The "craving for beauty," she told Etta in 1924, was "a vital function of the human soul," but saw collecting as "silly foolishness." She was deeply conflicted. "I find things so much more satisfactory than people," she said, sounding like a Henry James character, yet warned Etta "do not let things consume you."[20]

Mabel Dodge was the most interesting of Stein's followers. Heir to a banking fortune in Buffalo, New York, Dodge encountered Stein in Florence and was captivated by her charisma. Inspired by her independent spirit, Dodge embarked on her own journey of self-discovery, becoming one of Stein's patrons in the process. Spurred on by the house beautiful movement, Dodge bought and decorated the Villa Curonia at Arcetri outside Florence, throwing herself into its renovation and redecoration after her marriage failed. "In a lack of love," she wrote, "I had tried to pass out of longing into materials—and out of my passion I had built my house." But then she found that her house was in fact a prison, one "too powerful" to escape from because she had built it too well. Part of her cried out "'let's go!' but another part sank deeper into feathers ... in my beautiful shell."[21]

Serial seeker that she was, Dodge is fascinating because of the many different paths to self-realization she tried. Feeling trapped by the gilded domestic cage she built for herself, she turned from collecting and furnishing to psychoanalysis once back in New York, hosting some of the first psychoanalytic soirées in America, writing about her experience with analysis and popularizing Freud in the pages of the *New York Journal*. In the end,

Bettmann Collection via Getty Images

Mabel Dodge Luhan at the Villa Curonia (undated): Dodge (1879–1962) was a banking heiress from Buffalo who became a devotee of the house beautiful movement, decorated fine houses, and was inspired by Gertrude Stein to become an art collector, before taking up psychoanalysis, becoming disillusioned with material culture and relocating to the Taos art colony in New Mexico.

however, she settled in New Mexico, where she became deeply involved with the Taos art colony, as well as indigenous art and politics, marrying a Native American man named Tony Luhan.

The careers of other women collectors were living proof of the fallacy of Freud's notion that collecting was a substitute for sexual gratification. The colorful exploits of the New York heiress Peggy Guggenheim exemplified how sex and collecting could intertwine in an experimental modernist life. Like Stein before her, and benefiting from the counsel of Marcel Duchamp like a latter-day Gardner with her very own Berenson, Guggenheim collected what later became some of the most canonical works of modern art, including pieces by Constantin Brancusi, Max Ernst, Jackson Pollock, and others. Guggenheim not only collected their work, she collected *them*— having an affair with Ernst (among many others) and being one of Pollock's first patrons, cataloging her liaisons in her tell-all biography *Out of This Century* (1979) like a twentieth-century Don Giovanni. Despite great personal shyness and a botched surgery on her nose, she lived the life of a modern libertine, for whom artistic and sexual freedom went hand in hand—heir to the freethinking tradition of Queen Christina and Catherine the Great. Not everyone fawned with admiration at her prodigious acquisitiveness. In her short story, "The Cicerone," Mary McCarthy satirized Guggenheim mercilessly through an aptly named character called "Miss Grabbe," the proverbial American opportunist abroad, for whom "men were a continental commodity of which one naturally took advantage, along with the wine and the olives, the bitter coffee and the crusty bread." In rejecting the shackles of propriety, however, Guggenheim epitomized the new woman as a collector who pursued art and pleasure with abandon and without concern for respectable opinion.[22]

But such exemplary libertinism did little to deter Freudian views of collecting as a symptom of sexual repression. In the 1960s, the philosopher Jean Baudrillard spiced up his own take on collecting with some classic Freudian frissons. Baudrillard reckoned that people didn't collect for the joy of owning any one thing in itself, but rather for the satisfaction of repetition and building up entire series of objects. Collecting, he wrote, entailed a "system of objects": only by assembling sets of things was it possible to experience the pleasure of distinguishing one from another. Collectors strive to complete the set of objects to which they devote themselves, no matter what they are: first editions of Shakespeare, paintings featuring the color blue, porcelain hedgehogs. Subconsciously, however, collectors dread completion. "The acquisition of the final item," Baudrillard warned, "would in effect denote the death of the subject." By *not* assembling a complete set of objects, by continuing to collect, the collector hoped to defy the passage of time and cheat death itself.[23]

Baudrillard didn't quite say *collecting is therapy*, but he may as well have. Agreeing with Freud, he noted how almost all children adore collecting but abandon it at puberty, leaving open a possible return in middle age to compensate for carnal pleasures lost. There was a "strong whiff of the harem" about the collection, Baudrillard wrote, channeling *Vathek*. The collector was "the sultan of a secret seraglio" and his museum a petting zoo where the stroking of bibelots happily replaced all those oh so troublesome encounters with befuddling human beings. Bibliomaniacs, he thought, were assuaging their castration anxiety and maintaining "neurotic equilibrium" when they fondled their books. Writing around the same time, the American psychoanalyst Norman Weiner redefined bibliomania in proper Freudian fashion as a fetishistic antidote to castration anxiety that provided "gratification of oral, anal, and phallic strivings." Little had Leigh Hunt known.[24]

Baudrillard granted there was a certain "sublimity" to collectors, as the Ming had first suggested, because they grappled valiantly with the infinite. But in the end, collectors were sadly rather inadequate as people. "He who does collect can never entirely shake off an air of impoverishment and depleted humanity," he concluded. At some level, collectors aren't really alive. They're people who avoid death rather than live. The psychosexual compromises of modern life in a consumer society were perhaps regrettable, he conceded, yet necessary and perhaps unavoidable. After all, containment and control were preferable to dissolution and despair.[25]

But the true psychoanalytical godfather of collecting emerged later in the twentieth century. His name was Werner Muensterberger and his magnum opus—a veritable *summa* of psychohistory—was *Collecting: An Unruly Passion*, published in 1993. According to Muensterberger, collecting was not merely a symptom of repression but a response to trauma in each and every instance throughout history.

Born in Westphalia, Germany, in 1913, Muensterberger lived a long and full Freudian life until his death in 2011. Like Freud, Muensterberger fled the Nazis, escaping to the Netherlands in 1936 where he spent most of the Second World War. He then settled in the United States, where he apparently arrived with nothing but $100 and two African sculptures. Muensterberger went on to amass a sizable collection of African art and artifacts and published a volume called *Sculpture of Primitive Man*. Inspired by *Totem and Taboo*, he edited an anthology of essays by prominent psychoanalysts of anthropology such as Géza Róheim called *Man and His Culture*. Muensterberger established himself in private practice as a leading psychoanalyst in New York, as well as teaching at the State University of New York, becoming something of a celebrity analyst. James Dean, Marlon Brando, and Sir Lawrence Olivier are all said to have been clients of his. He also became friendly with Bruce Chatwin, author of *Utz*, with whom he shared a deep interest in anthropology and archaeology.

Muensterberger tells a vivid, engaging, and astonishingly totalizing story in *Collecting*. There's something wrong, he explains, deeply wrong, with every collector who has ever lived, because every collection is a manifestation of "severe inner problems" that relate to some form of childhood trauma. For Muensterberger, there is no other way to interpret a collection. The collector is somebody who procures relief from deep-seated neuroses through the possession of objects, though the sense of relief inevitably proves fleeting.

Muensterberger doesn't follow Freud to the letter. He rejects the link between collecting and anal retention, for example, as far too literal-minded. He makes the case instead that collecting is culturally rather than biologically universal. An experienced anthropologist, Muensterberger conducted fieldwork himself among Native American peoples such as the Pomo of California. Echoing Fenichel and drawing on the studies of Robert Codrington, Muensterberger regarded all collected objects as akin to the *mana* the Melanesian Islanders believe exist in certain objects: a powerful supernatural force. Collecting, therefore, involves "the transmigration of an intrinsic force." At some level, all collectors believe collections give them magical powers.[26]

Muensterberger was convinced that headhunters were bona fide collectors, too, just as rational and repressed as their Western counterparts. He conceded there *was* something of a difference between skull collectors and art collectors, yet there was also a "subliminal nexus as to the inner motivation" of both. A true Freudian egalitarian, he believed *all* human beings everywhere in the world made collections to assuage intense existential doubts about their place in the universe and establish a sense of control in an otherwise chaotic cosmos. He called this our "archaic need for reassertion."[27]

Muensterberger marched an army of past collectors onto his proverbial couch, as well as psychoanalyzing entire eras, the Middle Ages for instance. His was a tour de force of anachronism, analyzing individuals and epochs in terms they would never have understood. Relic collectors were driven not by theological concerns, he judged, but rather by a desire for "peace of mind." He defined the seventeenth-century Scientific Revolution not as a narrative about the discovery of dramatic new cosmologies but the story of "man . . . in search of himself."[28]

To be fair, there was a great vogue for psychohistory in Muensterberger's time, endorsed by the eminent Freud biographer Peter Gay among others. But consider Muensterberger's analysis of Rudolf II, one of his most insistent. He sweeps away the complex historical motives that drove Rudolf's collecting as Rudolf himself understood them—scientific experimentation, religious polemic, and his abiding interest in magic and the occult—and replaces them with psychoanalytic jargon. He calls Rudolf "a progressive paranoid type" and an "anal-obsessive," whose collecting was a response to childhood trauma and a search for "reassurance of all kinds." Muensterberger applied this same analysis to collectors across all periods of history, erasing the differences of context and motive that gave their collecting very different meanings. Bold psychoanalysis, but terrible history.[29]

It's easy to mock Muensterberger—rather *too* easy. He's almost a caricature like the parodic psychoanalyst Dr. Ludwig Brubaker in *The Seven Year Itch*—a monomaniac who looks at everyone and everything through the same foggy Freudian lens ("psychoanalysis does not recognize the *booboo* as such"). Few historians make much use of Freud these days, and Freudian interpretations of collecting are now decidedly out of fashion to say the least. There is, however, something truly majestic, if sorely misguided, about Muensterberger's grand historical narrative, weaving together as it does such a vast psychohistorical tapestry. No one before or since integrated the psychoanalysis of collecting into an overarching story, drawing together an array of ancient and modern collectors including Rudolf, Christina, Balzac, Sir Thomas Phillipps, and many more besides. *Collecting: An Unruly Passion* is an encyclopedic labor of love and one that feels highly personal. When one reads Muensterberger, his devotion to psychoanalysis is palpable. It's as though all the illustrious figures he describes really *are* patients on his couch and he desperately wants to cure every one.[30]

We'll return to the legacy of Freud, what has replaced him and what hasn't, at the end of the book. But next we meet one of the new kinds of collector the discovery of the "inner fire" of subconscious motives created. For Mabel Dodge and other modern art-lovers, collecting entailed the pursuit of beauty and the nourishment of the soul. But what if the collector's soul was a heart of darkness, driven by forces it couldn't control, as Guy de Maupassant and others had started to suggest in the late Victorian era? What if the collector was someone driven not by taste or reason, science or piety, but irrationality and a dangerous will to power over not only things but also people?

Enter a new kind of collector, who was also a new kind of magus—one who thought collecting was wrong, possibly evil and maybe even damned, but who kept collecting just the same, believing it promised spiritual liberation from the false modern gods of science, technology, and endless material progress. Enter the surrealist.

CHAPTER TEN

SURREALISTS, NATIVE COLLECTORS, AND THE COLONIAL CURSE

Do Not Visit the Colonial Exposition.

—SURREALIST SLOGAN (1931)

Several ghost stories by the Edwardian scholar M. R. James feature collectors who run afoul of mysterious forces guarding sacred treasures. A medievalist, bibliographer, and director of the Fitzwilliam Museum at Cambridge University—for which he collected books and manuscripts— James dramatized the perils of a haughty rationality that rejected the existence of the supernatural in the age of modern science. He did so through a series of tales he read out loud to his students at Cambridge, which were later published as short stories.

James's 1894 story "Canon Alberic's Scrap-Book" provides a vivid case in point. An archaeologist named Dennistoun travels from Cambridge to the town of Saint-Bertrand-de-Comminges in southern France, where he is given a tour of the local church. He eagerly makes notes and takes photographs. Noticing his interest, the church's sacristan—a strangely fearful man—shows Dennistoun an illuminated manuscript assembled by one Alberic de Mauléon, a clergyman there centuries earlier. The manuscript tells of treasure hunts and contains striking pictures. The most graphic

Illustration by James McBryde for M. R. James, "Canon Alberic's Scrap-Book"
(1894) in Ghost-Stories of an Antiquary *(London, 1904 ed.): Echoing Goya's*
Caprichos, *McBryde depicts the demonic visitation experienced by Dennistoun*
after he acquires a rare manuscript in southern France, one of many stories in
which the Cambridge medievalist James (1862–1936) portrayed collectors as cursed.

depicts "the dispute of [King] Solomon with a demon of the night": a skel-
etal, dark-haired entity resembling one of the "awful bird-catching spiders
of South America," only in human form. Would Dennistoun like to buy it?
The sacristan asks only 250 francs.[1]

Dennistoun is delighted, but doesn't want to take advantage of his host's
generosity. He knows the album is worth far more, yet the sacristan oddly
refuses to accept a larger sum. Dennistoun buys the album, and the sacristan's mood suddenly brightens. Mysteriously, the churchman insists his
daughter place a silver crucifix around Dennistoun's neck. Bemused, Dennistoun accepts this strange gift but has no idea what it means. Later that
night, alone in his room, he removes the crucifix. After doing so, he thinks
he spies a rat or a spider on his desk, only to recognize it a moment later as
the hand of the demon from the scrapbook he bought. Dennistoun grabs
the crucifix and screams.

"Canon Alberic's Scrap-Book" and many other of James's tales tell
of fussy antiquarians searching fusty manuscripts for glittering treasures

before they invariably find themselves in some obscure yet terrifying mortal peril because they have transgressed a moral law. They are modern stories on an ancient theme: the curse.

Curses are immemorial. Dating back to the ninth century BCE, to take but one example, the monolithic stela commemorating the Assyrian king Ashurnasirpal II at the Ninurta Temple in Nimrud threatened to "curse [the] destiny" of anyone who took it. By the nineteenth century, fear of curses resonated as an expression of Westerners' disquiet at their colonial conquests. Byron's mocking verses on the "noseless" Lord Elgin were just the tip of the iceberg. The Koh-i-Noor diamond, acquired and worn by Queen Victoria after 1849, was said to have a Hindu hex on it. In his 1868 novel *The Moonstone*, Wilkie Collins told the story of three Indians who travel to England to repossess a fabulous gemstone originally stolen by Mughal forces and subsequently seized by the British from Tipu Sultan during the Siege of Seringapatam. John Herncastle, the soldier who takes the stone, goes mad as a result of the theft.[2]

Yet, when M. R. James was writing at the end of the nineteenth century, exploiting this culture of the curse to sensationalistically eerie effect, collectors were also becoming a new kind of hero. What was new was the claim that collectors now possessed superior scientific methods and technological instruments that gave them the ability and the right to preserve civilizations they believed were disappearing. On this view, collectors weren't damned or doomed at all. Quite the opposite: they were saviors.

The collector had been imagined as a savior at least since the biblical story of Noah. The image of making order from chaos was reinforced time and again, as in Frans Francken's *The Cabinet of a Collector*. But in the Victorian era, this dream of salvation became technologized. Where Renaissance explorers had set out with pens and paper to laboriously write down information about exotic places, travelers after Humboldt armed themselves with an increasingly varied array of measuring instruments. The dream of scientific collecting, in other words, meant getting rid of the fallible and error-prone human collector as much as possible. If one could use a machine to measure phenomena such as temperature and humidity using numbers, it would be far more accurate and far more useful than a traveler penning such notes as *it is very hot and humid here.*

Anthropologists modeled their approach to collecting after biology. Just as Darwin had gathered specimens relating to the theory of evolution by natural selection, anthropologists now sought to gather objects that would demonstrate human evolution from allegedly simple to more complex societies. By the 1870s, specialized collectors, notably the army officer turned anthropologist Augustus Pitt Rivers—who founded Oxford's Pitt Rivers Museum in 1884—were dismissing "miscellaneous" curiosities of the kind Sir Hans Sloane had accumulated as far too randomly "procured by sailors at the seaports" and not "systematically collected, [so they] cannot be scientifically arranged." What was needed were "typological museums" to make clear how "simple forms have preceded complex ones." In archaeology, advances in techniques including stratigraphy allowed for more accurate dating of architectural remains. In his memoir *Digging up the Past* (1930), Leonard Woolley, who excavated Ur in southern Iraq with his wife, Katharine, insisted on distinguishing between the "casual digger and the plunderer" and the professional archaeologist. "Field Archaeology," he wrote, "is the application of scientific method to the excavation of ancient objects." The archaeologist was a modern "scientific worker" who noted provenance, took measurements and photos, and made extensive notes, although, indulging the proverbial opposition between the theoretical genius and the collector as dunce, Woolley added that those who excavate and document often lack "powers of synthesis and interpretation."[3]

Inspired by natural science, modern thinkers were recasting the act of collecting as one of unprecedented technological authority and endowing the figure of the collector with the heroism of a truly scientific savior. And yet, a profound reaction to this technocratic glorification of the collector very quickly set in. It was inspired by the insights of Freud, galvanized by the horrors of the First World War, and obsessed by the idea that collectors should reject scientific methods and be driven instead by the irrational impulses of a more sublime and humane unconscious instinct.

The Parisian poet and critic Guillaume Apollinaire became one of the first avatars of this new cultural movement. Apollinaire was one of the first commentators to promote the value of collecting art beyond the conventions of the Western canon and, indeed, as a way to subvert that canon. He haunted the Trocadéro—the leading Paris anthropological museum, which was later succeeded by the Musée de l'Homme and most recently by the Musée du quai Branly—in search of "savage" art and curiosities, in order to write about them and encourage the readers of his articles to follow suit and take them seriously in terms of aesthetics. Apollinaire surveyed the anthropology museum with the eyes of an artistic connoisseur and argued that masks, power figures, and sculptures from Oceania and Africa were comparable in merit and interest to the most sophisticated works of European art.

The idea was radical for the time. It influenced Picasso's fascination with African art and the emergence of cubism—a term Apollinaire coined—and, among many others, inspired a young Parisian named André Breton. From as young as twelve, Breton had begun collecting sculpture from Pacific Island peoples. And as he came of age, he masterminded an entire movement that questioned the meaning of art, the function of the collector, and all notions of reason, science, and progress, under the banner of another term invented by the ingenious Apollinaire: surrealism.

The watershed for surrealism was the First World War. During the conflict, Breton worked as a nurse in a neurology ward, witnessing firsthand the carnage that mangled the bodies of soldiers and derailed the course of European civilization, absorbing the full force of its cultural shock in the process. How could science and technology, the source of so much progress and optimism in the nineteenth century, be used to senselessly slaughter so many, seemingly to no purpose?

Regarding science and technology as amoral, the surrealists hoped instead to tap the power of the unconscious mind to deliver humanity from the disastrously false reassurances of reason. In 1920, Breton coauthored *Magnetic Fields*, an experiment in automatic writing, a form of composition so rapid, he claimed, it expressed pure thought unmediated by reason (interestingly, the phrase "as boring as a museum" appears in the book). Four years later, Breton launched the first of several manifestos in which he declared independence from what he saw as the false god of reason. Humanity was still laboring "under the reign of logic" and "absolute rationalism," he lamented, confining experience "in a cage." But now was the time to abandon the "pretense of civilization and progress" in favor of "superstition," dreams, even madness. "I could spend my whole life prying loose the secrets of the insane," he sighed. It was time to reject modern science and rediscover reverence for the marvelous rather than the factual, he urged, harking back to the cabinet of curiosities as a collection of riotous truths unstifled by the stultifying rigidity of modern classification systems. "Only the marvelous is beautiful," he wrote. It was the essence of what he called "surreality."[4]

Breton's touchstone was Freud, though his attitude to his hero mixed idolatry and misunderstanding. Freud regarded psychoanalysis as a rigorous science of mind, whereas Breton saw it as a path to irrational truths, almost approaching spiritualism. He defined surrealism as "psychic automatism" and "the absence of any control exercised by reason." Breton traveled to Vienna to interview Freud, but the admiration was not mutual. Breton felt that automatic writing and other surrealist techniques were making serious contributions to psychoanalysis; he even practiced psychiatry for a time. Freud, however, considered his visitor just another overblown and undisciplined artist infatuated with the new science of mind. But Breton was undeterred. When it was rumored in 1938 that the Nazis had kidnapped Freud, Breton published a prayer for his "illustrious master . . . from whom many of us derive our best reasons for existing and acting" and praised his "unswerving devotion to the cause of human emancipation."[5]

For Breton, the collector was a pivotal yet ambiguous figure. Like Apollinaire, he reviled art collectors as the pillars of a depressingly conservative establishment, busybodies who reduced the beauty and spirituality of great art into mere commodities of tastefulness and profit. But what if the collector could liberate art from the banalities and superficialities of the market and truly unleash its deeper spiritual potencies? Could the collector become a revolutionary?

Breton sought an escape from both modern industrial capitalism and the dead end of secular Marxist critique, as he and his fellow surrealists saw it. One path of creative subversion lay in finding beauty and value in common objects, not just what people labeled fine art. Freud, after all, had collected common things of seemingly no value to great psychological advantage: slips of the tongue, dreams, and jokes. Kurt Schwitters and other modern artists likewise began collecting ephemera, making collages from old newspapers and even refuse from the streets. Their examples inspired surrealists to find magic in the mundane.

Another exciting path lay in seeing exotic objects not as mere curiosities or even as art comparable to that of the West, therefore, but as portals to alternative forms of consciousness. Following Apollinaire, Breton developed a passionate interest in art from the Middle East, Africa, the Pacific, and the Caribbean. In the process, his version of surrealism became an anticolonial movement that opposed imperial rule and rejected European aesthetic sensibilities. After Breton was banished from France by the pro-Nazi Vichy government, he sailed to New York and the West Indies. He became friends with the Martinican anticolonial philosopher Aimé Césaire in Haiti and met the Russian revolutionary Leon Trotsky in Mexico. Returning to France in the 1950s, he became a leading critic of his country's Algerian war.

Like other collectors of his time, Breton thrived at the intersection of art and anthropology. Both in Paris and New York, the latter-day flaneur delighted in the jumble of mysterious objects he encountered from different cultures at local flea markets. Surrealist collecting involved recasting old traditions as new, so surrealists looked to the *Wunderkammer* and saw its curiosities not as expressions of divine wisdom, as did the Renaissance magus, but as playful jests. Surrealists reenvisioned the curiosity collector as an inspired prankster dissolving the limitations of the very categories *art* and *science*. To Breton, true curiosity was surreally uncategorizable.

Breton admired J.-K. Huysmans but balked at the antidemocratic snobbery of the genius responsible for *A Rebours*. He also differed with Freud. To Freud, the collector was a civilizational hero: someone whose repression of their violent instincts made possible the creation and preservation of art and culture. For Breton, by contrast, Western pretenses to civilization had been exploded forever by the mechanized atrocities and wholesale slaughter of the Great War. Non-Western art objects promised access to "primitive" consciousness, which Breton regarded as superior to Western rationalism. He believed that the collector who recognized the power of primitive art stood on the threshold of a momentous transformation from destructive bourgeois art-monger to an enlightened and emancipated shaman.

In reality, Breton's surrealism was shot through with contradictions of bureaucracy, market, and empire. His purpose was spiritual and his language mystical, yet his movement was cliquey and highly officious. It featured a Bureau of Surrealist Research, constant squabbles over who was in and who was out, and endlessly repetitive declarations and manifestos. Breton himself worked in the art market as an adviser to the impressionist collector Jacques Doucet. Many of the objects Breton collected came to France from its colonies. He spent enormous sums and amassed around 15,000 pieces, to the dismay of his wife, artist Jacqueline Lamba. In the end, he auctioned off many at the Hôtel Drouot after the Great Crash of 1929, though their remarkable variety can still be glimpsed at the Centre Pompidou in Paris.

Breton wanted to get rid of collectors and collecting. He dreamed of communing with objects as spiritual entities, liberating them from colonialism, the art market, and bourgeois taste. In his short book *Nadja* (1928), for example, he tells the story of his romance with a woman who suffers

André Breton and his curiosities by Ida Kar (1960): Inspired by Freud, Breton (1896–1966) was the leader of the surrealist movement and author of several surrealist manifestos, as well as a collector of sculpture by non-Western peoples, whose spiritual power he believed offered the possibility of transcending the limitations of Western consciousness.

from mental illness, but in whose mind objects resonate with brilliant vividness. He wrote that the first piece of art he ever acquired from Easter Island spoke to Nadja the words "I love you, I love you." For Breton, the true collector didn't possess the object, the object possessed the collector.[6]

His most treasured possession of all was a power figure made by the Pacific peoples of New Ireland called *Uli*. Breton saw Uli at auction in Paris in 1930 but couldn't afford to buy it, so instead he dreamed about it, wrote poems about it, and even named one of his dogs Uli. He had to have it and finally did, buying it in 1964, just two years before his death. Placing Uli on his desk at long last, he idolized it. "You are a great God," he addressed the figure before him, "your creation prostrates us." To Breton, the collector could indeed become a visionary and a revolutionary.[7]

No one confronted the moral quandaries of collecting more than Breton's fellow Parisian the anthropologist Michel Leiris. Like Breton, only more so, Leiris dismantled the idea of the collector as a scientific savior and replaced it with a fusion of Freud, surrealism, and anthropology that radically questioned whether the impulse to collect possessed any scientific or moral worth whatsoever—or the exact opposite.

Born in 1901, Leiris studied philosophy and chemistry before becoming inspired by cubism and joining the surrealist movement, though he was never close to Breton. In 1929, he suffered the onslaught of a profound personal crisis that would prove lifelong. He entered psychoanalysis; at one point, he attempted suicide. Like Breton, Leiris began to search for something more than critiques of power as a path to genuinely spiritual enlightenment. And like other surrealists, he found more inspiration in jazz and the dizzying dances of Josephine Baker in Montmartre than in the finer points of Marxist analysis.

Leiris soon became disillusioned with psychoanalysis, however. Instead, he turned to travel. After studying with the eminent anthropologist Marcel Mauss, he became secretary-archivist to the Mission Dakar-Djibouti during 1931–33 under Marcel Griaule. The mission was an expedition from northern Africa's west coast to its east coast, sponsored by the French government and the Rockefeller Foundation. It was colonial anthropology in action: an attempt to gather information to help French administrators govern African territories while collecting artifacts for the Trocadéro museum.

While in Africa, Leiris buried himself in his duties. The mission was heavily bureaucratic, generating countless notes and lists, and sending more than 3,500 objects back to Paris, as well as more than 6,000 photos, and sound recordings. Leiris also kept a journal that became the book *Phantom Africa* (1934), one of the first works of reflexive anthropology that analyzed the anthropologist on his travels. A self-consciously Freudian and Conradian work, Leiris explored his own personal heart of darkness in the book; it even includes a section that outlines a story about the mysterious death of a Kurtz-like colonial. And it embodies the contradiction of a surrealist critic of Western reason who remained a consummate bureaucrat, while he gathered countless self-observations with the goal of self-analysis.

Light years from Humboldt's heroics or Wallace's stoicism, *Phantom Africa* is an epic confession of existential doubt. Instead of supporting the scientific claims of his anthropological mission, Leiris confessed his dismay at the workings of both colonialism and collecting. He recorded his dreams and nightmares, his sexual encounters and masochistic longings, his insomnia and depression. The image of collecting he produced is one of collective cultural insanity. One day, he witnessed a "wacky colonial" who was "chasing little birds" like a demented hunter. Another time, when raiding a cave to obtain human skulls, he noted how his colleagues burst into "mad laughter" in the process. He felt appalled by how bizarre they doubtless appeared to the locals: "we must look like ultra-comic animals with our sun helmets, our shorts, and all our outlandish equipment."[8]

In theory, the expedition sought to pay fair prices for African artifacts, but in reality, the anthropologists resorted to chicanery. Griaule threatened those who refused to part with statues and paintings in Gonda, Ethiopia. He obtained the Kono fetish from the Bla people in present-day Mali by suggesting he'd call in the police if they didn't cooperate. To Leiris, this amounted to criminal plunder and blackmail. But he neither denounced nor resisted these activities. Such behavior left him "without remorse," he wrote to his wife Louise Godon back in Paris. He did not regard the seizures as "sacrilege," he went on—he was far too modern for such a "grandiose" notion—though he admitted they *felt* like sacrilege, indeed, thrillingly so. "I feel as if I have stolen fire," he wrote after he had spent some time handling the Kono fetish, comparing himself to Prometheus.[9]

Leiris was nonetheless clear-eyed about what he called the "vicious circle" of collecting. "We pillage the Negroes," he wrote, "under the pretext of teaching people to understand and appreciate them [only] to mold other ethnographers who will go in turn to 'appreciate' and to pillage them." Like Breton, Leiris wanted to get rid of the collector, but again found he couldn't quite stop collecting himself. He loathed colonialism and fantasized about leading Africans in a war against Europe. In the end, however, he was too preoccupied with his own quest for self-knowledge to commit fully to political action. Fascinated by the possibilities of trance, he participated in Dar possession ceremonies and drank the blood of sacrificial animals. But he was far too Western, he concluded, to transcend his sense of self, experiencing only "the sensation of being at the edge of something whose depths I will never touch . . . because I do not have the power to let myself go."[10]

After returning to Paris, Leiris took up a post at the Trocadéro, which he held for many years. Among other things, he became a Freudianized bibliomaniac, taking "almost fetishistic care of my books," he wrote, noting how he had "transferred" his tenderness for his mother to these volumes. He remained deeply conflicted over collecting and museums. He once wrote a story where his narrator fantasized about making love to women in the galleries, a Freudian vision of libertine sexuality rending the veil of civilization. In a dream he recorded, he imagined the Musée Guimet of Asian art in Paris as a slaughterhouse full of dead bodies, recalling Maupassant's bloody story about the Muséum national d'Histoire naturelle.[11]

Leiris was his own psychiatric bureaucrat. He may have disavowed psychoanalysis, but he continued to practice his own version of it, collecting every scrap of introspection he could about himself, as though he were assembling a gigantic collage of his own soul. Picasso, Alberto Giacometti, and Francis Bacon all painted his portrait in various states of psychic fragmentation. But as the titles of his published autobiographical self-analyses suggest—*Scratches, Scraps, Fibrils, Frail Riffs*—Leiris remained plagued by the suspicion that there was no overarching unity to his existence. Nor to the act of collecting. At one point, he tells the story of a silver pendant cross he obtained from a lover of his named Khadidja in Algeria. Leiris later gave the cross to his wife, who wore it until the Gestapo seized it from her in

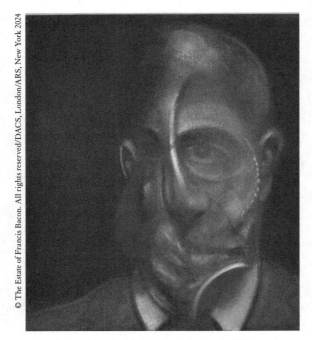

Portrait of Michel Leiris *by Francis Bacon (1978):*
Leiris (1901–90) was a Paris-trained anthropologist who
underwent psychoanalysis and worked on the Mission Dakar-
Djibouti in Africa seeking, like Breton, liberation from
Western consciousness. He was highly critical of French
collecting practices in Africa and published many self-critical
autobiographical works.

1943. Leiris's conclusion? Collecting was like writing in water, as Holbrook Jackson put it: an act of cosmic fragility, if not futility.

Leiris became an early hero of reflexive anthropology and an avatar of "showing showing": situating oneself in one's work as a participant rather than an observer. In an interview published in 1988, however, the American anthropologist Sally Price challenged Leiris by asking him whether it was wrong to collect African objects during the Mission Dakar-Djibouti as he did. "Some of what we did was very wrong," Leiris agreed and endorsed the idea that such objects should be repatriated to Africa. Surrealism was nonetheless radical for its time. As Leiris said, the surrealist cry was not merely "down with France" but supported a full-scale "rebellion against

Western civilization." In the end, surrealism was about much more than politics. It sought the liberation of the spirit and the creation of a new experimental self.[12]

Rejecting the idea that collectors were scientific saviors who produced order from chaos, surrealist-inspired visions of collecting flourished in many forms after the First World War. Instead, it was back to the Renaissance ideal of the collector as magus and to the nineteenth-century vision of the collector as an antimodern hero resisting the march of time, money, and progress, albeit with a mystical twist.

In his essay "Unpacking My Library," the German critic Walter Benjamin returned to these older images of the collector as a mystic and a magus. Written in 1931, it foreshadows Benjamin's status as a Jew who fled the Nazis and lived in exile, before he took his own life in 1940 to evade deportation to a concentration camp. Growing up in Berlin early in the century, Benjamin inhabited a world of industrial manufacturing, mass culture, and new technology including photography and cinema. A flaneur and student of Baudelaire, Benjamin embarked on an obsessive quest to find personal meaning in the increasingly impersonal landscape of mass consumer society. Turning to Marx to understand capitalism as the genie of modernity, he also became fascinated by mysticism, parting company with Freud as an atheist who regarded religion as a mere psychological opiate. Benjamin attended some surrealist meetings but never became a fully paid-up member of the movement. He was also a collector, accumulating works of modern art along with his wife Dora, as well as rare editions of Baudelaire, Balzac, and Goethe, and more than 200 children's books.

According to Benjamin, the collector creates a private magical realm out of a selfish impulse to retreat into a world of one's own. The "true collector," he writes, doesn't collect to advance knowledge or the public good but to create a world elsewhere. Reviving the image of the reclusive Rudolfine magus once more, he sees the collector as a secretive sorcerer who turns the collection into a "magic encyclopedia," investing its contents with deep personal meaning. He admits "this passion is behind the times," arcane and even self-absorbed, conceding that the collector's aim is to "disappear inside" the collection and leave the real world behind. But as such, collecting is therefore a noble quest to recapture the "enchantment" of life that the sociologist Max Weber thought the modern world had destroyed.[13]

Like the Ming collectors afflicted by *pǐ*, and like Oldbuck, Pons, and Des Esseintes, Benjamin's collector is an obsessive and an authentic who thrives precisely by turning inward and living out a childlike dream life. Benjamin comes back to life when he unpacks his crates of books, achieving a sense of "renewal" by reuniting with his possessions and their histories, while, like Pons and as William James warned, risking the annihilation of his identity should he lose them. To own was to live, but to lose was to die. A true collector senses the risk posed by the precariousness of his ownership all too keenly. "Every passion borders on the chaotic," Benjamin observes, "but the collector's passion borders on the chaos of memories." This is what Benjamin's books mean to him. Unpacking them sets off memories of ecstatic auction hunts where he bid for the thrill of possession. It's not that his books "come alive in him; it is he who lives in them."[14]

Like a true bibliomaniac, Benjamin did not actually read all his books. That was not the point. But unpacking his books allowed him to reconstitute himself through his possessions in a chaotic world. That was why keeping them together was so important, something Freud also understood when he shipped his antiquities from Vienna to London in 1938. Benjamin was not so fortunate, however. When he eventually took his life in the Pyrenees to evade the Nazis, the bag he was carrying contained a watch, some money, a passport, photos and newspapers but, it seems, no books.

Besides Benjamin, the other great interwar statement about collecting as a chaotic rather than orderly quest for knowledge and selfhood came from the Argentinian surrealist Jorge Luis Borges. Where Benjamin wrote a claustrophobically personal self-portrait, Borges was strikingly abstract and impersonal—so impersonal, in fact, that no collector as such appears in his stories. Like Benjamin, however, Borges believed collecting was an inherently irrational pursuit. Writing in the 1940s and influenced by Asian religion and philosophy, Borges proposed that every rational human endeavor possesses an irrational wellspring. Like the fantastical perspective-bending drawings of M. C. Escher, Borges's philosophical fables turn scientific premises of aggregating facts into accurate pictures of the world inside-out to reveal the pursuit of knowledge as a labyrinth in which we lose ourselves by seeking an objective truth whose reality turns out to be a matter of subjective perception.

"The Analytical Philosophy of John Wilkins" (1942) for example, argues that a truly scientific classification system is impossible. Describing a seventeenth-century philosopher's attempt to devise an objective or "natural" system for categorizing physical objects, Borges compares this project with an imaginary Chinese encyclopedia that overflows with amusingly arbitrary ways of classifying animals. These include animals "that belong to the emperor"; "embalmed ones"; "those drawn with a very fine camelhair brush"; and "those that look like flies from a long way off." Borges's point was that no classification system can ever be entirely rational, self-evident, or universal. All systems make assumptions that look illogical to outsiders. By implication, collectors who seek to impose order on their collections through classification inevitably impose personal preferences rather than applying strictly scientific criteria. Objective order is an illusion.[15]

Borges brings us a step closer to the collector through the figure of the librarian in his allegory "The Library of Babel" (1941)—but, typically for the elusive Borges, only a step. The Library of Babel is made up of a vast number of hexagonal galleries and is said to be total and infinite. It contains all possible combinations of characters and syntax, meaning that it holds all the books that ever have been written, as well as all the books that ever *could* be written. There is no guarantee, however, that anyone who enters the library will find the volume they are seeking, because man is inevitably an "imperfect librarian." There *is* an omniscient, godlike librarian somewhere in the library who has seen "the catalogue of catalogues" and who well might help us find what we're looking for. But this librarian cannot easily be found, so visitors have to make their own way through the library.[16]

"If," Borges writes, "an eternal traveler should journey in any direction, he would find after untold centuries that the same volumes are repeated in the same disorder—which, repeated, becomes order." Benjamin imagined himself fleeing modernity through the magic of the collection, but Borges's vision was more sublimely ironic: we may lose ourselves in the very systems we construct for making order. Where Breton and Leiris chafed at the moral and political contradictions of collecting, Borges was guided instead by a far deeper and rather gentler cosmic pathos: the dream of total scientific comprehension is Escher-like and merely leads us into the realm of the unknowable. This does not mean there is no such thing as order, but it may only exist in the eye of the beholder.[17]

Breton and Leiris wanted to get rid of the collector but couldn't. They objected to the exploitation they saw at work in collecting but continued to acquire objects and work with museums. In reality, however, Western anthropological collectors did not work alone, typically relying on "native collectors" to obtain objects for them from among indigenous communities. Native collectors assisted anthropologists because they agreed it was important to preserve artifacts from their societies. But by collecting across different worlds, native collectors had to endure the predicament of belonging at once to both and neither, even as they found new homes for objects from their cultures in Western museums.

The dominant anthropological assumption of the late nineteenth century was that many indigenous societies were on the verge of disappearance. Dwindling populations, rampant diseases including smallpox and tuberculosis, the encroachment of white traders, colonizers and missionaries, and the ascendancy of eugenics as an ideology of inevitable racial competition all combined to encourage the idea that collecting artifacts from indigenous peoples was a fitting way to create a record of vanishing cultures. For a range of complicated reasons, native collectors decided to assist in this effort.

Born in 1854 on Vancouver Island in Canada, George Hunt was of mixed parentage. His mother, Mary, was the daughter of a Tlingit chief, but his father was a Hudson's Bay Company fur trader. Hunt grew up bilingual and worked as a guide and interpreter for the eminent German anthropologist Franz Boas after 1886, helping Boas collect objects ranging from human skulls to sacred artifacts from the Kwakwaka'wakw people (then known as the Kwakiutl). Boas denounced eugenics and collected objects in order to understand their cultural meaning in the context of living indigenous cultures, rather than schematically tracing their evolution over time in order to prove any alleged theory about the development of complex societies from simple ones like Augusts Pitt Rivers. Hunt assisted Boas to this end, including reading out greetings from Boas to his native contacts while collecting among them. "My friend George Hunt," one letter read, "will show you a box in which some of your stories will be kept. . . . It is a good book, for in it are your laws and stories. Now they will not be forgotten."[18]

Hunt and Boas became great collaborators. They organized a live Tlingit exhibition together at the 1893 Chicago Exposition (these artifacts are still held at the Field Museum in Chicago). But Hunt got into trouble with his own people. Was the native collector a savior of indigenous culture or a traitor to his own kind? Many elders seemed to approve of Hunt, but on a visit to Alert Bay, British Columbia, in 1898, he found the local people were angry with him. "They say here is he who is finding out all our dances then he goes and tell it to Dr. Boas." Hunt was arrested in 1900 while observing ritual performances, tried, and fined $500 in Vancouver.[19]

Louis Shotridge was another high-born Tlingit man, from Kluckwan on the Alaska coast. Even more than Hunt's, his story dramatizes the predicament of the native collector. Born in 1883, Shotridge—also known as *Situwuka*, or "Astute One"—and his wife Florence were bicultural, attending missionary school and becoming bilingual. By the 1920s, they were collecting for George Byron Gordon, curator of American Archaeology at the University of Pennsylvania's Museum of Archaeology and Anthropology in Philadelphia, Louis drawing a full-time salary (he even enrolled in Penn's Wharton Business School). Louis and Florence collected numerous artifacts for Gordon and also recorded dances and songs.

Louis trained as an anthropologist under Boas at Columbia University before returning to British Columbia to buy pre-Contact objects as "authentic" examples of Tlingit culture. This concern with "authentic" objects was the anthropological equivalent of the Freudian idea that collections embodied an essential self, underpinning the assumption that it was possible to collect objects that captured the essential cultural identity of a society. In Shotridge's case, this included masks, utensils, and pipes, as well as compiling Tlingit grammars. He even hired his own native informant and referred to "the natives" in his letters to Gordon.

Shotridge's letters reveal a life lived between indigenous and Western societies, in which the native collector ultimately strove with difficulty to explain his actions both to himself and to posterity. Writing in 1923,

Shotridge wondered whether it was best for indigenous societies to retain all their own cultural possessions or instead "place them where they will continue . . . in the world of culture?" He feared such patrimony might genuinely be lost. "White men are not all the same," he believed. Some were "noble," collecting not for profit but to "present our history to the modern world."[20]

Shotridge was not wrong to argue that Western collecting created worldwide awareness of and interest in the culture and history of his people. But he could never quiet suspicions—including his own—that he was betraying his own people. In 1929, he wrote an article about the Kanguanton Shark Helmet, which he had collected. It was another collector's confession. "If only one of the true warriors of that clan" had been there to stop him, he conceded, he'd never have been able to remove it. "I took it in the presence of aged women," he recounted, who "could do nothing more than weep" at his audacity. "The modernized part of me rejoiced," he went on, but "in my heart I cannot but have the feeling of a traitor." Shotridge could not resolve the quandary of a divided self. Others resolved matters for him. After being let go by Penn, Shotridge returned to British Columbia to work as a river guard but was later found dead with his neck broken. Whether this was an accident or an act of revenge is unknown. Many of his artifacts remain at Penn, though some have been repatriated under NAGPRA, the 1990 Native American Graves Protection and Repatriation Act.[21]

But history's most unusual native collector may be Don Chuka Talayesva, a Hopi man from Oraibi, Arizona. This is because Talayesva not only helped anthropologists collect his culture; he helped them collect his self.

In the same way that Hunt is best known for his connection to Boas, Talayesva is rather less famous than the anthropologist associated with his people: Aby Warburg. An art historian and collector who founded a library and institute at the University of London, Warburg devoted his career to tracing cultural resonances across radically different traditions, from ancient Rome to indigenous societies including the Hopi. He traveled to Oraibi in 1896, where he was guided by the Mennonite missionary Heinrich Voth, who was fluent in Hopi and assisted many anthropologists seeking to document the era of the Ghost Dance, a period of unified Native American resistance to white settlers at century's end.

Held in the Smithsonian American Art Museum

Elias Grossman, Chief Don Talayesva *(1941): Talayesva (1890–1985) was a Hopi man from New Mexico who assisted anthropologists in collecting information from among his people, including recounting his own dreams and authoring a memoir called* Sun Chief *(1942), with the result that some Hopi alleged Talayesva sold sacred secrets for money and fame.*

Talayesva was also a Christianized Indian, who attended mission schools in Arizona and learned English. He was distinctive for the frankly commercial way he sold information to anthropologists about the innermost details of his personal life, ranging from his sexual habits to his dreams. One historian has called him anthropology's "most documented man": he's thought to have given 350 hours of interviews and reported 341 of his dreams, including ones about acquiring white friends and achieving fame in Europe. Talayesva's career thus marked a deepening of the Freudian encounter with anthropology. American social scientists wanted to collect his data to psychoanalyze him as an individual and to assess the evolution of "the primitive mind."[22]

Talayesva lived at a time when Hopi society was divided into *Friendlies* and *Hostiles*, rival groups who took very different views of the wisdom of accommodating white people. Talayesva's own family was torn, as his initial misgivings gave way to an eager embrace. In some ways, he got the recognition he craved for his collaboration. His autobiography *Sun Chief* (1942) was published to great acclaim. He even carried on a correspondence with André Breton, who traveled to Arizona and attended Hopi ceremonies in 1945, bringing Hopi *Kachina* dolls back for his collection in Paris. When *Sun Chief* came out in French, Breton eulogized Talayesva as a romantic hero fighting "all forms of oppression and [the] alienation of modern society." Talayesva, Breton wrote, embodied "*man* in his marvelously safeguarded original truth" and "the immortal genius of the American Indian."[23]

But like Hunt and Shotridge, Talayesva's collecting mired him in controversy. He admitted he'd happily "talk in the shade for cash" and charged seven cents for every diary page he wrote for anthropologists (who may have also bought him a car). His fellow Hopi eventually accused him of selling ceremonial secrets and sacred objects and of digging up Hopi dead to display them in the Field Museum. Here, Talayesva drew the line, insisting he knew the difference between information and secrets. Warburg's friend Voth was the real culprit, he claimed. That "damned missionary" was "wicked," he wrote, an "evil" invader who stole without permission. Worst of all, Voth was a hypocrite who "claimed that our gods were no good," yet disobeyed his own. He "told [us] to avoid all graven images; but you have stolen ours and set them up in your museum."[24]

Unsurprisingly, during these decades of archaeological and anthropological exploration, colonial tensions and world war, fears that collecting was a sacrilegious looting of the sacred were never dispelled by the claims of scientific salvation. As a result, Western popular culture became ever more fascinated by the idea that the collector was a sinner and cursed.

It wasn't just the ghost stories of M. R. James. In 1922, the so-called Curse of Tutankhamun was widely cited in the international press as causing the death of Lord Carnarvon shortly after the man he bankrolled, Howard Carter, entered Tutankhamun's tomb in the Valley of the Kings near Thebes in Egypt. Carnarvon died of pneumonia after sustaining a mosquito bite and razor cut that became infected, and toxic fungus in the tomb may also have played a role in his demise. But these facts proved no match for curse lore, reinforced by countless films beginning with *The Mummy* (1932) starring Boris Karloff. Curses rampaged through the popular imagination. In 1948, the Belgian cartoonist Hergé plunged his intrepid reporter Tintin into the mystery of *The Seven Crystal Balls*, where a team of anthropologists falls into a trance-like madness as punishment for violating the tombs of the Incas of Peru. "What would we say if the Egyptians or Peruvians came here to open the tombs of *our* kings?" Tintin is asked at the beginning of the story. He has no answer. As collecting became more modern, scientific, and heroic, the fear only grew that it in fact represented a primordial transgression that would be punished by ancient and supernatural forms of retribution.[25]

After the Second World War, as European empires were gradually dismantled by processes of retreat, decolonization, and emancipation, the idea crystallized that there was something fatally irredeemable about the Western collector as a central culprit in the sin of colonialism. In his

©Hergé/Tintinimaginatio 2025

Archaeologists plagued by madness in Hergé, The Seven Crystal Balls *(1948): the reporter Tintin investigates the mysterious madness that strikes members of the fictional Sanders-Hardiman expedition to excavate the Inca tombs of Peru, an expression of the culture of the curse in modern popular culture.*

1955 *Discourse on Colonialism*, Aimé Césaire—André Breton's Martinican comrade—was among the first to reject outright the idea that collecting was a positive act of civilizational salvation, seeing it instead as an act of reprehensible violence. Going well beyond the surrealists, Césaire stated categorically that the world would have been better off if museums had simply never existed.

To Césaire, the Western collector was not a savior but a butcher. It would have been far better to "tolerate the non-European civilizations," he wrote, "leaving them alive, dynamic and prosperous, whole and not mutilated," rather than try to collect them. Turning Maupassant and Leiris's nightmarish visions of the museum as slaughterhouse into a political denunciation, Césaire saw collectors as killers who "duly label" cultures after cutting them into "dead and scattered parts." At their core was racism: "the smug self-satisfaction" of those who have only contempt for other peoples. The museum "is nothing . . . it means nothing [and] . . . it can say nothing," he went on, concluding that "in the scales of knowledge, all the museums in the world will never weigh so much as one spark of human sympathy."[26]

Césaire gave full expression to the misgivings of Shotridge, Talayesva, and other native collectors, people who were cursed in their own fashion by their involvement in anthropology. It is one of the bitter ironies in the history of collecting, however, that in the same years anticolonial writers began to denounce collectors as sacrilegious invaders, totalitarian ideologues used almost exactly the same terms to persecute collectors as enemies of nation and state. In a bizarre twist of ideological fate, authoritarian regimes agreed that bourgeois selfhood was bad, collecting was decadent, and that collectors were evil intruders who had to be eliminated for the common good.

CHAPTER ELEVEN

HOW TO SAVE YOUR
PORCELAIN

Was the collector a class-enemy?

—BRUCE CHATWIN, *UTZ* (1988)

Shanghai, 1966. In the early stages of China's Cultural Revolution, the home of the affluent, London-educated collector Nien Cheng (real name Yao Nien-Yuan) is raided by Red Guards—the militant wing of Mao Zedong's ruling Communist Party. The Red Guards are young, zealous, and aggressive. They want to strike in the name of the people against enemies of the party and their leader by executing Mao's command to "smash the Four Olds": Old Ideas, Old Culture, Old Habits, Old Customs. This includes destroying antiques—as if a Marxist millennium might be realized by literally eradicating the past by smashing one Ming vase at a time.

The Red Guards menace Cheng, her daughter, and their servants as they turn the house over. Cheng looks worriedly at her paintings and her dining table, her lacquered screen, her gemstones, and her collection of porcelains. She knows they're in jeopardy. The Red Guards taunt her. She is "rich and lazy," they say, and in league with foreigners. She's a decadent Western-style bourgeoise, addicted to wealth and distinction—a "capitalist-roader" bent on corrupting Chinese Communism. Cheng isn't intimidated, however, and talks back. When the intruders insist everyone must be equal in the new era, she challenges them by pointing out that the illustrious Mao himself and his cronies enjoy many luxuries ordinary people do not. She is whipped for her trouble.[1]

The Red Guards start wrecking Cheng's possessions. They smash a mirror hanging over a vase from the time of the Kangxi emperor. They destroy the portrait of a lady above Cheng's sideboard. One of them holds a figure of the Buddhist deity Guanyin in the air and declares, "this is a figure of Buddhist superstition. I'm going to throw it in the trash." Then they turn to Cheng's collection of porcelains. There is no greater symbol than porcelain of the collector's fragile dream of loving preservation and, to the Red Guards, the collector's vanity.[2]

Cheng confronts the invaders. "No one in this world can make another winecup like this one," she tells them. "This is a part of our cultural heritage. Every Chinese should be proud of it." Such things certainly do belong to the past, she concedes, and the past must indeed make way for socialism. But they don't have to be destroyed. "Remember," she says, "they were not made by members of the capitalist class," but "by the hands of the workers. . . . Should you not respect the labor of those workers?" Would it not please Mao more to sell them, she reasons, use them to finance the revolution, and place them in the Shanghai Museum for the glory of the state? "You shut up!" one of the Red Guards yells at her. These things "belong to the old culture," they reply. "They are the useless toys of the feudal emperors and the modern capitalist class and have no significance to us." After all, Mao taught them that "if we do not destroy, we cannot establish. The old culture must be destroyed to make way for the new socialist culture."[3]

Did Cheng's retorts, made with such poise and courage, actually work? Did she succeed in saving her porcelains? The answer is best left until we see Cheng's plight in its full context: the singular predicament of the private collector seen as an enemy of the state by modern totalitarian regimes in the twentieth century.

There had always been religious iconoclasts, in China as elsewhere in the world, determined to discourage belief in false gods by smashing objects. But Cheng's encounter with Mao's secular iconoclasts marked a significant mutation and reversal in the cultural history of the collector. Writers from Ming China to Europe's fin de siècle had insisted that the *true* collector collected for love, passion, or obsession—not, to recall Walter Scott once more, through "force of money." Money was mercenary; monomania was authentic. The true collector was a counter-cultural hero who resisted the commercialization of beauty and the march of the almighty dollar symbolized by Keppler's cartoon lampooning J. P. Morgan's world-sucking dollar-shaped magnet.

In the twentieth century, Communist regimes in the Soviet Union, Eastern Europe, and China agreed with earlier writers from Balzac to André Breton and Aimé Césaire that bourgeois collecting for profit, status, and (imperial) power was fundamentally hollow, if not morally bankrupt. But these regimes went much further. They transformed the figure of the collector into an ideological foe and an enemy of the people—a class enemy. They turned Freudian psychoanalysis—the bourgeois science of self par excellence—inside out. The problem with collectors was not some kind of unresolved sexual neurosis, they supposed, but collectors' materialistic love of things and social status. Communist ideology, in other words, repudiated Romantic and Freudian ideas of collecting as an expression of individuality as an unpardonable violation of the new imperative of social egalitarianism. Private collectors became anathema, therefore. The ideological die was cast. But could totalitarians actually go one better than the surrealists and the postcolonialists and rid society of the bourgeois collector altogether? Or could the collector somehow survive?

The transformation of the private collector into an enemy of the people began in the late nineteenth century, with attacks on Jewish art collectors—not as class warfare but as a form of antisemitic racism. For centuries, despite their skill in various trades and professions, including money-lending or usury, and owing to their financial success despite being socially marginalized, Jews had been subject to criticism and calumny. By the late nineteenth century, however, a number of European Jews had amassed sizable fortunes, and their wealth became increasingly conspicuous. Jewish families among Europe's upper classes made fortunes in industrialization, finance, and banking, and took to collecting Old Masters and decorative arts, and buying up historic homes. The most renowned were the German-born Rothschild family, but they were only one of many living in France, including the Ukrainian-born Ephrussis and the Ottoman-born Camondos, whose stories have been poignantly retold in *The Hare with Amber Eyes* by Edmund de Waal, an Ephrussi descendant.

Antisemitic attacks on Jewish collectors became especially acute in France in the latter part of the nineteenth century. France had been soundly defeated by Prussia in the war of 1870–71, producing a deep and pervasive sense of humiliation. The country's lingering aristocratic order finally crumbled, making it into a permanent republic. But French pride was wounded, and several commentators seized upon wealthy Jewish collectors as scapegoats for the nation's malaise, portraying them as invaders who were criminally stealing and sapping Frenchness itself by acquiring the nation's patrimony.

The prominent conservative society writers Edmond and Jules Goncourt took the lead in launching these attacks. Collectors in their own right who were influential in promoting the appreciation of East Asian decorative arts, not to mention energetic salon-goers and indefatigable diarists of the fin de siècle, the Goncourts were deeply nostalgic nationalists who resented rising Jewish wealth and prominence. Encountering the Jewish collector Louise Cahen d'Anvers in 1880, for example, they described what they called the "lazy cat movements with which [she] fished her porcelain and her lacquer-ware out from the bottom of her vitrine." They fixated on the golden sheen of her blonde hair, as though it were a physical manifestation of Jews' allegedly unique obsession with money.[4]

Collectors had often been seen as arrivistes, of course. As an Ulster-born professional man in eighteenth-century London, even Sir Hans Sloane faced the charge that he was an ignorant outsider bulk-buying collections merely for status. Similar though rather more insidious attacks were made on Jewish collectors. Led by the Goncourts, critics insinuated that Jews were ignorant and therefore often bought fakes by mistake and spent absurdly, inflating prices beyond what real collectors (the envious Goncourts among them) could afford. They didn't simply see Jewish collectors as bourgeois money-grubbers or outsiders. They painted them as rootless cosmopolitans who could never really be French, no matter what they owned. They were alien invaders and always would be.

Published in 1886, Edouard Drumont's *La France juive* (Jewish France) promoted anti-Jewish financial conspiracy theories. In it, Drumont, an antiquarian, poured scorn on what he called Jews' "love of the bibelot" and "the Jewish sense of acquisition, of possessiveness." Drumont derided the "goût Rothschild" in particular for its eclecticism, to him the expression of a fatal lack of judgment and taste. Anticipating Mary Berenson's invidious tirade against Isabella Stewart Gardner and her highly varied collection, Drumont made his attack on what he saw as the indiscrimination of Jewish art collecting part of a larger smear that Jews were greedy, ignorant, and would never become truly respectable members of the upper echelons of French society. "These oppressive spoils of the universe do not harmonize," Drumont declared. They were "a mess, a trainwreck [and] an incredible junk store." It was "heartbreaking," he wrote of the Rothschilds' Louis XVI room, for example, to find Marie Antoinette's own harpsichord "in this house of Jews."[5]

In the same years that Henry James was rounding on the American robber barons of the Gilded Age as soulless art-magnets, Jewish collectors were also held up in almost identical terms as the antithesis of the true collector: all calculation and no passion, they were inauthentic, hollow, and disingenuous. Edmond Goncourt despised the "falseness" of the objects, paintings, and sculptures he saw at a Rothschild party in 1889—and, by extension, the falseness of their owners. The journalist Léon Daudet went even further, describing the Ephrussis as "truncated, hybrid beings . . . in search of an impossible nationality." The Jewish collector was not merely a fake connoisseur, but a fake person.[6]

The antipathy between polite society and the figure of the Jewish collector deepened over time. Marcel Proust's *Remembrance of Things Past* (1913) imagined with astonishing depth and vividness the world of Charles Swann, a character based in part on Charles Ephrussi. Both men were dandyish scholars of Renaissance art and collected impressionist paintings. They were also both Jewish. After the Jewish military officer Alfred Dreyfus was wrongly convicted of treason and sent to the Devil's Island prison colony in 1894–95, French society divided into Dreyfusard and anti-Dreyfusard camps. At one point, Proust has one of his characters, the Duc de Guermantes, confess his disappointment that Swann sympathizes with Dreyfus, something he finds especially regrettable because Swann is a collector. "I should never have believed it of him," says Guermantes, "an epicure, a man of practical judgment, a collector, a connoisseur of old books." While Jews might become collectors, in other words, a *true* collector should adopt respectably conservative stances—such as antisemitism.[7]

When the Wall Street Crash occurred in 1929, triggering the Great Depression, it was almost inevitable, therefore, that Jewish bankers and financiers would be blamed. In 1933, Adolf Hitler's National Socialists seized power in Germany and adopted racial laws to exclude Jews from German life, seizing much of their wealth and property. Jewish collectors, artists, and dealers immediately and unsurprisingly found themselves in significant peril. After annexing Austria, the Nazis sequestered the assets of bankers including the Ephrussis in Vienna, dissolving their businesses and confiscating their art collections. Some collectors fled, many had their property stolen outright, and others were obliged to live in exile and poverty. Some, such as Elisabeth de Rothschild, were arrested and died in concentration camps.

The Nazis' assault on Jewish collectors was part of a broader campaign against Jewish bankers and artists. Their most notorious anti-art stunt was the 1937 Munich exhibition they organized called "Entartete Kunst" (Degenerate Art). Reviving and instrumentalizing Max Nordau's diatribe against "degenerate" culture—ironically, the Jewish Nordau had been a leading Zionist—they denounced the modern art market as a "Judeo-Bolshevist" conspiracy designed to defraud honest Germans. They diagnosed Jewish artists, dealers, and collectors as the symptoms of a cultural and financial disease, bourgeois degenerates who got rich by imposing perverted foreign aesthetics on ordinary Germans.

In response to this alleged threat of cultural degeneracy, Hitler—who grew up in Linz, Austria, and began life as a frustrated painter of picturesque landscapes and urban scenes—declared all "non-obvious" art forbidden as acts of "artistic bolshevism," to be replaced by work "the average German" could understand without explanation. Antimilitarist painters of the Interwar period such as Otto Dix and Georg Grosz were repudiated on account of their being driven by Marxist ideology, or so the Nazis insisted, and works including the surrealist collages of Kurt Schwitters denounced as "Jewish trash" and "total madness." The Nazis banned such works as a form of cultural pollution, a degenerate parade of visual abnormality. A new

House of German Art was announced, which would canonize "Aryan" art instead. Jewish artists, editors, and curators were ostracized, and collectors were pressured into distancing themselves from international modern art and embracing state-approved German art.[8]

Jews involved in the German art world found themselves in an impossible position, in Germany and beyond. Consider the fate of Ludwig Pollak in Rome. Pollak was a Czech-born Jewish antiquarian, connoisseur, and curator at the Museo Barracco, and a collector devoted to Goethe, Judaism, and his native Prague. In 1906, he recognized and purchased the missing arm of the ancient statue of *Laocoön and His Sons*, which was later restored to the original sculpture in the Vatican, correcting the way the art world saw one of the most important works of classical art ever created. After the Nazis occupied Rome in 1943 and threatened to deport Jews to the concentration camps, the Vatican, recognizing Pollak's importance as a scholar, offered him and his family shelter from persecution. Tragically, and for reasons that are not clear, Pollak refused. He may simply not have believed the Nazis would go so far as to seize him or trusted that being in Rome would protect him, but he and his family were sent to Auschwitz and murdered in October 1943.

Even as they persecuted Jewish connoisseurs, prominent Nazis emerged as major art collectors in their own right with the outbreak of the Second World War, taking advantage of looting carried out around Europe by the German forces. As the Nazis occupied Poland, the Netherlands, and France, their armed forces took great care to preserve works of art in order to "safeguard" them. Like the English Puritans of the seventeenth century and the republicans of Revolutionary France, the Nazis faced the question of whether to destroy their booty in the name of ideological purity or, rather more pragmatically, to sell it off. Using utterly spurious criteria, they decided to draw a distinction between "Jewish art," which they deemed it acceptable to steal and sell (and also burn), and "Aryan art." Maintaining a veneer of commercial legality, they painstakingly documented the fact that technically they bought many works they seized, albeit at abnormally low prices.[9]

The leading Nazi collectors were Hitler himself and Hermann Göring, Hitler's *reichsminister* without portfolio and head of the Luftwaffe. Hitler's highly cherished personal dream was to establish a universal museum in Linz. Here, he was hoping to follow in Napoleon's footsteps by making his hometown a new center of world art, as well as arguably seeking to redeem both his sense of his own artistic failure as well as of Germany's contemporary aesthetic inferiority. As Hitler's armies conquered, they took photographs of works of art for his review, and he had first choice on acquisitions. Assisted by numerous art advisers, he used money earned from the sales of his autobiography *Mein Kampf* (1925) to purchase Old Masters, including Johannes Vermeer's *The Astronomer*, which had been owned by the Rothschilds, to cite but one example. One estimate is that the Nazis plundered art worth $100 million from the Rothschilds alone.

More than Hitler, however, Göring was the quintessential Nazi connoisseur. One of the few senior Nazis from the German upper class, Göring was corpulent and cunning, extravagant and epicurean. He lived as an aristocrat, residing in his ostentatious Carinhall country house like a baronial lord with his own hunting estate, and enjoyed showing off his hundreds of paintings. He also owned rare animals, several yachts and houses, and loved to dress in exotic costumes, once parading as an Oriental "sultan." In 1937, in his capacity as chief huntsman of the Reich, he organized an International Hunting Exposition, getting the British to bring him colonial trophies including a giant stuffed panda. Like the Führer, Göring bought masterpieces for a pittance and did not hesitate to free a Jewish art expert named Max Friedländer from a concentration camp so that he could work for the *reichsminister* as his personal art adviser.

As the war dragged on, the international press became increasingly aware of the considerable Nazi appetite for collecting. Observers, indeed, were bemused at the spectacle of Nazi commanders taking a keen interest in fine art. Just what were those "Nazi big shots," as the *New York Times* called them, doing with all those paintings? Wasn't it anomalous to say the least for such barbarous ruffians to carry on like the most civilized of connoisseurs?[10]

Douglas and Elizabeth Rigby, authors of several texts on collecting including a 1941 *Harper's* piece entitled "Embattled Collectors: How Treasures of Art and Culture Flee from War," tackled this question in the journal *American Scholar* that same year in an article entitled "Dictators and the Gentle Art of Collecting." One doesn't normally think of collectors as savage beasts of prey, the authors reflected, but refined, gentle, and studious. The very word *collecting*, the Rigbys observed, suggests a "tranquil activity." Yet, they pointed out, the "most ruthless tyrants" have often grabbed as much art as territory in the course of their conquests. They represent what the Rigbys called "the paradox of the destroyer-collector."[11]

The Rigbys took the common assumption to be that collectors are usually gentle or even weak people. The annals of history were full of rulers who "neglect[ed] their scepters" and the affairs of state because they lost themselves in their collecting: Nabonidus of Babylon; the emperor Huizong in China; the Mughal emperor Jahangir; King Charles I. Taking a ready example, the recently deposed king of Italy, Victor Emmanuel III, was yet another case in point. Benito Mussolini, Italy's self-declared Fascist *Duce*, all too predictably "shunted" aside the king, an "absorbed and excellent collector of coins," the Rigbys lamented. Somehow, unaccountable though it seems, the Rigbys failed to mention the legendary passivity of Rudolf II and the defenestration of his regime, but the point was made: a mere collector was no match for a brutal tyrant.[12]

Collectors were pigeons, the Rigbys averred, not hawks—an endless procession of Ponses, seemingly not a Verres among them. Yet history was also full of powerful men who became collectors in what the Rigbys, with memorably pointed whimsy, called "the paradox of hawk and pigeon nesting together." Hitler was only "the latest specimen of an ancient breed," preceded by an infamous succession of destroyer-collectors down through the ages: the medieval Chinese temple-smashers; King Ashurbanipal of the neo-Assyrian empire (whose agents were apparently "efficient in the manner of the Nazi Gestapo"); the ruling Ptolemies of Egypt; Augustus, Verres, and Julius Caesar in Rome; the emperor Charlemagne and the Renaissance banker Cosimo de' Medici; and, of course, that quintessential modern empire-builder Napoleon Bonaparte. Destroyer-collectors were, however, endowed with powerful creative impulses and not just a prodigious talent for laying waste. The Ptolemies filled the magnificent library of Alexandria with their loot; Napoleon founded the science of Egyptology; and the British solved the puzzle of the hieroglyphics by stealing the Rosetta Stone. There could be little doubt of the inconvenient fact that pillage meant progress.[13]

The Rigbys wrote before the Nazis decided upon the Final Solution and before the mass murder of Jews and others in the concentration camps. The true depths of Nazi depravity remained as yet unknown, therefore, and Nazi art collecting presented the German High Command in an oddly civilized light, notwithstanding their conquest of much of continental Europe. The paradox of the murderous collector was, however, already well established. The idea that collecting represented the repression of more violent urges in the name of civilization was well established after Freud, even though Oscar Wilde had already made the point in *The Picture of Dorian Gray* that aesthetes could easily turn out to be murderers. Art and beauty, Wilde suggested, had no necessary relation to morality. Henry James made a similar point in his novels: Gilded Age collectors were driven by power, not virtue. And the surrealists had also rejected the idea that collectors were pillars of civilization.

That the Nazis compiled careful catalogs of the art they looted is perhaps less a contradiction than a demonstration of the same bureaucratic mentality that underwrote their genocide of the Jews. In their *Dialectic of Enlightenment* (1944), Max Horkheimer and Theodor Adorno regarded the Nazis' combination of bureaucratic organization and mass murder as an example of instrumental rationality run amok. Reporting on the 1961 trial of Adolf Eichmann, who played a leading role in the Holocaust, Hannah Arendt described this mentality as an expression of the "banality of evil." "There were two things he could do well, better than others," Arendt wrote of Eichmann, "he could organize and he could negotiate."[14]

The question of how to interpret what contemporaries were already calling "German efficiency" remains highly complex. But one thing is clear. As the gravity of the Nazis' atrocities and the depth of their greed for art became more apparent later in the war—when the Allied Forces and "monuments men" tried to save art from them in occupied Europe—the Nazis contributed decisively to the growing perception of collectors' amorality. Indeed, it was the pretense of civilization that made the Nazi collector a particularly disturbing figure.

The early twentieth century witnessed revolutionary and military upheaval around the world, throwing the status of collecting and collectors into turmoil. When the Xinhai Revolution erupted in 1911, overthrowing the Qing Dynasty, China's august collecting tradition experienced a profound rupture. Emperors had acted as connoisseurs and guardians of the nation's heritage for centuries, supported by Mandarin scholars who maintained impressive collections of antiquities, texts, and catalogs. The Ming became the first society to develop the idea that collecting was not merely a form of affliction (*pǐ*) but a badge of cultural sophistication. Beware the person who is *not* devoted to an obsessive passion like collecting, they warned, for such people lack depth and truth to self.

A century of building frustration toppled the Qing after 1911. Nineteenth-century China suffered poverty, internal rebellions, and defeats to much smaller yet highly advanced industrialized countries: Britain in the Opium Wars of midcentury and Japan in the first Sino-Japanese War of 1894, fought for control of Korea. Doing away with China's long-lived imperial dynasties expressed an urgent desire to embrace modern industrial technology—lagging well behind the Meiji Restoration in Japan—and restore prosperity, security, and national pride. The value of highly traditional collections of cultural artifacts, especially those in the imperial palace in Beijing's Forbidden City, was therefore called into question. After Pu Yi, the Xuantong emperor, was deposed in 1912—he later became a humble gardener known merely as Pu Yi—the issue arose of what should be done with the royal collections. Who was their rightful owner, what was their purpose, and what was the value of the past itself in an era of revolutionary change?

Even before the last emperor was overthrown and new political ideologies declared the sovereignty of the people, prominent Chinese collectors found themselves to be enemies of the state. The downfall of Duanfang, a high-ranking Qing official, was especially dramatic. Duanfang's collections can be seen in museums around the world. The Metropolitan Museum of Art, for example, prominently displays a bronze altar set from an aristocrat's tomb dating to the Shang and Western Zhou Dynasties (1600–771 BCE) in its China galleries. The Met's caption identifies Duanfang as their source but omits the story of how the set came to the Upper East Side.

Born in 1861, Duanfang was a Manchu civil servant whose family was close to the emperor. Rising to become a leading diplomat and constitutional reformer, Duanfang was also deeply interested in antiquities. He formed an extensive collection, including bronzes, calligraphy, jades, and paintings. Becoming an esteemed connoisseur, he compiled an impressive catalog of his collection. He combined diplomacy with museology. Duanfang toured the United States and once gave the Field Museum a Daoist stone stele, in return for which he received a Tlingit artifact. Despite his devotion to antiquarianism, he advocated ardently for industrialization, becoming responsible for developing China's railroads in 1911.

The railroads, however, proved Duanfang's undoing. Their development intensified popular resentment toward the imperial household and its allies, leading to large-scale peasant revolts. Duanfang was sent to Sichuan Province with 500 troops to help put down an uprising in late 1911. His own men mutinied against him, however, and beheaded him. It was the start of the Xinhai Revolution. Desperate for money, Duanfang's family then sold off his collections, part of which made their way to New York.

Duanfang's fate foreshadowed the predicament of the Xuantong emperor's own collections. China's new republican government sought to take control of these collections in the name of the people, but the process was chaotic and marked by opportunism. The fact that the emperor remained in the Forbidden City for more than a decade after 1912 made it seem as though the royal holdings of antiquities and treasures were still his. At last, the government created a Committee for the Liquidation of the Qing Household in 1924, commissioning inventories and opening the Forbidden City up to the Chinese people. Even then, significant ambiguity remained. Officially, the republic would buy the royal collections, but it could not afford to, so they were to be "loaned" to the people instead. Much was stolen by government officials, much was sold, and the emperor took a sizable portion with him into exile in Taiwan, where it remains to this day in the National Palace Museum.

Uncertainty over the ownership of China's imperial collections and the value of antiquities in a modernizing society enabled looting and selling on the international market. The situation was part of a global moment that sent objects from all continents to Western museums in unprecedented numbers. It wasn't just a transatlantic moment where Duveens helped the likes of J. P. Morgan to hoover up Old European Masters, but a time of political revolution, intensive archaeological excavation, and anthropological collection that stretched from Egypt to Canada, Russia to China, and well beyond. It was a pivotal moment that created the international museum collections we know today.

Perhaps inevitably, the man most active in brokering the collection of Chinese antiquities abroad was called "China's Duveen." Like the Xuantong emperor, he too ended up on the wrong side of China's revolutions. Lu Huanwen, better known as Ching Tsai Loo, or C. T. Loo, sailed from China to Paris in 1902, aged twenty-two. There, he founded Ton-Ying and Company and began importing silk, tea, and antiquities to Europe. Using his links to Sun Yat-Sen's ruling Nationalist Party to overcome restrictions on exports, he established offices in Beijing and Shanghai, a brokerage house with a pagoda façade that still stands on the Rue de Courcelles in Paris, and later an office on Fifth Avenue in New York. As with Duanfang, objects sold by Loo can be found in many museums today.

Loo's specialty was the burgeoning international market in Chinese

C. T. Loo by Rudolph Burkhardt (1950): After looting brought many Chinese antiquities onto the open market in the Xinhai Revolution, the Paris-based Loo (1880–1957) became one of the leading exporters of Chinese antiquities but was forced to close down his business when Mao Zedong came to power in the 1940s, later expressing regret for his role in selling antiquities abroad.

antiquities and Buddhist artifacts, which wealthy Americans such as Isabella Stewart Gardner and John and Abby Rockefeller were beginning to collect in significant numbers. Loo was a suave cosmopolitan and dandyish yet astute businessman who helped kindle the new demand, brokering the sale of Buddhist art, including works from the renowned Longmen Grottoes near Luoyang in Henan Province, which contain thousands of ancient stone statues. Loo profited handsomely from exporting such materials. But when the Nationalists were deposed by the Communists, the political value of China's patrimony shifted. Within a year of Mao's proclamation of the founding of the People's Republic of China in 1949, Loo was forced to relinquish his business.

Today, in an era when China actively seeks to repatriate antiquities from abroad, and Luoyang is a protected UNESCO World Heritage site, some see Loo in retrospect as a traitor—someone who encouraged not just excavation but the looting of national treasures. Loo's predicament was similar to that of other collectors who straddled cultures during this same era of radical change and modernization: Louis Shotridge, Don Talayesva, and many others. Like Shotridge, Loo came to express remorse for his actions. "I feel so ashamed," he admitted in 1940, "to have been one of the sources by which these national treasures have been disbursed." But his actions have to be seen in the context of their time. Loo claimed to serve a larger purpose and insisted he was saving Chinese heritage from destruction, again not unlike Shotridge. "Art has no frontiers," Loo wrote, arguing that "because of [the] constant changes and upheavals" in his home country, Chinese art would be best preserved abroad as "messengers" to foster "love and better understanding of China." On this point at least, he was surely not wrong.[15]

Any retrospective judgment of Loo's conduct, moreover, must acknowledge the role many Chinese people later played in the destruction of their own patrimony, most strikingly during the Cultural Revolution. If the Xinhai Revolution was ambivalent about private collectors, the ultra-Marxist ideological fury of the 1960s vilified private collectors as reactionaries and counterrevolutionary enemies of the people and targeted them ruthlessly as enemies of the state whose possessions were to be destroyed.

Mao had ruled for almost two decades when he launched the Cultural Revolution in 1966. It originated as a tactical political maneuver designed to target and purge the Chinese Communist Party of political opponents, after the calamitous Great Leap Forward, a deeply ill-judged accelerated industrialization program that, due to the decimation of agricultural yields, led to 20 million deaths from starvation. The Cultural Revolution's determination to "smash the Four Olds" was not a spontaneous outburst of iconoclasm, therefore, but a calculated policy. Yet it acquired the character of a popular frenzy among the youthful Red Guards, who sought to identify elements of bourgeois, religious, and antiquarian culture for ritualistic destruction to prove their devotion to Communism. They modernized street names, attacked monuments including the Temple of Confucius in Qufu, Buddhist shrines, and the graves of Chinese converts to Christianity. In acts of ideologically blinded petty cruelty, they even killed pet dogs and cats as symbols of bourgeois decadence. They organized countless "struggle sessions," forcing declared enemies such as university professors to wear dunces' caps and sit in the stocks while they were forced to affirm their loyalty to Mao and the eternal glory of communist principles.

The Red Guards raided many homes, confiscating and destroying private property. They destroyed furniture, silk, books, and antiquities of all kinds. Ordinary people often tried to hide their possessions before the Red Guards arrived (stashing them behind pictures of Mao, for example) or to quickly destroy them in front of the Red Guards, in a desperate bid to save themselves from punishment and disavow their status as collectors, though such performances often failed to achieve their objectives.

Beyond Nien Cheng's *Life and Death in Shanghai* (1986), written in exile in the United States, there are few published tales of the trials ordinary people endured during the Cultural Revolution. Another notable exception to this silence, however, is *The Cowshed*. First published in 1998, it was written by the eminent Indologist and co-chair of the Peking University Eastern Languages Department Professor Ji Xianlin. In it, Ji recounts how he was at home reading one day in 1968 when some of his own students burst in to confront him. Wielding axes, they ransacked his home and destroyed his library. In an effort to mollify the purificationist fury of his highly agitated guests—whom he compared unfavorably with the Buddhist devils he studied—Ji obediently smashed a series of inoffensive little ornaments including "a black clay figurine of a smiling chubby baby" that came from

Wuxi, near Shanghai. But such obliging gestures of good-willed iconoclasm were for naught. The persecution Ji suffered at the hands of his own
students (and on other occasions his own colleagues) was vindictive and
ludicrous, but unstoppable. He was forced to construct a cowshed for his
own imprisonment, endure humiliating struggle sessions, and sentenced to
years of forced labor. His defiant sense of irony did not desert him in his
ordeal, however, and helped him to survive (he ultimately lived to be almost
a hundred). Ji mocked his persecutors' hollow crusade with withering wit.
After enjoying seeing some birds perching in a tree one day, for example,
he congratulated himself on internalizing the appropriate Maoist lesson: "I
immediately reflected on my incorrigible capitalist revisionist tendency to
take bourgeois delight in things around me."[16]

Like virtually every bout of revolutionary iconoclastic fervor, the
Maoist dream of smashing the Four Olds often degenerated into corruption and theft. In the city of Wuhan, according to some counts, 20,000
homes were raided, 679 antiques and 3,400 pieces of furniture taken, and
more than 3 million yuan stolen. In Shanghai, China's wealthiest city
where the collector Nien Cheng lived, a quarter of a million homes are
thought to have been raided and 3 million antiques and art objects seized.
Many were stored in warehouses to be inventoried, but some inevitably
found their way into eager private hands. The prominent Communist
official Kang Sheng, who worked in security and intelligence, built up
a large personal collection of art, seals, rubbings, and oracle bones from
these sources.

Like all revolutionaries, the Communists needed money badly and
confronted the perennial iconoclast's dilemma: smash or sell? Nien
Cheng's reasoning, as Red Guards stood poised to shatter her porcelain
to pieces, was sound enough. Even these utterly decadent bourgeois capitalist luxuries could be made to serve the revolution, she cunningly suggested to her tormentors, either as commodities to be sold or symbols of
the genius of Chinese labor to be preserved as such, in a state museum.
By 1967, the Shanghai Municipal Small Group for Sorting Cultural Relics was established to help preserve antiquities from destruction. The
revolutionary cause was best advanced, the Small Group argued, not by
destroying bourgeois collections but conserving them in order to exhibit

and critique politically inferior values, teaching the Chinese people yet another lesson about the genius of Communism in the process.

Nien Cheng prevailed over her antagonists. She succeeded in saving much of her porcelain. Initially, the Red Guards who'd burst into her house resisted the idea that any of her pieces should go to the Shanghai Museum and be assessed by experts, because experts were also "class enemies" in their view. Ultimately, however, fifteen of her porcelains became part of the Shanghai Museum, which even went so far as to financially compensate her for them. This act of "collecting" was, of course, coercive because Cheng could hardly have refused to cooperate. She observed, with the same ironically detached wryness as Ji Xianlin, that "on a large plate of [jade-colored] Ming celadon, some revolutionary had expressed his hatred for the rich by declaring in writing that collectors were bloodsuckers." Yet Cheng was ultimately praised in the local press for her "bequest" to the Shanghai Museum as an "honored donor to the people's collection." Through the strange mutations of Maoist self-justification, the bloodsucker had become a patriot.[17]

A few years after the Xinhai Revolution toppled China's last emperor, the Bolsheviks forced the abdication of Tsar Nicholas II in Russia in 1917, terminating Russia's imperial dynastic line. A similar pattern of state confiscation of private property in the name of the people ensued, including private collections. The Bolsheviks seized property from the Romanov royal family—whom they executed in summer 1918—the nobility, and the church. There were attacks on historical monuments and looting as Russia descended into civil war. Private art collections were seized and many works of art sold to raise desperately needed money for the Bolshevik cause, most famously the Romanovs' crown jewels and their Fabergé eggs, many of which were bought up by wealthy Americans. New journals emerged with titles like *Among Collectors*, which reflected the thriving new auction trade that then arose.

But, as in China, the question of how to manage national patrimony in a revolutionary moment was vexed and troubled. To deal with the issue, the Bolsheviks created Narkompros, the People's Commissariat for Education, which set about nationalizing the nation's collections in a program known as *muzeefikatsiia* (museification), creating many new state museums. Vladimir Lenin's revolutionary government issued a flurry of decrees to advance this process. The first concerned the remarkable museum of modernist art assembled by Sergei Shchukin. Shchukin came from a family of merchants and collectors and was among the first to buy works by Picasso, Matisse, and Gaugin. By 1909, members of the public could visit the "Picasso Room" in his private Moscow mansion, where he displayed fifty of Picasso's works—then the largest such collection in the world. The renowned "Shchukin eye" was so avant-garde, it was rumored by some that Shchukin's entire family had in fact gone insane, driven berserk by the visionary madness of "decadent" art—a label almost inevitably applied to everything that wasn't socialist realism.

The fate of Shchukin's collection epitomizes the profound ambivalence over modern art in the Soviet Union. The authorities couldn't decide whether to destroy or store Shchukin's art, and whether to tout it or sell it off. In 1918, Lenin signed a decree declaring it the property of the Russian people, making it part of the new State Museum of New Western Art. Like the surrealists, Russian constructivists (spearheaded by Alexander Rodchenko) dreamed of abolishing the art object and the art market as such, consigning private collectors to the dustbin of history. But Soviet Marxists went further. Art should never be treated as a capitalist commodity, they argued, but promote socialist values and national glory instead. It was a position that echoed the hostility to Jewish art collectors and the art market in Nazi Germany. In 1948, Josef Stalin ordered that Shchukin's collection be closed to the public as an example of "decadent bourgeois imperialist culture," deriding it as the work of "Muscovite capitalists." Yet, just a few years later in 1956, during a thaw in the Cold War, Saint Petersburg's Pushkin Museum was once again dazzling Russian audiences with its display of Shchukin's Picassos, even as it refused to credit the man who collected them.[18]

Shchukin fled Moscow for Paris and later died in exile. But other collectors stayed and reached accommodations with the Communist dictators taking over Eastern Europe. In Romania, in one of many such instances, the monarchy was abolished in 1947 and, once more, private collections were nationalized. The newly created Ministry of Arts and Information

predictably declared an end to "capitalist aesthetics" and the "decadent culture of the Western bourgeoisie." To create new public museums, however,
once again required the cooperation of experts, including collectors. Among
the most prominent was a canny businessman named Krikor Zambaccian.
Zambaccian was a collector of Romanian modernist art. He managed to
remain active under the new regime by giving the state half his collection in
1947 and promising them the remainder on his death, in return for offering
his services to the government as an art adviser.[19]

Such negotiations meant that, for all the ideological fury directed at
them, private collectors were never entirely wiped out by totalitarian
regimes. Like the surrealists, totalitarians could never quite do away with
the bourgeois decadent they so often denounced in the name of Marxist
egalitarianism. The most poignant tale of a collector who survived totalitarianism in this way is about one who never existed, but who mimics
the experiences of many who endured the trials of collecting under Communism: Bruce Chatwin's fictional creation Kaspar Utz, a porcelain lover
who is forced to choose between his collection and his freedom in Cold
War Czechoslovakia.

Bruce Chatwin studied archaeology at Oxford before becoming a denizen of the auction house and the art world. Beginning in 1958, he worked
at Sotheby's in London, where he acquired a reputation as a dashing storyteller, able to describe objects and their histories with captivating charisma.
Inspired as a child by a cabinet of curiosities owned by his grandmother,
Chatwin adored objects of all kinds and yearned to collect fine art, though
this ambition was blunted by the lack of a requisite fortune.

More significant than what he collected, however, was what Chatwin
gave away. Chatwin loved things not for their collectability but for the stories
they could tell about faraway places and people. Travel was his true passion.
He has been called the world's last great explorer and is best known for
writing *In Patagonia* (1977), which describes his journeys in South America,
and *The Songlines* (1987), based on his time among the Aborigines of Australia. Chatwin saw the urge to move and the urge to own as diametrically
opposed impulses. He was convinced travel was the source of all vigor. The
"nomadic alternative" to civilization, as he called it, nourished the brain and
stimulated the mind. Accumulation, by contrast, was symptomatic of the ills

Bettmann Collection via Getty Images

Bruce Chatwin at Sotheby's in London (ca. 1960): Chatwin (1940–89) trained in archaeology at Oxford before working at Sotheby's and becoming a renowned travel writer who argued that nomadism represented freedom and creativity, whereas collecting embodied the ills of property-owning civilization. His novel Utz (1988) tells the story of a man forced to choose between his collection and his freedom.

of civilization. Possessions enchained the spirit and bred inequality, neurosis, and strife. Though Chatwin became friends with the psychoanalyst Werner Muensterberger, he came to reject Freudian interpretations of collecting and scorned the idea that collections were expressions of an essential personal identity. If "my objects expressed my personality," he quipped, "then I hate my personality." He came to loathe the denizens and passions of the art world, too, though maybe because he understood them all too well. Like William Beckford and Walter Benjamin before him, Chatwin acknowledged the ecstasy of the collector's chase but rejected what he called "the morality of things," admitting that the "adoring [of each] new fetish" only lasted until the next "more desirable thing." This was perhaps why, late in life, prior to his untimely death from AIDS in 1989, Chatwin gave away to friends the last few treasures he owned, including a red lacquer snuffbox from Japan, some Eskimo walrus ivory, and a funerary mask from Argentina.[20]

For all his ambivalence about collecting, Chatwin's story of the fictional Utz is intensely sympathetic to its hero. First published in 1988, the novel was inspired by a trip Chatwin made to an archaeological dig in Czechoslovakia in 1967, during the liberalizing period of the Prague Spring. In *Utz*, a journalist also visits the Czech capital and becomes fascinated by the legends surrounding Rudolf II and "the psychopathology of the compulsive collector." A colleague tells the journalist that if he wants to meet a modern-day Rudolf, he should meet Utz. When he does so, he sees that Utz owns a fantastical collection of porcelain figurines made at the storied Meissen manufactory, near Dresden, dating to the early eighteenth century. How Utz manages to retain his collection under a political regime that has, in theory, banished personal property is a mystery, however. Utz is an enigma. He's a Ponsian nobody: physically unprepossessing, secretive, and self-effacing, yet strangely intense. Solitary, bespectacled, and utterly forgettable, he's the man who wasn't there—only, somehow, he's still there.[21]

Slowly, the narrator gathers fragments concerning the relationship between collector and collection. Utz's grandmother is Jewish, so he considers himself one-quarter Jewish. But when the Jews are persecuted by the Nazis, robbed, and forced to flee Germany, Utz opportunistically buys up their porcelain, traveling to Berlin right after Kristallnacht in order to do so. Collectors always benefit from others' tragedies, he frankly admits. Utz tolerates a Nazi cousin of his and acquiesces to Nazi aggression. Some rumors have it he was even part of Göring's "art squad," though Utz also helps Jews to escape the Nazis' clutches. Jews, Utz believes, make the best collectors because they simply love things too much and cannot resist them. They're not supposed to idolize graven images, of course, but they absolutely do. He says this with more than a hint of pride, as though he sees himself as a Jewish idolater, too. In the end, Utz is neither hero nor rebel.

He just wants to survive and keep his porcelains. He's subversive, but quietly and sheepishly, and only insofar as he lives his life pretending that the state does not exist and carrying on as if it didn't.

Like Shchukin, Zambaccian, and Nien Cheng in real life, Utz is faced with the dilemma of the private collector under Communism. Is Benjamin's dream of retreating into a magically private realm of things possible when the state forbids you to *have* a private life? Utz gets to keep his collection, it turns out, because he has made a deal with the authorities: they'll get it when he dies. He has to check in with them like a parolee, but he doesn't flee, even when he has the chance to. In one key part of the story, Utz obtains permission for health reasons to visit Vichy, former home of the pro-Nazi French government. He could easily escape to the West, should he choose to make the attempt. But that would mean leaving his collection behind. Instead, he goes home to Prague and back to his porcelains.

Utz's decision looks mad. Why would anyone give up their freedom for a collection? Except that the madness of collecting is what has kept Utz going all this time. His collection *is* his life. Rudolf's legendary flaw becomes Utz's salvation: he lives through his things, and in a brutal century racked by Nazi atrocity and Communist oppression, where the individual is hounded almost to extinction, the only way to survive is to fly from reality. There's no evidence Chatwin drew inspiration from the story of Ludwig Pollak's apprehension by the Nazis in Rome, but he does compare Utz to Augustus the Strong, the eighteenth-century elector of Saxony whose own legendary "porcelain-mania" once led him to exchange real men for porcelain figurines. He makes the point that Utz's "world of little figures *was* the real world," crucial precisely because it kept the horrors of real-life Nazi and Communist tyranny at bay.[22]

Why do the authorities allow Utz to keep his collection if private collectors represented the antithesis of communist ideals? In part, Utz thinks, because they never understood themselves whether collections are private property or just goods. "Marxist-Leninism," he observes, "had never got to grips with the concept of the private collection. . . . No one had ever decided if the ownership of a work of art damned its owner in the eyes of the proletariat. Was the collector a class-enemy?" Was porcelain art, was it ideologically significant, or was it just kitsch crockery?[23]

Utz's secret weapon against the Marxist view of the world is magic. He never mentions Walter Benjamin, but he shares Benjamin's belief that collecting is an act of mystical significance and that ownership both confers the right to touch objects and creates the possibility of a true bond between owner and owned. He authors a pamphlet on "The Private Collector" in which he reaffirms the idea that collections live only through individuals. "The collector's enemy is the museum curator," he writes. Museums are where objects go to "die," so they need to be looted so they can live again. And when he says *live*, he means it, because he agrees with the alchemists, going back to the time of porcelain's inventor Johannes Böttger, that porcelain is not inanimate but imbued with spirit. He asks: Isn't all clay alive? Didn't God create life from Adam's clay rib? Isn't the Golem of Jewish folklore mud made animate? Utz wasn't a class enemy, he was a magus: a spiritual collector in the ancient tradition.[24]

But there is a twist in store. Utz is not Shchukin, Zambaccian, or Nien Cheng. He is not desperate to save his porcelain at all costs. In the end, he smashes his entire collection, or so it seems—it is suggested but not confirmed that he does so. Unlike the Shanghai Museum, Narkompros, or the Romanian Ministry of Arts, the Czechoslovakian state never gets its hands on Utz's figurines.

Nor is Utz the sexless Ponsian bachelor he first appears. His maid Marta turns out to be his wife, and he seems to have carried on several affairs over the years. He's no Freudian husk, but a harlequin jester—like one of his shape-shifting porcelains—a canny chameleon with many a trick up his sleeve. By smashing his porcelains, he ensures the Communists never take from him what is his and his alone. The idolater becomes the iconoclast. Utz denies the state possession of his soul by denying them the collection that defined his life. This was Chatwin's ultimate commentary on collecting as a form of slavery from which the spirit is only set free by rejecting its trammels.

Utz's dates are telling. The book came out in 1988, one year before Chatwin's death, the fall of the Berlin Wall, the collapse of the Soviet Union, and the end of Communist rule. In Czechoslovakia, the Velvet Revolution reinstituted democratic rule. In 1992, when a film based on *Utz* directed by George Sluizer came out, the American political scientist Francis Fukuyama published *The End of History and the Last Man*, declaring that Western liberal democracy and free-market capitalism would displace all other systems of political economy across the world.

Utz, in other words, was a novel on the cusp of profound historical change, albeit ironically so. Like the surrealists before them, the Communists failed to get rid of the collector or the role of money in collecting. The bourgeois decadent had not been liquidated, but survived. Under Communism, it seemed natural to yearn for the moment when private property and personal freedom would finally be restored and usher in a new era of individual self-expression, of which the collector would surely be a prime example.

Western societies, above all the United States, embodied the dream to emulate. In the West, the figure of the collector was rapidly becoming democratized. By the middle of the twentieth century, there were collectors not only of fine art, books, or sculpture, but also of mass-produced collectibles from bubble-gum cards and children's soft toys to old newspapers and even product packaging—and just about everything else in between. In the modern West, there was nothing you couldn't collect, and virtually anyone could be a collector, regardless of wealth, education, or social class—it was just a matter of taste and tastes were changing and broadening all the time. The democratization of taste was not only the dream of twentieth-century collecting; it was the reality. The only problem with this brave new world was that the Freudian idea that there was something wrong with the collector—something repressed, sinister, even potentially dangerous—remained deeply ingrained in the popular imagination. If the collector was now an everyman, that everyman might just turn out to be a psycho.

CHAPTER TWELVE

CROSSING THE
CREEP THRESHOLD

I have invented a new sensation.

—COUNT ZAROFF IN *THE MOST DANGEROUS GAME* (1932)

A big-game hunter named Bob Rainsford (played by Joel McCrea) finds himself shipwrecked on a mysterious island with an enigmatic host named Count Zaroff (Leslie Banks). When Rainsford regains his strength, he finds he is not alone, and encounters survivors from previous shipwrecks including a woman named Eve Trowbridge. He is glad to be alive, yet the atmosphere among the assembled company in Zaroff's Gothic abode is oddly strained. Just *where* has Rainsford landed?

His host Zaroff is a sinister patrician with a peculiar proposition for his guest. Like Rainsford, Zaroff happens to be a big-game hunter and has discovered the pleasures of hunting what he calls "the most dangerous game" of all: human beings. "I have invented a new sensation," he confesses, showing Rainsford his trophy room of human heads: the remains of those he has hunted down. The shipwrecks are no accident; they are engineered by Zaroff to trap people he can hunt for sport with a bow and arrow. He invites Rainsford to join him as a partner in this fiendish enterprise. Naturally, Rainsford refuses and flees, so Zaroff hunts after him and Eve as they attempt to flee. In the end, it is Zaroff who meets a grisly end, eaten alive by his own hunting dogs, as our heroes escape to freedom.[1]

The Most Dangerous Game is a 1932 film based on a Richard Connell short story and occupies a peculiar place in cinema history. Shot at the same time as *King Kong*, made by the same producers Ernest Schoedsack and Merian C. Cooper, it uses *Kong*'s jungle for the hunt scenes on Zaroff's island and features several *Kong* actors including Fay Wray.

The Most Dangerous Game is also one of the first films to depict a serial murderer as a collector, illustrated by the heads in Zaroff's trophy room. It's 1932 and Zaroff exudes every period pathology imaginable. He's Prospero ensnaring victims on his enchanted island; a decadent with a love of the crueler sports and a penchant for pleasure of the most twisted kind; a vaguely Nazified Darwinian who decides who lives or dies; an imperial huntsman; and a vampiric cannibal showman who derives his vitality from his human trophies—not to mention a lonesome Freudian homoerotic who craves a fellow hunter.

Throughout history, collectors have, of course, been killers of various kinds. The golden age of natural history was a saga of Victorian animal-killing, driven by religious and scientific purpose, until an awareness of the very real possibilities of extinction emerged with the conservationist movement, and the idea of scientific animal slaughter thus began to seem horrific, not least to Guy de Maupassant. Grave robbers in Europe and the Americas furnished craniological specialists with skulls for comparative phrenological research.

As the nineteenth century drew to a close, however, psychologists were starting to connect collecting with potentially life-threatening sexual psychoses. In his *Psychopathia Sexualis*, under the heading *Fetish*, Richard Krafft-Ebing documented the singular case of someone he termed a Parisian "hair-despoiler." Referred to simply as "P.," the individual in question was a forty-year-old locksmith of an extremely nervous disposition who cut off and saved women's hair, together with their hairpins. The locksmith's "mania for collecting" involved fondling the hair he stole, then wrapping his genitals in the hair in order to achieve orgasms of such intensity the he had "only imperfect apperception and subsequent memory of what he does." Indeed, "P." felt himself "possessed by a supernatural power and unable to give up his booty." The man had been arrested and sent to an insane asylum. Krafft-Ebing also discussed the "girl-cutter of Augsburg," a man who derived sexual gratification from handling the knives and daggers he used to commit acts of violence against women.[2]

It was around this time that decadent novelists, notably J.-K. Huysmans, Gabriele D'Annunzio, and Oscar Wilde, were starting to imagine the collector as a potential murderer. Freud's vision of the collector, which he started to articulate just a few years later, was rather tamer, of course. His aging Don Juan was repressed, not dangerous; retiring, not frightening. But other psychoanalytical views of the collector were more disturbing. In Victor Fleischer's novel *The Collector*, the protagonist Baumgartner lashes out at himself and his rival. Karl Abraham and Otto Fenichel saw collectors as supernaturally sinister: vampiric cannibals seeking to incorporate other people by owning their things.

Enter the figure we began our story with, Norman Bates—not in the suavely charming person of Anthony Perkins in Hitchcock's 1960 movie, but the original Norman Bates as created by novelist Robert Bloch in his 1959 pulp-fiction classic *Psycho*. Collecting features only obliquely in *Psycho*, yet Bates is a pivotal figure in the cultural history of the collector, marking a decisive shift from the decadents' aristocratic obsession with class status to the new democratic obsession with individual sexuality. *Psycho* was Freud democratized into a pop culture shocker.

Bloch was a prolific producer of pulp fiction. A protégé of the imaginative horror writer H. P. Lovecraft, he published countless short stories and novels in the crime, horror, and supernatural genres. In *Psycho*, Bloch blended true crime with psychoanalysis, a story "based on the notion," he said, "that the man next-door may be a monster, unsuspected even in the gossip-ridden microcosm of small town life." He drew in particular on the sensational stories of serial killers who became a new media fixation in 1950s America. He acknowledges as much at the end of *Psycho*, when TV reporters insist on comparing Bates to the real-life rural Wisconsin serial killer Ed Gein, on whom Bloch partly based him. Gein impersonated his mother after she died, carried out the murders of several women, and adorned his house with their remains as trophies after the fact.[3]

In Bloch's pacy, punchy, and tormented novella, Bates is a singular motel-keeper with a multiple personality. It appears that Bates's ailing and unhinged mother Norma has murdered several recent visitors to the

Bates Motel, although in reality, Bates himself committed the crimes while dressed as his mother, whom he in fact murdered years ago, fearing that she would leave him for another man and carefully preserving her corpse to maintain the illusion she is still alive. In the end, Norma's dominant personality takes over and Norman—a pun on *normal*—ceases to exist in any meaningful psychological terms.

In Hitchcock's film, the photogenic Perkins plays Bates with guile, yet warmth and charm. The early scenes, where he is attracted to Marion Crane (Janet Leigh), are touching. They look like the beginnings of a romance, before Norma/Norman murders Crane while she is taking a shower. But Bloch's original Bates is different from the handsome and sensitive Perkins. He's rather more like Pons or Utz: a chubby, bespectacled, and homely recluse with barely any charm to speak of. He's also a hobbyist and a serious reader. The first time we meet him, right at the beginning of the story, he's absorbed by a passage he's reading on human sacrifice in the Inca Empire featuring a description of a man being flayed alive, complete with notes on how to preserve the corpse.

Bloch reveals the range of Bates's library in the course of the novel. It's a wonderful surprise for anyone who thinks they know Bates from Hitchcock's movie. He possesses works on "abnormal psychology," *Justine* by the Marquis de Sade, and pornography. He also owns *Là-Bas* (*The Damned*), Huysmans's novel about a scholar immersed in researching both devil worship and one of the first known serial killers, the fifteenth-century French child-murderer Gilles de Rais. Bates also reads about cosmology, witch cults, and the occult. Bates, in other words, is as interested in exotic cultures and magical practices as he is in psychology. As such, he's nothing less than a child of *Totem and Taboo*, a devotee of anthropology as well as psychoanalysis. Stop reading those "nasty bits about those dirty savages," Norma yells at him in his head. He doesn't.[4]

Psychoanalysis is central to the explanations of Bates's behavior in both the novel and the movie. Bloch characterizes him as a neurotic schizophrenic, stressing his deep-seated fears of castrating motherhood, a dominant theme in American pop psychology during the Cold War. Bates himself is a keen Freudian, well up on the Oedipus complex, and actually wants to discuss it with Norma in hopes it might help them both. At the same time, he labors painfully under the labels he imagines others apply to him, especially the word *impotent*. But the original Bates is not merely an amateur psychologist: he's also an occultist. He believes that taxidermy is a form of magic with the power of reanimation. To him, Mother really *is* alive. In the movie, however, Hitchcock and screenwriter Joseph Stefano stripped away all mention of Bates's belief in magic, getting rid of the anthropology and leaving just the psychology, allowing audiences to embrace Bates as a thoroughly modern maniac.

They did leave in the collecting, however, and it was Freudian psychoanalysis that made it seem natural and logical to hint that Bates was dangerous *because* he stuffed animals. In Bloch's novel, Bates stuffs squirrels, but Hitchcock and Stefano shrewdly changed this to birds to emphasize Bates's voyeurism. As Hitchcock told François Truffaut, the birds reflect Bates's guilt "in their knowing eyes." They also changed his victim's name to *Crane* and put pictures of birds in her motel room to frame Bates as a hunter.[5]

Bates's taxidermy is also intended to symbolize the sexual neurosis and arrested development produced by his incestuous relationship with his mother. One of the most revealing scenes in the film shows Bates spying on Marion through a peephole behind a painting in his parlor as she undresses in her room. These are Bates's two worlds: the world of a collector versus the world of a lover. Bates wants to enter Marion's world but can't. The stillness, voyeurism, and taxidermy of the parlor are incompatible with the flesh-and-blood desire of the boudoir.

Bates looks for all the world like a classic collector weakling. He's especially creepy when he tells Marion about his taxidermy and how the chemicals are the only thing that cost anything, before he criticizes her for insinuating that Mother should be institutionalized. At this point, it's Norma we fear, not Norman. The twist, however, is that Norman is the killer. He's so weak, he's dangerous. As such, Bates explodes Freud's notion that collecting acts as a safety valve for dangerous passions. In *Psycho*, the collector murders anyone who threatens his carefully constructed world.

The *Psycho* house is another manifestation of Bates's pathological collecting. Bloch tells us the Victorian-style house dates to the 1890s—taxidermy was, of course, a favored pastime of Victorian families—and he likens it to a museum. As well as her old clothes, Mrs. Bates's bedroom contains clocks, figurines, carpets, and furniture from the previous century. Hitchcock films it like a museum, too, showing us one object at a time, repeating the technique when Marion's sister Lila investigates Norman's bedroom. Bates will do anything to preserve the past as it was before his mother died, and what horrifies Lila above all is the sense that the past is indeed still alive in the house.

Like Dorian Gray, Norman Bates is a reincarnation of collectors past. He's the reclusive magus of his own private museum, a Renaissance melancholic suffocating in memento mori. But Bloch and Hitchcock twisted the murderous collector into a new twentieth-century nightmare, moving the madman from the city to the country, from the elevated pleasures of art to the brutally clinical techniques of science, and from anxieties over class status to an overwhelming obsession with sex. The genius of *Psycho*'s casting, however, meant that although Bates was creepy and his murderousness stunned audiences, leading them to shriek with terror in cinemas, he became one of the most beloved antiheroes of screen history. Casting the attractive and intelligent Perkins mainstreamed the menace. Bates may be troubled and lethal, but he seduces with his boyish charisma. And he might just be us. "We *all* go a little mad sometimes," Perkins tells Janet Leigh, whose character has committed crimes of her own. She dares not disagree.[6]

The invention of Norman Bates marked a profoundly ironic democratization of the collector: the boy next door might turn out to be a collector *and* a killer—a killer *because* he was a collector. But not all psychos are alike, of course. Hot on the heels of *Psycho* came *The Collector*, a novel published by the British writer John Fowles in 1963 and made into a 1965 film by director William Wyler, starring Terence Stamp and Samantha Eggar. Where Bates is a mere hobbyist, Fowles's protagonist Frederick Clegg is an obsessive butterfly collector and, unlike his American counterpart, preoccupied not by sex, but that perennial British obsession, class.

Fowles based Clegg in part on his own experience and, it seems, his own personality. Fowles preserved butterflies, collected books and Chinaware, and enjoyed shooting and hunting, though he later renounced the pleasures of the hunt for ethical reasons after injuring himself. Fowles was also evidently something of a recluse who idealized beautiful women and fan-

Poster for The Collector, *directed by William Wyler (1965):
Based on a novel by John Fowles,* The Collector *tells the story of
a young man who collects butterflies and abducts women, a fable
that associates the killing of animals for science with a dangerous
form of psychopathy.*

tasized about possessing them. *The Collector*'s original dust jacket even mentioned that he had been a butterfly collector as part of its promotional blurb.

Both novel and movie tell the story of Clegg, a young bank clerk who wins a fortune on the football pools. The money allows Clegg to move out of his auntie's house and buy a Tudor cottage, dating back to 1621, outside London. Clegg is dangerously delusional, however. He "collects" a young woman called Miranda, a student at the Slade School of Fine Art, and holds her captive in his house's dungeon-like cellar. After she eventually falls ill and dies, Clegg is distraught, yet makes up his mind to "collect" another woman in his demented quest to find a mate.

The Collector is a study in the psychopathology of the scientific collector. Clegg is a dangerous individual, but he's also a type, and Fowles uses
a series of lengthy discussions between him and Miranda to explore the
conflict between science and art. Clegg scorns his hostage. To him, she is a
pretentious middle-class art student, while he by contrast is a humble and
honest working-class scientist. And yet, he yearns for her to embrace him,
fantasizing that they will live together someday, Miranda loving him and
appreciating his collections. Miranda repeatedly asks Clegg *why* he collects
butterflies but by the end comes to see his devotion to arranging dead insects
as typical of what's wrong with all scientists and collectors. Her sentiments
recall those of Darwin a century earlier when he reflected on the capacity of
scientific collecting to deaden the collector to the beauty of the world. "How
many butterflies have you killed?" Miranda asks Clegg, thinking "of all the
living beauty you've ended" by hoarding it up in drawers and seeing herself
in these "fellow-victims." "I hate scientists," she comments, "I hate people
who collect things, and classify things and give them names and forget all
about them." That's the "great dead thing" about Clegg, she concludes. In
her view, all collectors are "anti-life, anti-heart, anti-everything." Collecting
is the opposite of living: to collect is not only to kill but to be dead inside.[7]

Clegg hates what Miranda represents just as much. Her devotion to art
torments him. When she tries to teach him about the hidden meanings of
modern art—Pollock in the book, Picasso in the film—he erupts in fury
at the very idea of having to grasp something he cannot immediately see.
It's an eerie echo of Hitler's ban on "non-obvious" art and frighteningly
dogmatic in its literal-mindedness. Even Miranda's name taunts him: a
reference to Prospero's daughter in *The Tempest*, and she duly calls Clegg
Caliban—Prospero's savage slave—to indicate his monstrosity. Naturally,
all such references elude the militantly philistine Clegg. "I never had your
advantages," he sulks resentfully. Like Bates with Marion, the collector can
again see a world of flesh and beauty but is powerless to enter it.[8]

For all his devotion to collecting, Clegg is not a practicing professional scientist. He enjoys some connection to the London Natural History
Museum and corresponds with lepidopterists in other countries, though he
happens to think his own amateur butterfly specimens (he also raises live
specimens from larvae) are rather more impressive than theirs. A classic

outsider, Clegg oscillates between idealism and rage. Wyler's first scene in the movie captures his dangerous childishness well: armed with a net like Wallace's statue inside the Natural History Museum, Clegg traps a butterfly in a state of stupefied rapture. Other scenes show "beautifully arranged" specimens with, as Miranda observes in the book, "their poor little wings all stretched out at the same angle." They make for a classic image of scientific order as madness, when scientific work becomes detached from any actual scientific purpose.[9]

Abducting Miranda looks like a sexually motivated crime at first, but Clegg turns out to be disgusted by everything to do with sex. He does try to force himself on Miranda at one point but soon abandons the attempt and redoubles his efforts to act "proper." I'm not Christie, he tells her at one point, referring to the serial killer John Christie who raped and killed several women in West London in the 1940s and kept a collection of their pubic hair. Clegg's "absolutely sexless," Miranda realizes. "Are you a queer?" she asks him at one point. Like Norman Bates, he seems unsure of the answer.[10]

Fowles casts the struggle between Clegg and Miranda as a conflict steeped in history, too. He mentions that the house Clegg buys was used to hide Catholics from the Puritans during the seventeenth century. We've returned to the struggle between Puritan science and Catholic art in early modern English culture: Clegg's a latter-day descendant of the sexless scientific pedant, a secularized zealot who scorns the corrupting pleasures of art. The ghost of Charles I stalks his pursuit of Miranda and she, too, becomes a martyr to art, like the connoisseur king beheaded in the name of piety.

Clegg may be a Puritan, but he lives in the era of Freud and the nuclear age. So Miranda psychoanalyzes him and debates him over the Campaign for Nuclear Disarmament (CND). Since Dorian Gray, fictional collectors had used science to get away with murder: in Wilde's story, Dorian blackmails his college friend Alan into dissolving a corpse. But by the 1960s, after the dropping of the atom bomb on Hiroshima and the onset of the nuclear arms race, the scientific collector's ease with the act of killing assumed ominous new overtones. Even science's most innocent pursuits—chasing a butterfly with a net—now seemed portentous. Miranda tries to convince Clegg he should oppose the nuclear arms race as if the fate of the world depends on his stance, urging him to send a cheque to CND. He refuses. Unlike the idealistic Miranda, Clegg is resigned to a world of nuclear peril. "You're a part of it," she judges him. The collector's instinct is an instinct for death. "Everything free and decent in life is being locked away in filthy little cellars by beastly people who don't care."[11]

Here, we come back to Edgar Anderson's view of Alfred Kinsey and the "inner significance" of the closing of a specimen box. The person who kills beautiful living things in the name of science possesses an instinct so destructive, Fowles suggests in *The Collector*, it threatens the entire world. Clegg's butterfly displays are beautiful, Miranda concedes, but because they exist independent of any scientific institutions, they lack scientific meaning and embody mere personal obsession as chilling embodiments of Clegg's closed world. Scientific methods divorced from scientific purpose don't represent reason but rather danger. The heroic animal serial killing of intrepid Victorian field collectors like Alfred Russel Wallace had become little more than a sick murderous psychopathy.

The notion that scientific collectors are killers whose willingness to take animal lives makes them sick or evil may sound extreme, but it endures. The need to kill animals to collect specimens for biology is not without its critics. A 2014 article in the journal *Science* entitled "Avoiding (Re)Extinction" by American zoologist Ben Minteer argued that recording technologies, especially digital photography, are now sufficiently advanced as to make the taking of actual specimens unnecessary. A large number of scientists replied to Minteer in print, insisting that only physical specimens can provide the full range of information scientists require to monitor population fluctuations among species and so help preserve them.

This debate may or may not be closed, but consider the case of Christopher Filardi. In 2015, Filardi, a professional ornithologist at the American Museum of Natural History, went on an expedition to Guadalcanal, one of the Solomon Islands in the South Pacific. On Guadalcanal's Chupukama Ridge, Filardi heard the following sound: "kokoko-kiew." It was the call of the mustached forest kingfisher bird, and it was an extraordinary moment: Western scientists had not encountered a living mustached kingfisher for years and feared for its survival. The bird was stunningly beautiful, a rapturous combination of orange, purple, and blue. Filardi's heart leapt.[12]

Filardi took a photograph of the kingfisher, posted it online, and admirers were soon swooning at its exquisite plumage. Shortly afterward, however, some of those admirers realized what was to them a chilling scientific fact: Filardi had taken out his mist net to collect one of the birds as a specimen for the museum. In other words, he killed it. The kingfisher's admirers turned on him. Online posts, including some by scientific researchers, denounced taking the bird's life as scientifically unnecessary and cruel. The most outraged respondents called Filardi a murderer and threatened him. A petition stating "Chris Filardi is a disgrace and frankly does not deserve to breathe another breath" obtained almost 4,000 signatures. Fearing for his safety, Filardi went to ground.[13]

Today's scientists emphasize that specimen collection is now infrequent, governed by strict protocols, and vital for bio-geographical conservation. It does not threaten endangered species but monitors them precisely in order to protect them. This is how Filardi understood his killing of the kingfisher: taking a single life as a means to safeguard an entire population. Filardi's harshest critics, however, zeroed in novelist John Fowles's idea, expressed half a century earlier in *The Collector,* that there is something deeply wrong with people who kill animals to collect them and Maupassant's fin de siècle vision of zoology as a slaughter of innocents and a crime against nature deserving retribution. The animal-killing scientific collector was a psycho who had to be stopped.

In the wake of *Psycho* and *The Collector,* serial killers who collected and curated trophies of their murders became proverbial in pop culture. In a vicious cultural loop, real life began imitating pop art. In 1966, a man kidnapped a woman in Tokyo after seeing Wyler's movie of Fowles's novel. In 1985, Leonard Lake and Charles Ng were convicted of murdering eleven men and women outside San Francisco (with more than twice as many suspected victims) in a rare case of serial killers working together. Lake invoked the character of Clegg, grimly referring to his crimes with Ng as "Operation Miranda."[14]

Between 1978 and 1991, Jeffrey Dahmer, a Wisconsin native like Ed Gein, killed seventeen boys and men and was subsequently found guilty of murder. He was sentenced to life in prison and eventually killed by a fellow inmate. Science, collecting, and trophyism figure prominently both in Dahmer's crimes and how psychologists have interpreted them.

As with other serial murderers, both real and imagined, killing and collecting animals proved a formative background to Dahmer's many murders. His father Lionel was a chemist who exposed his son to laboratory techniques as a youngster and stimulated his interest in corrosive acids. Like Norman Bates, Dahmer was also deeply interested in the occult and satanism—a family member once found cult objects in his room—and he was obsessed with death. As a youth, he once killed tadpoles by pouring motor oil on them, and he killed/collected rodents and insects. He liked to see the effects of chemicals on chickens. "I know it's stupid," he once told his father, "but I just like to experiment."[15]

After he began killing people, Dahmer bought a large freezer where he liked to store parts of his victims' bodies. He'd select young men, mostly black and Latino, primarily for their physical attractiveness, drug them, have sex with them, kill them, then preserve their corpses. In some instances, he perpetrated acts of cannibalism, cooking and eating muscle tissue. While committing these acts, he would look at photos of his victims he had taken while they were still alive.

One of the most grotesque yet significant aspects of Dahmer's activities is the highly ritualistic way in which he planned to curate his victims' remains. This plan, which he illustrated in sketch form, involved arranging these remains in what he called a "temple." Dahmer intended to arrange ten skulls on a long table, next to two complete skeletons, so that he could sit with them and experience feelings of power before going out cruising for new lovers and victims. He experimented with preservation methods, drying and baking, and many chemicals were later found in his apartment when the police finally raided it.[16]

Those seeking to explain Dahmer's actions have often drawn strikingly similar conclusions. With gruesome literalness, Dahmer's trophyism and cannibalism fit the early psychoanalytic insights of Karl Abraham and Otto Fenichel, who viewed collecting as a means of physically incorporating other people and deriving vampiric power from doing so. Dahmer's father and several psychologists argued that his trophyism was driven by a fear of loneliness and a desire to keep the dead present and in some sense alive, just as Norman Bates does with his mother. Dahmer had a "dread of people leaving him," Lionel observed, and wanted to "make them literally a part of him . . . forever."[17]

The psychological literature analyzing Dahmer emphasizes collecting not merely as a feature but even a primary motivation for his crimes. One 2002 article calls him "essentially a cadaver collector" and explores the role Asperger syndrome may have played in his actions, observing that it often induces people to collect, from innocent pastimes on the order of stamp collecting to horrific cases of ritualized serial slaughter of the kind Dahmer engaged in. An article from 2013 insists that collecting is no mere by-product of serial killing but forms the greatest motive force driving the commission of such crimes. Its authors suggest that collecting offers a more lasting psychological pleasure than either the acts of sex or killing. "The collection," they write, "serves to weld together an experience of self that is of paramount importance to the offender and possibly constitutes the single most fundamental motivation for their crimes."[18]

This argument may or may not be convincing. One thing is clear, however. The equation of collecting and selfhood shows just how indebted current psychological analysis of serial killing remains to Freudian psychoanalysis, even though neither of these articles on Jeffrey Dahmer goes so far as to even mention Freud, let alone Abraham or Fenichel. Fascinatingly, however, the 2013 article uses both Walter Benjamin and Werner Muensterberger's analyses of collecting to analyze Dahmer's killing. It brings in Benjamin after describing Dahmer's grisly temple to explain how the collector "lives in" his things. Serial killers and ordinary collectors might not be entirely different kinds of people, it suggests, because they share the "collecting impulse." The popular Freudian link between murder, collecting, and trophyism has become so ingrained, in other words, and so proverbial, it seems perfectly reasonable to use collecting studies to carry out psychological studies of serial killers. Such analyses have become a form of cultural common sense.[19]

As the twentieth century drew to a close, fiction and film kept pace with real-life horrors by designing ever more stylized killers, who displayed their style as a form of personal signature more often than not through collecting. Arguably the most stylized of all was Thomas Harris's 1988 novel

The Silence of the Lambs, filmed by Jonathan Demme in 1991. Dr. Hannibal Lecter, played with unforgettable menace by Anthony Hopkins in Demme's film, is a highly sophisticated psychopath and a throwback to the paradox of the civilized Nazi—a savage killer with refined tastes. A brilliant psychiatrist who both reads (hence the name *Lecter*) and eats people (his nickname is Hannibal the Cannibal), Lecter is part psychopathic decadent, part amoral connoisseur, and enjoys reading, art and music, and killing in style.

In the story, Lecter helps a young FBI agent named Clarice Starling (played by Jodie Foster in the movie) decode the murderous collecting habits of a rural loner called Jame Gumb. Gumb's character (nicknamed Buffalo Bill) revisits the pathological insect obsessions of *The Collector*, taking them to new extremes. Where Clegg turns out to be "sexless," Gumb is fixated on his quest to become a woman at all costs. He has applied for surgery to achieve his objective but his requests have been denied. Bitterly frustrated, he has taken to breeding moths from pupae, a symbol of his own longed-for transformation, kidnapping and killing women in order to make himself a suit of female skin. He used to work in a "curio store" that made butterfly ornaments, and he has become obsessed with the death's-head moth, whose natural patterning resembles a skull. "The significance of the chrysalis is change," Lecter tells Starling, who researches the creatures at the Smithsonian Institution in Washington, D.C.[20]

Brilliantly gruesome and psychologically incisive, *The Silence of the Lambs* was virtually the last major work of its kind, a summa of Freudian obsessions linking sex, collecting, and violence. In the book, Lecter scorns "the dead religion of psychoanalysis," but he's still playing a Freudian game. He helps Starling analyze Gumb—like Bates, a rural drifter plagued by repressed yearning—to help make sense of his behavior and track him down in order to save his current captive, a senator's daughter. At its core, the story is still a search for the meaning of a collection in all its terrifying darkness.[21]

The twentieth century seemed in infinite supply of psycho collectors. It was as if any boy next door who collected anything at all, from cookie jars to Beanie Babies, could turn out to be a murderous sociopath if you caught him on the wrong day. By the 1990s, after a century of Freudian psychoanalysis, the search for meaning in the psycho collector's story was, however, burning itself out and becoming culturally exhausted. There was just time for one more tale—a satire on the whole genre of serial killing. Like Clegg, and unlike Bates, the century's culminating psycho was obsessed by class, not sex. After decades of fascination with sexually tormented psycho-collector nobodies marooned in the middle of the great American nowhere, the psycho got a top job and moved back to the city in the age of Reagan to embark on a joyride of quasi-cannibal consumerist mayhem.

Bret Easton Ellis's novel *American Psycho* (1991) tells the story of Patrick Bateman, played by Christian Bale in Mary Harron's darkly humorous 2000 film adaptation. A Wall Street trader by day, Bateman is well heeled and well chiseled, adorned by a beautiful fiancée and powered by a fat paycheck. By night, however, Bateman is a somewhat different proposition, bedding call-girls and committing a series of truly horrific murders. His business? "Murders and executions," he jokes (mergers and acquisitions), though oddly no one seems to notice his pun when he does so. Gratuitous sex and lethal violence give him an outrageous outlet for the monumental insecurities that plague every fiber of his neurotic being. As a Harvard graduate, he's naturally viciously status-conscious, driven by mortal dread of embarrassment and a pathological need to conform. "I want to fit in," he pleads. Constantly teetering on the edge of humiliation, he fears his friends will outdo him, by getting swankier dinner reservations, having a sexier business card and pretty much any other marker of social distinction.[22]

Bateman is the ultimate Reaganite hedonist. He eats at the hippest Manhattan restaurants, daubs himself with the finest skin-care products, buys designer brands, and acquires expensive contemporary art. He accumulates instinctively, which is to say, ignorantly. He often has no idea what he's doing, like when he accidentally hangs a pricey David Onica canvas upside down without even noticing. He knows nothing about either contemporary or classic art but buys both. When he puzzles over what luxury goods his eighteenth-century George Stubbs painting looks best next to, he blandly decides the picture looks fine in either place he contemplated.

Bateman delights in contemplative yet utterly vacuous consumer soliloquies, delivered in perfect deadpan by Bale in the movie. A satire on pop culture connoisseurship, these include deep musings on the songs of Phil Collins, Huey Lewis, and Whitney Houston (Genesis's best album is "an epic meditation on intangibility," he reckons) before he beds a prostitute or rains an axe down on a colleague's skull. But the music, the paintings, and the restaurants all fail to satisfy. So, too, do the orgies and the orgiastic killing sprees. In the end, no one actually believes Bateman has committed them, and, worst of all, he can't convince them that he's done so. His terrible crimes are the one meaningful thing in his life, but ultimately even he comes to doubt he has committed them. Is *anything* in his life real?[23]

A manic rampage through Wall Street materialism as collective cultural insanity, *American Psycho* is emphatically a tale of the eighties. But this psycho has historical form, too. The name Bateman, of course, recalls Norman Bates, and Bateman leads a double-life like Dorian Gray, living it up at New York's best restaurants while slumming it on the skuzziest Manhattan streets. He's an American Clegg, whose frenzied narcissism is driven not by sex but by ferocious status anxiety. His sexual adventures offer releases of a sort, but he suffers no brooding Freudian crisis like Bates or Gumb—he's far too shallow for that. He is what he buys, and it turns out there's nothing really there.

The story is a warning. America, as so many love to point out, is the new Rome. Bret Easton Ellis is Cicero and Bateman the new American Verres: the maniac whose appetites will devour the republic itself. America is being decimated by the corruption and madness of its own elite. Bateman's touchstone isn't Ronald Reagan, however, but Donald Trump, whose pathological playboy entrepreneur eighties persona he worships above all else. Bateman thinks he sees his idol everywhere around Manhattan, much to the chagrin of his companions. "Not Donald Trump again," his fiancée moans at one point, "this obsession has got to end."[24]

Is the chilling story of the serial trophyist culturally dead? There are still serial killers, of course, real and imagined, roaming pop culture and Netflix—not least a resurgent Jeffrey Dahmer—but their stories no longer seem to shock us quite the way they used to. Killers may still collect trophies in a desperate quest for meaning, but that quest has hollowed itself out, at least as a cultural narrative. They no longer seize our imagination in quite the same way. That was Bret Easton Ellis's point about Bateman back in 1991: in the end, nobody actually cares about his supposed crimes or the haunting meaning he himself sees in them. That's life these days. It's not really possible to be evil anymore. Everyone's too distracted or too narcissistic to notice.

The view from the suburbs looks different, however. The suburbs are still awash in meaning and harbor plenty of collectors who flirt with the dark in a quest for true selfhood. They're not murderers or psychos, of course. They're just a bit creepy. But they're also cool. Many of them now have their own intriguing Instagram pages. A few years ago, a select few were curated into a book called *Morbid Curiosities* (2016). Its editor, Paul Gambino, calls them "collectors of the macabre" and arranged them into an admiring portrait gallery, featuring lavish photos of them and their collections along with interviews in their own words. Gambino's purpose? To probe the inevitable question—Freud's question—of why these "monsters" collect what they collect, what their collections mean, what they say about them as people, and show that they're not monsters at all.[25]

Nicole Angemi is one of them. A former biology student, Nicole hails from outside Philadelphia. She became a pathologist's assistant who developed a passion for gross pathology and collecting and displaying corpses, both human and animal. In her highly striking portrait in *Morbid Curiosities*, she stares straight at the camera, wearing blue glasses that match the spidery bluish tattoos covering her arms and neck, holding a hairless cat. Behind her we can see a pair of antlers and specimens in jars. Other pictures featuring Nicole's collections include the taxidermic specimen of a mouse; human and animal bones, including the skull of a lynx; a fetal pig she received as a wedding gift; IUDs; diseased organs; brains, a uterus, and an ovary; and one of Nicole's placentas.

A true postmodern Victorian, Nicole finds beauty in death, challenging present-day taboos on mortality. Her collecting also marks a return to the early modern tradition of the memento mori. *I collect to confront you*, she seems to say, *with what you most want to forget: that you will die.* But Nicole's collecting is more than this. Her tattoos and her collection are acts of defiant self-expression. "I really don't care what people think about me," she says, "I don't do anything in my life to please other people." She explains that her collection and her home are an expression of her and (her hus-

Maria Q. Kane

*Nicole Angemi (2024): A New Jersey pathologist's
assistant, Angemi is a defiantly proud contemporary
collector and online exhibitor of gross anatomy specimens
and cadavers, both human and animal. In this photo, she
holds a jar containing her youngest daughter's placenta.*

band's) "personalities" and "creativity." Their friends and family think she's weird but also accept that she's "cool." Anyway, "if someone is offended, they do not have to look." By one count, she has almost 2 million followers on Instagram.[26]

Brent S. is another of Gambino's featured collectors. He works as a registered nurse in a Northern California hospital and started out by collecting baseball cards and knives. But when Brent came upon the complete skeleton of a deer, the true glory of collecting's possibilities revealed themselves to him. He now focuses his efforts on osteology, but also enjoys forensic anthropology and archaeology as collecting fields. One picture in *Morbid Curiosities* is labeled *trophy skulls* and includes trepanned, hydrocephalic, and elongated crania. A gentle tattoo-less giant with a rather jolly-seeming demeanor, Brent's portrait features him holding a human skull in each hand with a cheerful smile.

Like Nicole, Brent believes his collecting is countercultural and therefore unique. He explains that it's about seeing beauty in what "the general population finds bizarre." It all took off for him when he bought a weapon used by the Dayak people of Borneo at a flea market, and since then he has gone on to correspond with dealers in all sorts of medical oddities including at Philadelphia's Mutter Museum, the mecca of anatomical abnormality. "In the beginning, it was pretty cool just to have a human bone," Brent remembers, but he has obtained so many, he can now "do comparative studies on anomalies." His family doesn't understand, and most people just call him "the skull guy." But he approaches his hobby with happy innocence. "Many assume the collectors of the macabre are all in it for the histrionics," he says. As for him, he associates mainly with those who "are constantly educating themselves" in fields such as craniometry and anthropology. "Nobody has to like my collection," Brent comments, echoing Nicole. "I don't collect for them."[27]

Then there's Jessika M., who has no portrait in *Morbid Curiosities*. Jessika lives in Indiana and she's a "dark collector." True crime is her area, not pathology. She's driven by a deep curiosity about criminals and their deeds. She owns a knife used to kill a prison inmate, as well as the victim's prison ID card. "I keep those depressing items together," she says, they're "very special." But the object that really "creeps me out"—"and that is pretty hard to do"—is the hammer a man called John Robinson used to kill eight people in Missouri. "It had been cleaned in bleach," she explains, and "I've never smelled anything quite like that hammer in the towel that it was wrapped in. It definitely creeps me out!"[28]

Jessika collects in order to cross what another collector in *Morbid Curiosities*, Jack Kump, calls "the creep threshold." To her, collecting is transgressive thrill-seeking. This becomes clear from the photos Gambino includes from her collection: Robinson's hammer in its towel; letters from serial killers (including Ted Bundy) and their admirers; Polaroids of infamous murderers including Aileen Wuornos; locks of killers' hair; and art and objects (such as necklaces) made by killers in prison. Jessika also writes to convicted murderers and dreams of acquiring material associated with Jim Jones,

Gary Gilmore, or other truly notorious murderers. The more infamous the killer, the more alluring their relics.[29]

Some objects, however, are too far over the creep threshold, even for Jessika. She has refused to collect the underwear of female inmates, for example. It's odd for her, she admits, but these specific items leave her "morally conflicted." The same goes for killers' tombstones, like Ed Gein's, which was in fact stolen in Wisconsin. Thefts like these, Jessika says, makes the public think "there's something inherently wrong with people who collect things considered 'dark.'" People thought she was probably going to become a killer herself, she says, and she concedes many might find her collecting "offensive," but "that's what makes it so interesting."[30]

Gambino's gang of misfits is surprisingly uniform. They're all idiosyncratic individuals who collect in the conviction that their families, friends, and the public think there's something wrong with them. They collect exactly what they want to and don't care what others think. Actually, they do care: they *like* it when others disapprove. It reaffirms their sense of self.

In this respect, Nicole, Brent, Jessika, and other macabre collectors may look alternative or creepy, but they represent a powerful continuity with the nineteenth-century cult of the collector as a charismatic countercultural antihero. Like the Victorian eccentric Charles Kirkpatrick Sharpe and Huysmans's fin de siècle misanthrope Des Esseintes, they collect not for gain or status but are driven by an overwhelming need to express themselves, thumbing their noses at polite society, financial reward, and the mores of their times—all in the name of realizing the dream of the Romantic collecting self. Like the Ming literati who suffered from *pǐ*, like Pons and Walter Benjamin, they are *true* collectors who collect in order to be themselves and nothing *but* themselves, defying every norm of respectability they can identify. Whether you're an aesthete and an urbanite or a working-class suburbanite, the dark heart of collecting is redeemed by the promise of authenticity and truth to self. Whatever your collection is, it is good, insofar as it is *you*.

It's hard not look at collectors of the macabre through Freudian eyes. Hannibal Lecter was wrong: the dead religion of psychoanalysis isn't really dead at all. *Why* do people collect morbid curiosities? That is Gambino's question. We still want to know and we still want meaning. We assume that accumulating skulls *must* say something about what kind of people collectors are, allowing us to wonder as well what they might be capable of. Because without meaning, all would be *too* random and the carefully constructed world of the collection not merely dark but unfathomable. Dark collectors know this all too well and dare us to judge or dismiss them.

But we don't, do we? Not anymore. We don't dare. Because something has changed. We don't really assume Nicole or Brent or Jessika are like Norman Bates or Frederick Clegg or Jeffrey Dahmer. In a sense, whether they know it or not, their defiance now looks out of date. Being a dark collector may be creepy, but we now realize it's cool. That's because attitudes to collecting have changed in the twenty-first century. But how? An answer is to be found in the final chapter, which introduces us to the culminating figure in our story: the hoarder. Hoarders aren't just a new type of collector; they're part of a new era in which we have learned to see collectors as people driven by an innate biological urge to accumulate, one we now locate not in sexual neurosis, past trauma, or status anxiety, but in the human brain. Because to one degree or another, we're all hoarders now.

CHAPTER THIRTEEN

ALL HOARDERS NOW

He doesn't throw anything away.

—REPORTER COMMENTING ON CHARLES FOSTER KANE
IN *CITIZEN KANE* (1941)

Bothell is a small town in Washington State. A former logging community, it's now a Seattle suburb that has been colonized by the city's biomedical, technology, and engineering industries. Bothell is also home to Shanna: an ordinary person with extraordinary habits. Shanna's home is so filled with clothing, newspapers, boxes, and trash, she can barely move. She eats her meals in cramped corners close to large plastic buckets. The buckets loom quietly, yet ominously. They contain urine and excrement—her own.

Shanna didn't always live by herself. She used to live with her mother, but her mother died from cancer, a cancer that may just possibly have been caused by the squalor of the house they shared. It's possible, in other words, that Shanna's constant accumulation and inability to throw anything away may have inadvertently resulted in her mother's death. And this may also be the reason why her brother and sister are angry with her. But she continues to gather junk all around her, and she refuses to move.

Representatives from social services are brought in by Shanna's family and visit her at home. They interview her and try to explain that they're going to try to save her, whether she likes it or not. Having dealt with similar cases, they take suitable precautions, donning hazmat suits to begin the process of clearing Shanna's house of its most scabrous contents.

Shanna looks on, bemused, as if it were all happening to somebody else. She wants to refuse their help but finds she can't. Finally, she agrees to leave her home to be rehoused and start a new life. Family reconciliation and emotional closure appear at hand. But there's a lot going on behind Shanna's eyes as she acquiesces to the salvation her family, the state, and the medical services insist on. Removed from her home, she looks bewildered, not relieved. She doesn't want to die, but she doesn't want to leave. Because Shanna is a hoarder.

Shanna is a person *and* a persona. This is her story as presented by the American TV show *Hoarders*, which began airing on the Arts & Entertainment Network in 2009 and originally ran for 118 episodes. It inspired many similar shows around the world. But where and how did the modern concept of the hoarder originally emerge?

In 2013, the world's most powerful medical institutions began catching up with the keen psychological insights of Reality TV. That year, the American Psychiatric Association included hoarding disorder (HD) for the first time in the fifth edition of its *Diagnostic and Statistical Manual of Mental Disorders* (*DSM-5*). Then, in 2018, HD went global when the World Health Organization (WHO) included it in the eleventh edition of its International Classification of Diseases (ICD-11). According to these organizations, people like Shanna need professional medical care—not just professional de-cluttering, but psychiatric intervention. Since then, an increasing number of psychologists have defined hoarders as people afflicted by compulsive accumulation or extreme collecting, treating HD as a mental disorder. Rather than a physical illness with a cause and a cure, it's defined as a chronic behavior whose symptoms require cognitive therapy and anti-anxiety drugs.

The hoarder isn't just the most recent incarnation of the idea that accumulating too many things is a form of illness, therefore, but also continues the shift in focus on *who* is doing the accumulating. The educated upper-middle-class subject of Freudian psychoanalysis has given way to the economically marginal lower-class hoarder who is to be treated not by talking cures but by drugs and social services. Medical intervention has replaced psychological explanation. Treatment is the goal with Shanna on *Hoarders*, not explaining why she does what she does. We've moved from the twentieth century's obsession with the collecting self as an intricate labyrinth of meaning to standardized diagnoses and pharmaceutical care in the twenty-first.

Perhaps the simplest definition of a hoarder is someone who accumulates things of no value and is unable to throw worthless things away: junk mail, product packaging, and, in extreme cases like Shanna's, their own excrement. In the process, their homes become physically hazardous and they withdraw from the world, placing themselves in jeopardy.

Hoarding disorder may be a new phrase, but the term *hoard* goes back centuries. *Hoard* denotes the hiding of valuable treasures, often by burying them in the earth. Relatedly, hoarding is an economic term to describe the act of keeping currency out of circulation. Google's N-Gram tracker shows that use of the word *hoard* has in fact declined since the nineteenth century; the word *hoarding* has stayed in fairly consistent use since the sixteenth; but *hoarder* and *hoarding disorder* have spiked since the year 2000. They go together: the invention of hoarding disorder brought about the invention of the modern hoarder as a new category of person.

But shouldn't one distinguish between *collectors* and *hoarders*? Collectors, one might assume, act with an orderly purpose in mind, contributing to art or science or a meaningful personal life, gathering things of value; whereas hoarders are driven by an unreasoning and potentially self-destructive inability to throw out junk.

Yet, as a matter of historical fact, the distinction between *collecting* and *hoarding* has never been as easy to draw as it seems. No one would call Shanna a collector, of course, yet her hoarding of her own feces recalls Freudian theories that the urge to collect universally originates in the act of anal retention. And although no one psychoanalyzes Shanna on *Hoarders*, the narrative about her bears unmistakable traces of Freudian interpretation, as it's also suggested that her mother's death may have reinforced Shanna's hoarding behavior, recalling Werner Muensterberger's insistence that collecting is always a response to some form of trauma.

We also think of hoarders as people who fill their houses with worthless objects to the point of physical collapse. But something similar has very often been observed of collectors. Sir Hans Sloane built up a huge natural history collection, but critics often derided it as worthless, and he had to acquire the house next door to store it. Robert Opie mystified people in the 1970s by collecting consumer packaging, such as cereal boxes and chocolate wrappers. Like Sloane, Opie stuffed his London home to bursting until eventually moving his collection into the Museum of Brands. In Germany, Kurt Schwitters literally collected rubbish from the streets to make his collages, the kind of work the Nazis later denounced as "Jewish trash." The history of collecting is thus full of "rubbish," a notion often invoked when collectors are ahead of their time or others fail to see the value of their collections.[1]

From the beginning, Freudians were fascinated by people who could not throw things away. In his 1921 essay on "the anal character," Karl Abraham compared the satisfaction he believed many people experience on looking at their feces to an inability to separate oneself from objects of no value. He discussed individuals who accumulate broken objects in their attics, telling themselves they might need them one day; people who keep pieces of paper, envelopes, and worn-out pens; clerks who collect used blotting paper; and an old woman who would carry in her pocket toilet paper she had used. Abraham concluded such people were marked by "a strong regression of libido to the anal stage," though he did acknowledge the satisfaction they felt in effecting the occasional evacuation. In one remarkable instance, Abraham described a woman who could not willingly throw any single thing away. She was so fixated on retention that she had to trick herself into getting rid of things. She would go to another neighborhood and shed certain objects "accidentally" by letting them drop from the back of her body, so as not to witness the otherwise intolerable act of separation.[2]

Today, one crucial yet often unstated distinction between hoarders and collectors is not in fact psychological but the matter of social class. *Hoarders* are those who can't afford to buy that second house as the first overflows, while *collectors* can. But in the early twentieth century, before the rise of Bates and Clegg as embodiments of the democratic collector nobody, popular culture was fascinated by the figure of the upper-class hoarder.

The subject of Orson Welles's masterpiece *Citizen Kane* (1941) is Charles Foster Kane. Loosely based on newspaper tycoon William Randolph Hearst, the mighty Kane is an upper-class melancholic, yet another Rudolf who turns inward in his castle: a gigantic mansion and estate named Xanadu in imitation of Kublai Khan. Finding himself alone at the end of his life, friendless and separated from his two wives, Kane is surrounded only by his things, his vast art collection, accumulated at great expense from his time in Europe. It is "a collection of everything, so big it can never be catalogued or appraised, enough for ten museums . . . the loot of the world." It includes the "biggest private zoo since Noah" and is "the costliest monument man has built to himself."[3]

But what does it all mean? Welles opens the film with the most famous dying words in cinema history—"Rosebud"—but what does *that* mean? The question becomes a quest: newsmen covering Kane's demise want a story for their reels. Can you distill the meaning of an entire life down to a single phrase, asks *Citizen Kane*, or the things someone accumulates? That's what they're hoping to show.

Kane began buying art on a grand European tour, sending countless crates back to America without even bothering to open them all. He keeps them not because he loves them but simply because, as someone observes, "He doesn't throw anything away." In the end, the newsmen fail. In the film's immortal final shot, the camera pans over hundreds of crates before the removal men burn the undiscovered "Rosebud" without realizing it. Smoke rises from Xanadu's chimney like a funeral pyre, keeping the meaning of Kane's melancholy secret forever.[4]

The tragedy was intended as parody. In interviews, Welles revealed that he meant to mock the Freudian idea that you can diagnose the essence of a person's life from their things. He saw Kane's story not as one of trauma and psychoanalytic depth but as a Henry Jamesian "attack on the acquisitive society," the hollowness of American materialism and money's self-defeating soullessness.[5]

Kane's other target was Hearst. If you visit the tycoon's modestly named Hearst Castle at San Simeon near San Luis Obispo on the California coast, the stark difference between Welles's vision of Kane as a gloomy Rudolfian recluse and the reality of Hearst's life becomes clear. Hearst didn't flee from the world at San Simeon, he brought it with him: he ran his newspaper empire from his castle while inviting Charlie Chaplin and Cary Grant and a constant stream of rather glamorous guests to swim, play tennis, dine, and generally pay homage. Hearst was furious that Welles's film convinced the world he was some kind of depressive—no doubt to Welles's great amusement—and the two men launched into a lengthy feud.

Americans at midcentury were enthralled by the figure of the aristo-cratic hoarder and the more Gothic, the better. Its most infamous exemplars were Homer and Langley Collyer, who were found dead in their Harlem townhouse in 1947, entombed in a building filled with old newspapers and junk, including booby traps they'd set for burglars. The two brothers made tragic front-page news and became the object of morbid fascination, not least because they claimed to be original blue-blooded descendants of the original Pilgrim settlers on the *Mayflower*. E. L. Doctorow later immortal-ized them in a 2009 novel called *Homer and Langley*.

In 1975, the documentary filmmakers Albert and David Maysles released their swansong for the upper-class hoarder, *Grey Gardens*. The movie show-cased the reclusive lives of "Big" and "Little" Edie Bouvier Beale—relatives of Jackie Kennedy—who hoarded cats and raccoons and lived amidst gar-bage in a derelict mansion without running water on Long Island.

Beginning in the 1960s, however, an egalitarian cultural revolution began to sweep aside the figure of the aristocratic hoarder. It wasn't just that American pop culture's fascination with hoarders slid from upper-class somebodies like Charles Foster Kane down to nobodies like Norman Bates. A broader revolution in aesthetic and cultural tastes was taking place in which mass-produced industrial commodities were beginning their improbable rise to the status of million-dollar art object. The avatar of what became known as Pop Art was a conceptual artist and entrepreneur who just happened to be an insatiable collector as well.

Today, Andy Warhol is heralded as the genius (or villain) who champi-oned the aesthetic beauty of industrial consumer goods and their packag-ing, from Campbell's soup cans to Brillo Pads, and their commodification as works of art. A cultural subversive, aesthete, and sexually ambiguous latter-day decadent who cut against hierarchies of education, class, and taste, Warhol advanced the idea that every kind of thing in the world pos-sesses a unique value.

Born and raised in Pittsburgh by Slovak parents, Warhol became a com-mercial illustrator before moving to New York in 1949 and embarking on a career as an artist. Warhol conquered the Manhattan art scene and the New York social scene as a modern-day flaneur. He was a countercultural dandy for the democratic age. Making art out of industrial commodities and photographs of movie stars would have been Des Esseintes's worst nightmare, but, in reality, Warhol was a refined if anarchic connoisseur similar to Huysmans's fictional decadent. Like Des Esseintes, for example, Warhol was a connoisseur of scents and owned his own perfume museum. In *The Philosophy of Andy Warhol* (1975), he even discusses what he considers the great smells of New York, listing them in catalog style like a true connoisseur: "neighborhood grocery stores . . . the wood chairs and tables in the N.Y. Public Library . . . the good cheap candy smell in the front of Woolworth's."[6]

Warhol's philosophy of accumulation was, however, conflicted. He liked to declare his adherence to minimalism. It was best not to accumulate too much, he warned, at least not where you live. If you live in New York, for example, and you end up with too much stuff, you'd better "send it over to Jersey." But Warhol didn't follow his own advice. Instead, he kept a vast collection in his apartment at 57 East Sixty-Sixth Street, safely hidden under lock and key, guarded by maids and a security system. His collection constantly expanded and he monitored it every day. Perhaps this was why he was so keen on the idea of minimalism and storage, because he could not contain himself.[7]

After Warhol died in 1987, the extraordinary range of his collections suddenly became public when they came up for auction at Sotheby's in New York. He'd collected Picassos and Native American sculptures, but also Kermit the Frog telephones and air-sickness bags, crockery, and product packaging. High art and Old Masters, modern classics and ethnographic artifacts, ephemera and quotidiana jostled together with apparent indiscrimination.

Several of his acquaintances later explained how Warhol became obsessed with money, status, and shopping. Sometimes he'd go on collecting trips in a Rolls Royce; sometimes he'd go antiquing with fellow celebrities including John Lennon and Yoko Ono. Shy by nature, Warhol also dispatched friends and agents to bid on his behalf at auctions. He *loved* not being at these auctions, he quipped. By the late 1960s, he was reputedly spending about $1 million a year this way. He liked antiques, a friend observed, because they made him feel rich. Starting the day meant buying something, another commented, packing it up in cartons or shopping bags and locking it up.

Andy Warhol, self-portrait with fright wig (1986): Warhol (1928–87)
spent lavishly, collecting everything from fine art and anthropological
artifacts to toys and air sickness bags, leading some observers to label him
an undisciplined and even deranged hoarder.

Warhol is particularly hard to classify, and much ink has been spilled in the attempt. Was he a shopper or a collector, a hoarder or an investor? "He collected as an investment," observed the New York collector Stuart Pivar, and "looked upon spotting trends as an industry," finding "aesthetic interest in everything." He loathed compartmentalization. But the sight of radically different things jumbled together proved shocking to some, as if Warhol thought they were all somehow of equal value. "Andy Warhol's collection," Stuart Greenspan judged in the magazine *Art and Auction*, "is more the result of his compulsive shopping and hoarding than of any calculated, orderly plan of acquisition." When it came time to auction it off,

Sotheby's took care to sort Warhol's collection into different categories, to allow for separate bidding on each.[8]

Whether we call this kind of mixed collecting *camp*, as Susan Sontag did in her 1964 essay "Notes on Camp," *queer*, or simply *eclectic*, it was part of a larger revolution in value. Warhol wasn't just the avatar of Pop Art but also preoccupied by trash. When it came to disposing of garbage, he stuffed it into trash bags, which he left outside other people's buildings on different city blocks, assuming people would naturally go scavenging among his discards if they knew they were his. "Virtually everything that came through [his] mail box was carefully conserved," observes the art historian John Richardson. It ended up being taped, bagged, or boxed and dated: junk mail, fan letters, documents, old magazines. This was Warhol the "recording angel," whose legacy remains on view in Pittsburgh's Warhol Museum, which devotedly preserves the artist's "time capsules": boxes of ephemera whose contents document countless moments in time. To this day, Warhol's curators continue to unpack his time capsules. Like the clinical de-clutterers who cleared Shanna's house, they wear hazmat suits to shield themselves from the toxins that might potentially be released when they open the great recording angel's hoard.[9]

Lionized by many, Warhol's collecting seemed creepy to others, and the "creep threshold" is precisely where some of his most notable heirs are to be found. Consider the case of Ward Harrison. Harrison was not an art collector or a hoarder but an expert at scavenging in the trash cans of Hollywood stars, finding brass in muck and selling off his ill-gotten treasures. A former debt collector, the self-described "garbologist" and "shitehawk" started bin-diving in Beverly Hills in the 1970s. "I'm collecting history," he once explained to an interviewer. Among his dubious trophies are the guest log from actor Jimmy Stewart's wedding; a Barbra Streisand gold bracelet; love letters written to the Rat-Packer and friend of JFK Peter Lawford; and actress Natalie Wood's diaphragm, which Harrison stole despite being accosted by her husband, Robert Wagner. The diaphragm sold for $35. Harrison bin-dived for the money, but like any true collector, it was also for the thrill. "There's no greater high," he explained. "Especially when you idolize these people . . . you're touching their lives in a very intimate way."[10]

Those who idolize Warhol praise him as the person who more than any other democratized aesthetic value. But inflating the monetary value of consumer goods as an art commodity doesn't seem quite so democratic today; quite the opposite. Harrison selling Natalie Wood's diaphragm for $35 was a sign of things to come, a world Warhol envisioned and where the collection of absolutely anything can be monetized. Toys from Star Wars figures to Beanie Babies have gone from children's playthings to investments traded by pop connoisseurs like commodities on the stock exchange. In 2022, Warhol's Marilyn Monroe portrait *Shot Sage Blue Marilyn* sold for $195 million at Christie's, becoming the most expensive work of American art ever sold at the time. Who bought it? The buyer remained anonymous. Like Warhol, the collector never showed at the auction.

If some called Warhol a hoarder, nobody suggested he had hoarding disorder. That is because HD was not invented until 2013, when the American Psychiatric Association coined and defined the term. But how easy is it really to diagnose HD?

According to the American Psychiatric Association's *DSM-5*, HD belongs to the family of obsessive-compulsive disorders and is characterized by a "difficulty discarding or parting with possessions, regardless of their actual value." Discarding items causes distress, and the resulting inability to throw things away produces a cluttering effect that poses a threat to the individual's well-being. This is the essence of the diagnosis. HD is not an offshoot of depression or caused by brain injuries and cannot be explained as a generic form of obsessive behavior. It is its own peculiar disorder.[11]

In 2018, the WHO offered a more nuanced definition in the ICD-11. Again, the telltale sign is clutter that poses a threat to safety, which the individual fails to recognize and which usually starts in childhood but can also come on with dementia in old age. Unlike the American Psychiatric Association, however, the WHO blurs the distinction between HD and collecting in interesting fashion.

"Amassment," the ICD-11 authors explain, can be "passive" or "active" in HD. It's more acquisitive than not throwing things out. They explain that HD shares a "threshold" with normal collecting—we could call it the hoarding threshold—which is often unclear. "Collecting and saving items" is a perfectly normal behavior among children, for example. Like HD sufferers, "collectors acquire many items that they report being attached to and reluctant to discard," though collectors are more "organized." Some studies suggest women are more likely to suffer from HD than men.[12]

But the WHO then muddies the distinction between collecting and hoarding, referring to "excessive collecting and accumulation of clutter" in the same sentence. It goes on to explain that it would be wrong to see HD's symptoms always as signs of illness. "The nature of what is collected and the meaning, emotional valence, and value that people with Hoarding Disorder assign to their possessions may have cultural significance." Not throwing things away means different things in different places, including "cultural values of thriftiness" and "saving items for later use" in "contexts of scarcity."[13]

Like the American Psychiatric Association, the WHO shows little interest in explaining why people have HD. Again, it's a far cry from Freudians looking to understand what collections reveal about collectors' inner lives. Others go quite a bit further, however, believing they can explain HD as a form of extreme collecting by use of brain scans. We may have given up trying to explain why people love things too much, but some now believe we can see what's wrong with the brain that does so.

In 2005, in the journal *Brain*, neuroscientists Steven Anderson and Hanna and Antonio Damasio published an article entitled "A Neural Basis for Collecting Behavior in Humans." Was it possible, the authors wanted to know, to correlate "abnormal collecting behavior," as well as normal collecting, with forms of brain damage?[14]

In the article, Anderson and the Damasios define collecting broadly, scientifically, but also idiosyncratically, to mean the accumulation of objects beyond a "normal" amount, without ever specifying what they consider "normal." In their view, collectors collect things that possess no utility: no aesthetic value, no financial value, and no practical function. They are mere collectors. Yet in doing so, the authors overlook personal value and self-expression as rational motivations for collecting. Collecting, to them, is instead a peculiar activity because—so defined—it serves no real purpose. It is an end in itself. And they compare the collector to the proverbial packrat who hoards—they use the word *hoard*—not because such accumulation is necessary but purely out of instinct.[15]

The three neuroscientists carried out trials on eighty-six human subjects. They found that all had lesions of the telencephalon, which includes the cerebral cortex and is the largest part of the brain and the focus of the central nervous system. They found more specifically that all subjects with what they called "pathological collecting behavior . . . had damage to the mesial frontal region." They concluded that such damage disinhibits the impulse to accumulate: it "disrupts a mechanism which normally modulates subcortically driven predispositions to acquire and collect." They made clear that each subject began collecting only after sustaining a lesion. This included a student who started accumulating can openers after undergoing surgery and a man who bought so many clothes after a surgical procedure that he went bankrupt (he also gained eighty pounds).[16]

The notion that collecting is related to brain damage is a striking if not subversive idea. Should we see *all* collectors and hoarders as neurologically compromised or neurodivergent to some degree? Have the complex personal stories explaining why people collect finally run their course, because neuroscience may now be taken to suggest that the reasons for collecting and/or hoarding are essentially biological?

In her 2019 book *Inside the Head of a Collector: Neuropsychological Forces at Play*, the American neurologist and porcelain collector Shirley Mueller seeks to establish a link between collecting and the field of neuro-economics. Her principal argument is that collecting is in no way an odd or peculiar behavior but an activity that simply makes our brains happy. Mueller recounts how stressed she was by her medical career until she found that reading about Chinese porcelain made her feel better. Mueller began collecting porcelain and then felt even better. Drawing both on her knowledge of porcelain and her experience as an investment adviser, she believes the neuropsychology of investing can be readily applied to collecting.

In her book, Mueller uses several simplified diagrams of brains to illustrate the neuropsychology of collecting. She discusses how triumphs at the auction house create a powerful sense of pleasure in the collector's brain, while disappointments produce pain. Mueller rejects Anderson and the Damasios' brain damage thesis, arguing that the mesial prefrontal cortex is also associated with the perception of beauty. She suggests that our love of beauty, rather than the disinhibition of the urge to accumulate, better explains why collectors love collecting.

Mueller also dismisses Werner Muensterberger's Freudian view of collecting as outmoded and misguided. Rather like Muensterberger, however, she imposes current scientific theory on past collectors as though it can provide a definitive perspective on what was happening when collectors collected, going back almost a century. When, for example, Mueller discusses how the Indiana pharmaceutical executive Eli Lilly negotiated to buy Chinese antiquities in 1947 from C. T. Loo, she describes the interaction between the two men not according to what it meant to buy and sell such antiquities in that time and place, nor by way of the personal motivations of the individuals concerned, but instead in strictly neurological terms. Mueller speaks of dueling "pleasure centers," "reward probabilities," the activity of the mesial prefrontal cortex, "primitive emotions," and the workings of the "executive modern brain."[17]

The result is a highly reductive analysis, but one quite revealing of our times. Mueller's approach reflects the trajectory of psychology since the end of the twentieth century, as "soft" psychoanalysis has yielded to "hard" neurology, and talking cures to pharmaceuticals. In Mueller's perspective, Muensterberger's psychoanalysis of collectors was hopelessly cluttered by endless tales of childhood, abusive parents, and sexual pathology—cluttered, in other words, with an excess of individual causal explanation and personal meaning. For Mueller, by contrast, the cultural meaning of collecting has been eclipsed by its alleged biological drives. The pivotal Freudian question "Why collect?" no longer turns on the specific case history of a complex individual but on the competition between the pleasure of acquisition and the pain of disappointment in all human brains, regardless of time or place. The collecting self no longer merits a story, merely a brain scan.

Clearing out all the errors of psychoanalysis, leaving only neural networks in their wake, Mueller's neurological view of why collectors collect is like a positive take on hoarding. Some brains might be more disinhibited than others, but the suggestion is that we are all innately driven to accumulate. The impulse to obtain wealth and fine objects, not to mention the urge to make shrewd investments therefore, is natural, universal, and healthy. There's nothing *wrong* with collecting at all.

Whatever the precise scientific merits of Mueller's neurological perspective, from a historical perspective at least one thing seems clear enough: her analysis forms part of a long and ongoing reaction against Freudian psychoanalysis favoring hard-wired explanations of human behavior. Mueller may be right; or what she says may simply be what passes for scientific truth today. But what are the cultural implications of her analysis? If neurology now seems more scientifically authoritative than psychoanalysis, it is also more impersonal, reducing the collecting self to a set of physiological impulses rather than deeper personal motivations rooted in the life of the individual. Muensterberger, too, was reductive, of course, and many of Freud's ideas and practices now stand rejected. But as a matter of cultural history, psychoanalysis produced rather more humane, intricate, and interesting stories about the collecting self and its search for meaning than pictures of brains that reduce collectors to crude drives.

Are we "all hoarders now," as a 2007 article in the magazine *Mother Jones* put it? There's no question the word *hoarding* has become ubiquitous in recent years, from psychology journals to popular magazines. Even *The Economist*'s 2017 review of a biography of Sir Hans Sloane called the great collector a "hoarder extraordinaire." But if Shanna is a hoarder and Sloane is a hoarder, who *isn't* a hoarder?[18]

Psychological studies of hoarding disorder have now been conducted in North America, Europe, East and South Asia, South America, the Middle East, and beyond. Psychologists have tried to devise globally valid tests to diagnose whether someone is a hoarder, regardless of cultural context. Is it possible, for example, to define a standard diagnostic test that would make it possible to look at a photograph of someone's room—whether that room is in Shanghai or Istanbul, Rio de Janeiro or Rome—and diagnose its occupant as someone suffering from hoarding disorder?

Some think it is. Perhaps as a result, hoarding disorder now seems more and more like a global phenomenon, one whose universality we previously failed to grasp, leading some to want to explain its apparent intensification. Yet the phenomenon also appears different in different contexts. In Spanish, hoarders are *acaparadores*; in Italian, *accapparatori*. It's not just a question of language. A British reality TV show called *The Hoarder Next Door*

(2012–14) was rather less tragic than its American counterpart, treating its stars as lovable eccentrics instead of deranged loners on the verge of self-destruction. They're British, after all, not American.

Pursuing a different path to standardized diagnostics, one 2015 study used an American clinical questionnaire to attempt to diagnose hoarding disorder in people in China but found in the process that the very notion of hoarding possesses distinctive and positive connotations in China. In a society where Confucianism has long instilled values of restraint and where memories linger of mass starvation under Mao during the Great Leap Forward, clinging to things that look old or useless but that may prove useful someday, the authors of this study realized, is associated with the virtue of thrift and contrasted with the vice of wastefulness.

In Japan, what we now call hoarding has similarly been seen as a positive response to specific historical problems and conditioned by distinctive cultural traditions. After the bursting of the asset price bubble in 1989–91 ended a period of spectacular postwar economic growth, Japanese traditions of minimalism enjoyed a conspicuous revival. Some Japanese discussions of hoarding are moralistic. They focus on the figure of the *woman who cannot tidy up* and blame her for a lack of virtue. But Japanese attitudes to hoarding can also be forgiving. Japanese law allows hoarders to avoid eviction from their "rubbish houses," as they call them, if they take the initiative to seek help.

Minimalism has its roots in ancient Buddhist traditions, but more recent economic downturns have spawned revivals spreading the gospel of de-cluttering across the globe. In his 2015 manifesto *Goodbye, Things*, for example, the Tokyo minimalist Fumio Sasaki recounts how getting rid of the vast majority of his possessions not only de-cluttered his apartment but also led him to lose weight. Accumulation is hard not just on one's pocketbook, his story implies, but also on one's waist. Sasaki put as much of his life as possible on his phone—music, books, and so on—though he doesn't discuss whether spending much more time on his phone is healthy or not. Nor does he discuss the problem of digital clutter and storing so much virtually that we forget where we put it or that we even have it.

The world's most famous professional de-clutterer of recent years, Marie Kondo, claimed she was inspired by ancient Japanese Shinto tradition. Her bestselling Netflix-backed *KonMari* method prescribed such ingenious techniques as folding trousers vertically rather than horizontally to save as much space as possible. Kondo urged her followers to retain only those possessions that truly "spark joy." But what if *everything* one owns "sparks joy"? Kondo appears not to have read up on Andy Warhol's philosophy that almost every kind of object imaginable possesses its own special beauty. Most recently, however, she has changed her tune. Having three children has led her to embrace a little more clutter.

Not everyone agrees with the minimalists, of course, that when you get rid of your things, you find your true self. Some remain utterly convinced of the opposite: the more you have, the more you *are*—even when those things are plastic saltshakers or discarded cigarette butts. This is what the protagonist of Orhan Pamuk's 2008 novel *The Museum of Innocence* believes. He feels sure that the more he collects or hoards—he isn't sure which—the closer he will come to his true self. In his view, the humbler the objects, the better. He dreams of curating them in a museum to heal the pain of his tortured existence. But will they?

The Museum of Innocence is the most recent great portrait of a deranged collector in fiction. In it, Pamuk tells the story of Kemal Bey, a middle-class man in 1970s Istanbul, due to marry his bride-to-be Sibel. Instead, however, Kemal falls in love with Füsun, a shop girl who dreams of being a movie star. The affair between Kemal and Füsun is passionate and lasts many years but is also clandestine and ultimately doomed. The two are separated by social class and eventually death, when Füsun is killed in a car accident.

Even before Füsun's death, the relationship is strained because of Kemal's struggles to free himself from the expectations of his middle-class world that he marry the more respectable Sibel. In this sense, Kemal and Füsun often feel on the verge of losing each other well before her death. This is why Kemal starts collecting objects associated with her to assuage his yearnings for her when they are apart. To Kemal, these objects are more than souvenirs of trysts, they're like pieces of Füsun herself, which he cherishes with deep melancholy hunger.

The objects are common enough: plastic saltshakers, lighters, and the butts of the many cigarettes Füsun smoked. Like Walter Benjamin, Kemal is looking for personal meaning in a world of mass-produced commodities; echoing Sperelli in D'Annunzio's *Pleasure*, he finds an erotic charge in anything physically associated with his lover. Kemal fondles his keepsakes, presses them to his skin, and even inserts them in his mouth. He is a man possessed who marvels at the "astonishing powers of consolation that objects held." At one point, he quips, he isn't sure whether the Freudian subconscious or the jinn—the old Arab spirits from the days of the *Arabian Nights*—makes the better explanation of his strange obsession.[19]

Kemal's quip is doubly meaningful because he finds himself caught between East and West. He lives in the era of Atatürk's secular Turkish republic, before the advent of Recep Tayyip Erdoğan's nationalist regime in 2014, which has sought to remake Turkey in the image of the Islamic Ottoman Empire. Living in the era before Erdoğan, Pamuk's characters see the Westernization of Turkish society as a foregone conclusion, albeit one that threatens to undermine the essence of Turkish identity. Kemal loves to drink rakı, for example, but wants Turkish women to adopt liberal Western attitudes to sex. He subjects himself to psychoanalysis but doesn't really believe in it.

After Füsun is gone and only her objects remain, Kemal's new obsession becomes the creation of a museum to honor his lost love. And it's at this point that Pamuk, through Kemal, confronts the question of what it means to collect and create a personal museum specifically in a country such as Turkey, poised between East and West.

Kemal asks himself why only Westerners appear to have the confidence to create personal collections and museums that reveal their true selves. It is a confidence that he, as an Istanbulite, feels he sorely lacks. But why shouldn't he create a museum to Füsun? He travels the world and visits countless museums in search of inspiration, from the Camondo house in Paris to Freud's abandoned Vienna home to the Museum of Jurassic Technology. In the process, he becomes convinced that he must not create a Western-style museum, objectively scientific and coldly impersonal, but fashion one that exposes his deepest flaws as an individual. If the people of Istanbul are to realize their cultural destiny, they need museums that "show us our own lives," rather than aping Western institutions or producing official temples of national glory on the order of Istanbul's illustrious Topkapı Palace.[20]

Is Kemal a lowly hoarder of junk or a true collector? Or are all collectors really just glorified hoarders, he wonders? If there *is* something fatally wrong with Kemal's obsessive, romantic and doomed collection, his answer is to put it all on public display just the same, so the world can at least judge him as he is, and so he can be true to himself. Once again, we return to the dream of the Romantic collecting self revealing the essence of the individual—of collecting as the dream of the "self loving the self," as the Ming scholar Yuan Hongdao put it. Maybe what Kemal does is just hoarding, compulsive and even pathological, but it's authentic. For Kemal, the true collector is not the expert connoisseur or the skilled naturalist but rather the abject hoarder of what others consider trash. Can't we just admit, once and for all, that the truest collector of all *is* a garbologist?

Here *The Museum of Innocence* ends, but not the story of Kemal's collection. While Erdoğan was mayor of Istanbul during the 1990s and, ironically, establishing his political profile by streamlining the city's rubbish collection, Pamuk began collecting objects from around the city for a *real* museum based on his novel. Years later, the museum opened in 2012 in Istanbul's

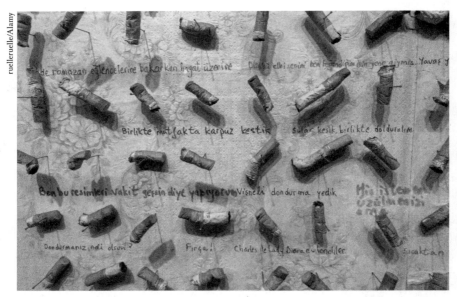

Füsun's cigarettes in Orhan Pamuk's Istanbul Museum (2012): This remarkable wall of used cigarettes can be found in the real museum Orhan Pamuk (1952–) created to memorialize the fictional love story he tells in The Museum of Innocence *(2008), illustrating his argument that even the basest objects can become treasured keepsakes for the obsessive collector.*

Çukurcuma neighborhood. To this day, visitors can gain admission for free if they bring a copy of *The Museum of Innocence* with them, which has a ticket printed inside. Pride of place in the museum goes to Füsun's cigarette butts, fixed in a vast grid anatomizing the depth of Kemal's tortured devotion, a wailing wall of adoration.

In a strange twist of fate, however, Pamuk went on to become a real-life Utz. As Turkey began its slide into authoritarianism under a regime that is hostile to artists and journalists, Pamuk had to employ bodyguards to guarantee his safety. Where Czechoslovakia moved toward freedom at the end of the 1980s, the liberties enjoyed by Kemal, Pamuk, and ordinary Turks became an increasingly distant memory. The story of the collector under totalitarianism, in other words, is far from over.

In other ways, however, Pamuk's *Museum of Innocence* suggests that we may have reached the end of the history of collecting as we have known it, or at least a dramatic watershed in that story. Has the age-old idea that there is something wrong with people who collect things now finally run its course?

THE GREAT COLLECTORS

*"Don't buy what you love, buy what makes you
slightly uncomfortable."*

—EVAN BEARD AT THE GREAT COLLECTORS SYMPOSIUM (2018)

Some years ago, I received the distinct honor of an invitation to a symposium organized by the Preservation Society of Newport County, Rhode Island. The symposium was called *The Great Collectors*. The spring weather was brilliant, the assembled company sparkling, the atmosphere positively Gatsbyish. Our venue was the Jane Pickens Theater, which originated as a church in the 1830s, though we were also regaled by tours of historic houses like The Breakers, built by Cornelius Vanderbilt II in the 1890s using his steamboat and railroad fortune. Rather more than an academic affair in both style and substance, the symposium featured not merely scholars but also curators, art advisers, bankers, philanthropists, collectors—and no doubt more than a few squillionaires, as Mary Berenson baptized the denizens of Newport a century ago.

There were a number of noteworthy presentations, but three stood out for the way they embodied the shifting cultural identity of the collector—past, present, and future. The first was a lecture by Inge Reist, art historian and founding director of the Frick Collection's Center for the History of Collecting. Brilliantly knowledgeable and incomparably elegant, Reist treated her audience to a tour de force. Her lecture was a whistlestop not of collectors but of tastemakers in modern art: the brokers and dealers who have an eye for the beautiful and know what collectors want before collectors themselves do, bending their ears and prying open their pocketbooks to realize their patrons' dreams of connoisseurial immortality.

As befit the magnificence of our surroundings, Reist's cast of characters was nothing if not illustrious. The Earl of Arundel and Charles I; Bernard Berenson and Isabella Stewart Gardner; Mary Cassatt; Louisine Havemeyer; Ileana Sonnabend and Leo Castelli; and many besides. It was a glittering history of a long Gilded Age—a very long Gilded Age—but not the Gilded Age as Henry James saw it. Reist rather differed from the Master in that there were no mechanical Adam Ververs in her portrait gallery, nor soulless J. P. Morgans hoovering up the world's treasures like unthinking magnetic machines. Great collections, Reist allowed, *are* built on great wealth, but a truly great collection only comes together when money is spent with love. Money doesn't prove the absence of a collector's passion; it is, rather, the precondition for the expression of a personal vision.

The second memorable presentation was delivered by the suavely understated Amin Jaffer. Jaffer worked at the Victoria and Albert Museum and at Christie's in London before becoming senior curator to the Al Thani Collection, which belongs to Sheikh Tamim bin Hamad Al Thani, the emir of Qatar. Jaffer described for his listeners how the sheikh has gone about emulating the Mughal emperors by amassing a truly extraordinary collection of gemstones. Showing pictures of Shah Jahan, Jaffer explained that in the Mughal era, gems such as spinels were thought to possess magical properties, as well as symbolizing both kinship and divinity. Like his predecessors, Jaffer observed, the sheikh "has a great appetite and love for stones" and collects "almost with a sense of destiny." But when the audience asked what drove the sheikh at a personal level to collect, Jaffer was the soul of discretion. What was the sheikh actually like? "Very bashful," was all Jaffer would say.[1]

The sheikh's gems were the real star of the show, however, not the sheikh, and Jaffer's slides left his audience quite breathless. Diamonds, emeralds, sapphires, rubies, spinels, and a shockingly stunning feast of other gems made them gasp at the splendor of the sheikh's tastes, if not the glory of his very soul. It were as though the finery of Newport with its Breakers and industrial fortunes were mere gewgaws that paled by comparison, and one were witnessing some ineluctable changing of the civilizational guard, with the old new money of Newport paying an indubitably cowed homage to the new old money of Doha.

But the last gasp of the day belonged to Evan Beard. Beard was a different kind of speaker from a different kind of world: that of art finance, Beard being a national art services executive at U.S. Trust, part of Bank of America's private wealth management operation. Bracing and brusque with more than a hint of Patrick Bateman—he was a U.S. naval officer in a former life—Beard bounded onto the stage like a man possessed and immediately rattled off the economically titillating tale of *Salvator Mundi*, the long-lost da Vinci that had recently been discovered and acquired for a cool $450 million by an anonymous Middle Eastern buyer. Explaining that investment opportunities now permeate art collecting at virtually every level, Beard recounted how short-selling bets were placed by third parties on the outcome even of the original auction-house sale.

Beard's objective was to school a genteel audience in the ways of today's market whether they liked it or not. He explained that there were a range of social issues that might make some of us uncomfortable these days—the question of gender, for example—but they also presented significant investment opportunities in today's art market ignored at one's financial peril. An essential part of his work, he went on, lay in assisting those with especially high-value collections get the very most out of them as assets, for example by deploying them as collateral in order to secure loans for additional investments or even leveraging their financial value to support the making of political campaign contributions. There was nothing new about manipulating the value of art in such ways, Beard observed. Perhaps some in the audience had heard tell of the buying and selling of shares in individual works of art as a dastardly innovation of the so-called neoliberal art market. But, like Reist, he pointed out that art and money have always gone together since at least the time of the Medici. Really, there was nothing new under the sun.

Unlike Reist, however, Beard explained that today's collectors are far less apt to get hung up on the art they hang up, unlike the great collectors of yesteryear. Collecting today is *so* not a passion thing. No, today's contemporary art collectors don't cry, they click. They're not latter-day Walter Benjamins seeking some kind of mad ecstasy and not the kind of passionate obsessive we carry around in our minds as our Romanticized ideal type of the *true* collector. The Romantic collecting self? A wonderful notion, but really . . . Instead, we had to understand that the new generation of contemporary collectors grew up on banking, trading and e-commerce, so that "flipping" art—buying to make a tidy profit—is second nature to them. It's just the way we collect now. If you want to become a collector, "don't buy what you love," Beard advised us, be smart, not passionate: "buy what makes you slightly uncomfortable." Think hot-button issues. What's going to get under people's skin in the coming years?

The audience in the Jane Pickens Theater gasped for the second time that day, but not the way they gasped at the sheikh's spinels. Beard's barbs rankled them. His message was rather too Wall Street for the Newporters who, after all, had just been so sweetly wooed by tales of the sheikh, not to mention Reist's impeccably genial tastemakers. Beard's Gen Z touchscreen flipper was not the Newporters' idea of a "Great Collector." They had no problem with money, but they evidently wanted and needed something more: Reist's passion and Jaffer's mystique. They didn't want collecting unmasked and reduced to mere numbers, they wanted beauty and love, mystery and romance. They wanted above all to be reassured that collecting represents not merely the pursuit of profit but also the expression of a personal vision. They wanted to hear something that Beard set out to deny, as if he were a Reformation iconoclast gleefully smashing a false idol in the name of an absolute materialistic truth. They wanted to hear that even the wealthiest and most powerful collector has a *soul*.

A Noble Madness has told the story of the idea that there's something questionable and possibly even dangerous about those who seem to prefer the company of things to that of people. The notion of an obsessive collecting self emerged first in premodern Asia and blossomed again in nineteenth-century Europe, when the Romantic idea that a collection was like a fingerprint, the unique expression of a complex individual, developed with unprecedented force as a counterpoise to the impersonality of modern industrial mass society. The idea that you could look at someone's collection, see their true self, and diagnose their personality—no matter how warped—then achieved a full-blown apotheosis through Freudian psychoanalysis and its many expressions in Western popular culture.

But the dark obsessive side of collecting has often been thought to possess an ironic silver lining. From Ming China to the modern West and beyond, obsessive collectors have been viewed as charismatic and authentic because, whether their actions are good or evil, they are *true* collectors who are true to themselves, doing what they do out of passion, not calculation. Norman Bates may be a murderer and a schizophrenic, but we can empathize with him. We may recoil at his collection of stuffed birds, but his madness proves his authenticity. As the psychoanalyst comments at the end of Hitchcock's movie, Bates's are "crimes of passion, not profit." That is the enduring appeal of the character and the idea of the mad collector more generally. Even though such collectors are mad—no, *because* they are mad—they are themselves.[2]

The 2020s are a peculiar moment from which to assess the sequel of this history, however. This is because the idea that there is something wrong with collectors seems to be vanishing in some quarters, while in others it has never been stronger.

If one listens to Evan Beard, collecting has nothing to do with selfhood or the soul anymore. It's not a matter of virtue or vice, philanthropy or villainy, obsession or mania. Like so many other areas of life, collecting is now purely a question of economics. Beard's recent project, Masterworks, has used data-driven approaches to selling fractional shares in single works of art. Now, in 2024, investors are beginning to bid on works of art generated by artificial intelligence, with an image of pioneer computer scientist Alan Turing by AI robot Ai-Da selling for more than $1 million. The Warholization of the world, where virtually any cultural object can now possess commodity value, means everything has its price and the collector is increasingly a calculator. Up until roughly the 1970s, if you collected ceramic hedgehogs or stuffed birds or Liberace dolls, let's say—and why not?—the first question you would have been asked is "Why?" It's Freud's question: What does a collection mean? What does it say about the kind of person you are? Assuming you weren't a kid, you'd have likely been considered eccentric or weird or, yes, maybe even creepy.

Today, you may well get the question "Why?" but, likely as not, you'll also be asked "How much is that worth?" If you look up your Ty Beanie Baby in the Beanie Baby Database, you might find out that your 1996 Peace

Bear is in fact now worth several thousand dollars. Not bad at all as a return on your investment. For better or worse, eccentric passions align more and more with economic motivations and canny monetizations. Nicole Angemi, the New Jersey corpse and placenta collector, has a new website to display her phantasmagorical wares called The Gross Room. It's pay-walled. Dark collectors of Nazi memorabilia and true-crime relics have their own flourishing markets where fascist keepsakes and murderous mementos fetch a pretty penny. Such collecting may strike many as morally questionable, but it's certainly financially rational. From Ming China to Walter Benjamin, the true collector was a cultural hero in no small part because he collected against his financial self-interest. From Lady Sloane to André Breton's wife, Jacqueline Lamba, the proverbial collector's spouse has always been appalled at their partner's moreish profligacy. But financial self-interest now seems to attach to virtually every kind of collectible object in the world. Today's collectors aren't crazy, they're savvy.

In some ways, we live at a time when the figure of the mad collector is disappearing altogether. We might explain this vanishing act through that somewhat nebulous and overused phrase *neoliberal economics*, therefore, but the symptoms of this disappearance are easier to discern than its causes. The emphasis on using brain scans to reduce the collecting urge to neurological impulses is telling. Freudian talking cures and analyses of complex individual selfhood have given way to encephalograms believed by some at least to reveal that the impulse to collect is no individual idiosyncratic foible, after all, but biologically innate.

Instead of telling stories, we're now taking photographs. Collectors aren't greedy or mad or malevolent, they're just doing what their brains are telling them to do. Recent scholarship argues that collectors aren't reclusive, either, but just the opposite: most are sociable and outgoing. There's no dark story about the self to tell and it's no big deal. If we listen to Evan Beard and Shirley Mueller, it's normal and natural, biologically as well as technologically, for people to collect for profit. There's nothing especially personal about it and certainly nothing to be done about it. If we're all hoarders now, and all have hoarding disorder to some degree, then is it really a disorder at all? Isn't that what science and medicine are now telling us—that no collector is *mad*? Perish the thought in all its Gothic self-indulgence.

Consider the example of another recent novel about a collector and a highly curious one at that. In Finnish writer Arto Paasilinna's comic masterpiece *Volomari Volotinen's First Wife and Assorted Old Things* (1994), Paasilinna's protagonist Volomari is an insurance man and compulsive collector who has a taste for decidedly dubious treasures. He comes to own (and wear) the dentures of nuns; a working guillotine; the world's oldest pubic hair; mortars and weapons left in the Finnish countryside during the war; skeletons of dead soldiers; and a relic (false, he is convinced) of Christ's clavicle, which he stole. Volomari's beloved wife, Laura, can never quite bring herself to think ill of her husband for any of this—in fact, she assists him in his collecting—and nor, seemingly, does Paasilinna. The implication seems to be—not unlike the way Orhan Pamuk presents Kemal Bey in *The Museum of Innocence*—that much collecting may be dubious and many collectors questionable in their motivations, passions, and methods. But who are we to judge?

Not everyone adopts this stance in every instance, of course. If it is true that we no longer see collectors as mad—or openly say they are—that does not mean we have lost the ability to say they are bad, and there are many zealous current attempts to eliminate the figure of the bad collector from historical and cultural discussion. The idea that scientific, anthropological, and archaeological collectors embody some form of political and/or moral evil has revived with notable intensity in recent years in a renewed wave of iconoclasm that has toppled many figures, both literally and figuratively, from public pedestals and public favor. The ghost of Verres has returned in a very specific form through the insistence that colonial and imperial collectors have in effect often stolen the very identities of subject peoples by seizing sacred objects, as Sicily's governor did to its subjects in the first century BCE.

The iconoclastic wave that struck in the early 2020s in the wake of the death of George Floyd in the United States, and framed by the Black Lives Matter movement, was not new but marked a return. As we have seen in this long and twisted history of collecting, the dream of getting rid of the collector as an evil decadent/bourgeois/imperial looter has assumed many different guises: targeting Jews in France during the Third Republic and in Nazi Germany; targeting commercial art collectors and anthropologists, the scourge of surrealist and postcolonial critics of empire; and targeting private collectors of all kinds under modern totalitarian regimes. These campaigns were by no means morally equivalent, of course, but they did assert a common claim: that some collectors at least should be suppressed if not eliminated for the good of society, in the name of progress and justice. In a context of recent campaigns to repatriate looted objects, monuments to collectors have, therefore, been rethought, where they have not been removed outright. The equestrian statue of Theodore Roosevelt leading an African and a Native American outside the American Museum of Natural History has been taken down, though visitors can still learn about TR's career inside. At the British Museum, a bust of Sir Hans Sloane was not removed (as some London newspapers erroneously reported) but made *more* visible in order to contextualize Sloane's collecting within the history of the Atlantic slave trade. At London's Wellcome Collection, meanwhile, all materials regarding its founder, the American pharmaceutical entrepreneur Sir Henry Wellcome, have for the time being been removed from the public galleries, affording visitors the bizarre experience of being able to learn nothing about him. This stance is myopic: the Wellcome's abdication of its duty to educate visitors about its origins denies the public the chance to make up its own mind about its past. For now, at least, however, the Wellcome has succeeded where many have failed: it has erased its founding collector.

The classic scientific hunting expedition is now a thing of the past. There have been calls for an end to killing animals as specimens and outrage at collectors like Chris Filardi, whose routine scientific work was denounced by a small but vocal minority as an evil and immoral act when he "murdered" a kingfisher. There *are* bioprospectors who have signed agreements to allow them to collect genetic information and enjoy unique rights to that information, as the American corporation Diversa did with the University of Hawai'i in 2002. In response, indigenous Hawai'ians have sought the passage of legislation to deny the abrogation of *their* rights to their own biodiverse genetic heritage.

Since 1990, NAGPRA has advanced the restitution of Amerindian artifacts and recently recommended the removal of sacred objects and, in the case of the American Museum of Natural History, resulted in the closure of entire galleries of indigenous displays judged unfit for purpose. Since 2021, an initiative known as Indigidata—the title of a conference organized by the Navajo genetics researcher Krystal Tsosie—has aimed to train Native Americans to collect and manage their own data in the future so that it cannot be used without consent by others. Such movements are a far cry from the world of Don Talayesva, when Native collectors sold information, artifacts, specimens, and even their dreams to Western collectors.

One might well assume that most "great collectors" of the past were white Western men. But this is why Pamuk's portrayal of Kemal Bey is so revealing. Kemal hopes that collectors in countries like Turkey, caught between the pull of local tradition and Western modernity, will create museums that "show us our own lives"—damaged, narcissistic, shameful, yet authentic lives. Don't copy Western museums' pretense of scientific neutrality, Kemal urges his fellow countrymen, but *do* emulate Westerners' confidence to collect with passion, even obsession, like the lowliest hoarder

Native BioData Consortium | Andrew Drexel (Nlaka'pamux Nation)

Indigidata (2021): Indigidata is a project launched by Vanderbilt University Navajo bio-geneticist Krystal Tsosie designed to indigenize the process of biological data collection and reverse centuries of data appropriation by Western scientific collectors.

and dare to put *that* kind of collection on display, even if it looks like a wall of common cigarette butts—even if it looks like rubbish. Kemal, of course, assumes collecting and displaying one's obsession is a Western tradition, but he's wrong about that. The question is not whether Kemal has the confidence to reveal his true self through his most intimate possessions like a Western-style obsessive, but whether, like his precursors in Ming China, he has the courage to display his *pi*?[3]

Kemal's quest to put his personal obsessions on display is especially hazardous in an era when authoritarian regimes (Erdoğan in Turkey, Putin in Russia, Xi in China) often speak of Western collectors as plunderers of patrimony in order to reinforce ideas of heroic national destiny and state authority. Is there any end to the usefulness of the evil decadent/bourgeois/ imperial Western looter as a foil for those looking to defend the honor of the homeland and the integrity of its culture against the barbarous cosmopolitanism that would break it apart by collecting it? Elgin's noseless ghost haunts us still. In China today, strict laws mandate the protection and return of antiquities, even while state museums remain silent on the more controversial periods of the nation's history. In a singular paradox, memorabilia from the Cultural Revolution, which sought to "smash the Four Olds," have become collector's items, not least the millions of badges produced that ordinary people wore to venerate Mao Zedong. Real estate magnate Fan Jianchuan has created a Cultural Revolution Museum near Chengdu, exhibiting many Mao badges as objects of historical curiosity. But the status of Fan's museum is decidedly ambiguous under a government that remains silent on the turbulent events of the 1960s that turned the lives of Nien Cheng, Ji Xianlin, and countless others upside down. Utz-like, Fan collects under a shadow but carries on.

"Don't buy what you love, buy what makes you slightly uncomfortable"— that was Evan Beard's message to his audience in Newport. Today's smart collector doesn't collect for himself but with an eye to the main chance. Collecting shouldn't be about what you love; in fact, it shouldn't be about *you* at all. Yet what the audience in Newport wanted was precisely to hear stories about collecting driven by love and passion, even obsession. They wanted to hear Inge Reist discuss the personal vision behind great art collections. And they wanted to ask Amin Jaffer what drove the emir of Qatar as a collector on an individual level. When they saw his gems, they thought they were seeing *him* and wanted to know what kind of person he really was.

What the audience wanted was Romantic, the stuff of myth and legend: the idea that behind every great collection there's a mysterious, complex, and charismatic collector—rather than a soulless automaton, a touch-screen flipper, a hollow imperialist, a brain scan or a medical diagnosis. They wanted, indeed needed, to see the person behind that collection and hear stories about their *pī*. For all its shortcomings, the Freudian impulse to understand *why* collectors collect remains uniquely powerful, because it tells stories about the pursuit of meaning by singular individuals. That storytelling impulse is humane—rather more humane than recent explanatory rivals like neuroscience—because it paints complex portraits of collectors, their lives and their behavior, rather than trying to explain them away.

This is why the figure of the mad collector has always served a vital cultural purpose. Myths and legends endure not because they are true, but because their power is real and abiding. Dark tales of the twisted exploits of mad collectors have always done two things: they've served as a warning about the personal and social perils of excessive passion; but they've also dramatized the cause of being oneself, as Huysmans put it, *against the grain*. The Romantic collecting self is not dead. Many have tried to kill it, but none have quite succeeded. Indeed, it may now be immortal. The figures described in this book embody this ideal. They are the great collectors of our cultural history. Their love of objects may be mad, bad, even dangerous. But we want to believe their love's a noble madness because by expressing that love, they are themselves.

ACKNOWLEDGMENTS

The idea for this book occurred to me while strolling one afternoon on Oranienstraße in Berlin during the autumn of 2013; it evolved in classrooms and museums, especially the galleries of the British Museum and the Metropolitan Museum of Art; and crystallized on various modes of transportation, above all the New York subway, in particular the B train to Brighton Beach.

For financial and logistical support, thanks go to the School of Arts and Sciences at Rutgers University and the staff of the Rutgers History Department; for bibliographical support, to the librarians of Rutgers's Alexander Library (Tom Glynn and Jim Niessen), the Harvard History of Science Department for access to Harvard's library resources, the British Library, the Warburg Institute Library at the University of London, the Bibliotheca Hertziana in Rome, Strand Books in New York, Nicole Ann Mira of The Last Bookstore in Los Angeles, and above all Carolyn Waters and her staff at the New York Society Library on the Upper East Side of Manhattan—one of the best libraries in the world and where much of the work was conceived.

For encouragement and discussion, I thank Ardeta Gjikola, Samaa Elimam, Justin Smith-Ruiu, Adina Ruiu, Cathy Gere, Hartwig Fischer, Léa Kuhn, Ulrike Keuper, Judith Zeitlin, Xiaohong Hou (my Mandarin teacher), Guangchen Chen, Ninon Vinsonneau, Jona Magidoff, Paul Sampson, Fortnum Hatchard, Alexander Petrusek (who performed several acts of translation), Javier González Cortés, Jackson Lears, Alastair Bellany, Seth Koven, Silverio Bellavista, Steven Shapin, Nancy Sladek, Spencer Weinreich, Melany Park, Stephane Van Damme, Simon Schaffer, Hongjia Pan, Silvia Chiaraviglio Sassoli, Richard Delbourgo, Elizabeth Fleure, and Laura Kopp.

My research assistant Laura Robbins, currently a PhD candidate in medieval art history at Rutgers, was a brilliant reader and conversationalist throughout, indefatigable in art research, fact-checking and permissions work—a true collaborator. Caspian Dennis of Abner Stein and Jon Riley of Quercus proved stalwart advocates and trusted confidantes in London. My editor, Amy Cherry, has my undying gratitude for her support and kindness, not to mention placing her faith in this book when many others did not; working with her and the Norton team, especially Wick Hallos and Huneeya Siddiqui, as well as Carolyn Levin and Christopher Curioli, has been a delight. My agent the formidable Jennifer Lyons has driven everything forward from the start with indomitable spirit, vigorous benevolence, and the deepest possible friendship.

Finishing this book coincided with the passing of a beloved generation in my family, who came of age during an era of great style and elegance, not to say historical transformation. My mother Rosella Maria Properzi Delbourgo of Ancona, Marche, Italy (1934–2024), and my "auntie" Annie Walker of Ossining, New York (1935–2024), died just before the book was completed. They were two beautiful women, full of life and now much missed. But I dedicate *A Noble Madness* to my father-in-law, the artist Dieter Kopp (1939–2022), a man who painted beauty and truth with a visionary eye, without bothering himself too much about collectors and their foibles. For more than a quarter of a century, Dieter welcomed me into his home in the heart of Rome, where we discussed countless subjects during countless hours with his daughter, my wife, Laura. When Dieter died, I was filled with regret, wishing I'd asked him to teach me about art. Later, I realized he had. *Grazie, tutti, ci vediamo.*

BIBLIOGRAPHICAL ESSAY: FURTHER READING

The literature on the history of collectors and collecting is vast, rich, and rewarding. As a work of synthesis and narrative history, this book relies on numerous specialist books and articles on many different times and places. I happily acknowledge the wealth of brilliant scholarship without which it would have been impossible to tell this story. All direct quotations in the text are attributed in the endnotes that follow this bibliographical essay below, but because this is a work intended for general readers, it seemed best to pick out the essential works on which I have relied chapter by chapter, both by way of acknowledgment and so readers may explore the world of collectors and collecting for themselves.

Readers interested in previous general treatments of collectors may wish to consult Susan Pearce, *On Collecting: An Investigation into Collecting in the European Tradition* (New York: Routledge, 1995), and her coedited rich anthology of primary sources, *The Collector's Voice: Critical Readings in the Practice of Collecting*, 4 vols. (Burlington, VT: Ashgate, 2000–2002). For older, stylish interpretations, Maurice Rheims, *The Strange Life of Objects: 35 Centuries of Art Collecting and Collectors*, trans. David Pryce-Jones (1959; New York: Atheneum, 1961), and Philippe Jullian, *Les Collectionneurs* (Paris: Flammarion, 1966); Douglas and Elizabeth Rigby, *Lock, Stock and Barrel: The Story of Collecting* (Philadelphia: Lippincott, 1944). For a range of different scholarly approaches to collecting, John Elsner and Roger Cardinal, eds., *The Cultures of Collecting* (Cambridge, MA: Harvard University Press, 1994), and Michael Camille and Adrian Rifkin, eds., *Other Objects of Desire: Collectors and Collecting Queerly* (Oxford: Wiley-Blackwell, 2002). On the evolution of concepts of madness across the centuries, Andrew Scull, *Madness in Civilization: A Cultural History of Insanity from the Bible to Freud, from the Madhouse to Modern Medicine* (Princeton, NJ: Princeton University Press, 2015). On consumer culture in the modern world, Frank Trentmann, *Empire of Things: How We Became a World of Consumers, from the Fifteenth Century to the Twenty-First* (London: Allen Lane, 2016). For a general history of empire and trade oriented to the East rather than the West, Peter Frankopan, *The Silk Roads: A New History of the World* (New York: Bloomsbury, 2015).

CHAPTER ONE: STATUE LOVE

On Verres and Cicero, Margaret Miles, *Art as Plunder: The Ancient Origins of Debate About Cultural Property* (Cambridge: Cambridge University Press, 2008), and Ann Vasaly, *Representations: Images of the World in Ciceronian Oratory* (Berkeley: University of California Press, 1993). On the culture of collecting in ancient Rome, Alexandra Bounia, *The Nature of Classical Collecting: Collectors and Collections, 100 BCE–100 CE* (Burlington, VT: Ashgate, 2004); Steven Rutledge, *Ancient Rome as a Museum: Power, Identity, and the Culture of Collecting* (Oxford: Oxford University Press, 2012); and Mary Beard, *The Roman Triumph* (Cambridge, MA: Belknap Press, 2007). On Rome and its wider context, Mary Beard, *SPQR: A History of Ancient Rome* (New York: Liveright, 2015); and Jerry Toner, "Decadence in Ancient Rome," in *Decadence and Literature*, ed. Jane Desmarais and David Weir (Cambridge: Cambridge University Press, 2019), 15–29.

On Mesopotamian antiquities, Zainab Bahrani, "The Biopolitics of Collecting: Empires of Mesopotamia," in *Collecting and Empires: An Historical and Global Perspective*, ed. Maia Gahtan and Eva-Maria Troelenberg (London: Harvey Miller, 2019), 38–49; on ancient Jewish object legends, Jason von Ehrenkrook, "Image and Desire in the *Wisdom of Solomon*," *Zutot* 7 (2010): 41–50. For the Caligula debate, D. Thomas Benediktson, "Caligula's Madness: Madness or Interictal Temporal Lobe Epilepsy?," *Classical World* 82 (1989): 370–75; David Woods, "Caligula's Seashells," *Greece & Rome* 47 (2000): 80–87; and Aloys Winterling, "Imperial Madness in Ancient Rome," in *Evil Lords: Theories and Representations of Tyranny from Antiquity to the Renaissance*, ed. Nikos Panou and Hester Schadee (Oxford: Oxford University Press, 2018), 61–80. On collecting ancient sculpture across the centuries, Erin Thompson, *Possession: The Curious History of Private Collectors from Antiquity to the Present* (New Haven, CT: Yale University Press, 2016); on animate statues, Kenneth Gross, *The Dream of the Moving Statue* (Ithaca, NY: Cornell University Press, 1992), and Jana Funke, ed., *Sculpture, Sexuality and History: Encounters in Literature, Culture and the Arts from the Eighteenth Century to Today* (Houndmills, UK: Palgrave MacMillan, 2019); for Antinoüs and his cheek, Caroline Vout, "Antinous" (video, 2020), Faculty of Classics, Museum of Classical Archaeology, University of Cambridge, https://www.youtube.com/watch?v=APMoQU7U9qU (accessed November 30, 2024).

CHAPTER TWO: THE IDOLATER'S FOLLY

On iconoclasm in general, Bruno Latour's essay "Iconoclash: Or Is There a World Beyond the Image Wars?," in *Iconoclash: Beyond the Image Wars in Science, Religion and Art*, ed. Bruno Latour and Peter Weibel (Cambridge, MA: MIT Press, 2002), 14–38; on Albrecht and the Halle Reliquary, Dagmar Eichberger, "A Renaissance Reliquary Collection in Halle, and Its Illustrated Inventories," *Art Bulletin of Victoria* 37 (2014); on Jewish aniconism, Jason von Ehrenkrook, "Image and Desire in the *Wisdom of Solomon*," *Zutot* 7 (2010): 41–50; on Confucian thought, Roel Sterckx, *Chinese Thought from Confucius to*

Cook Ding (London: Penguin, 2019); on Buddhism in China, John Kieschnick, *The Impact of Buddhism on Chinese Material Culture* (Princeton, NJ: Princeton University Press, 2003), Pema Konchok, "Buddhism as a Focus of Iconoclash in Asia," and Heather Stoddard, "The Religion of Golden Idols," in Latour and Weibel, *Iconoclash*, 40–59 and 436–55.

On Byzantium, Leslie Brubaker, *Inventing Byzantine Iconoclasm* (Bristol, UK: Bristol Classical Press, 2012); on Islam, Finbarr Barry Flood, *Objects of Translation: Material Culture and Medieval "Hindu-Muslim" Encounter* (Princeton, NJ: Princeton University Press, 2009); on the Mughals, Ebba Koch, "Jahangir's Hazelnut and Shah Jahan's Chini Khana: The Collections of the Mughal Emperors," in Gahtan and Troelenberg, eds., *Collecting and Empires*, 134–61, and Jack Weatherford, *Genghis Khan and the Making of the Modern World* (New York: Broadway, 2004); on relics in medieval Europe, Patrick Geary, *Furta Sacra: Thefts of Relics in the Central Middle Ages* (Princeton, NJ: Princeton University Press, 1978), Jay Rubenstein, *Guibert of Nogent: Portrait of a Medieval Mind* (New York: Routledge, 2002), and Carol Bynum, *Christian Materiality: An Essay on Religion in Medieval Europe* (New York: Zone, 1998); on the Protestant Reformation, Carlos Eire, *War Against the Idols: The Reformation of Worship from Erasmus to Calvin* (Cambridge: Cambridge University Press, 1986), Eamon Duffy, *The Stripping of the Altars: Traditional Religion in England, c. 1400–c. 1580* (New Haven, CT: Yale University Press, 1992), and Joseph Koerner, *The Reformation of the Image* (Chicago: University of Chicago Press, 2004).

CHAPTER THREE: BEWARE THE UNOBSESSED

Fundamental to this chapter and its discussion of obsessive collecting in Ming China is Judith Zeitlin, "The Petrified Heart: Obsession in Chinese Literature, Art and Medicine," *Late Imperial China* 12 (1991): 1–26; Wai-Yee Lee, "The Collector, The Connoisseur and Late-Ming Sensibility," *T'oung Pao* 81 (1995): 269–302; on obsession in the modern West, Lennard Davis, *Obsession: A History* (Chicago: University of Chicago Press, 2008). Contemporary definitions of 癖 (*pǐ*) may be found in the Pleco Software Chinese Dictionary app. On early dynastic Chinese collecting, Jeannette Shambaugh Elliott and David Shambaugh, *The Odyssey of China's Imperial Art Treasures* (Seattle: University of Washington Press, 2005); on Ming material culture, Craig Clunas, *Superfluous Things: Material Culture and Social Status in Early Modern China* (Urbana: University of Illinois Press, 1991); Timothy Brook, *The Confusions of Pleasure: Commerce and Culture in Ming China* (Berkeley: University of California Press, 1998); and *The Elegant Life of the Chinese Literati: From the Chinese Classic, Treatise on Superfluous Things—Finding Harmony and Joy in Everyday Objects*, trans. Tony Blishen (Shanghai: Shanghai Press, 2019). For the debate on Ming decadence, the essays in Katharine Burnett, ed., "Decadence (or not) in the Ming Dynasty," *Ming Studies* 71 (2015): 3–57; on Li Shizhen, Carla Nappi, *The Monkey and the Inkpot: Natural History and Its Transformations in Early Modern China* (Cambridge, MA: Harvard University Press, 2009). On Korean collecting culture, Confucianism, *pyŏk*, and *ch'aekkŏri* paintings, Sunglim Kim, *Flowering Plums and Curio Cabinets: The Culture of Objects in Late Chosŏn Korean Art* (Seattle: University of Washington Press, 2018).

CHAPTER FOUR: THE MAGUS AND THE MERCHANT

On the Museum of Jurassic Technology, Lawrence Weschler, *Mr. Wilson's Cabinet of Wonder: Pronged Ants, Horned Humans, Mice on Toast and Other Marvels of Jurassic Technology* (New York: Pantheon, 1995). On Rudolf II, Robert Evans, *Rudolf II and His World: A Study in Intellectual History, 1576–1612* (Oxford: Oxford University Press, 1973); Peter Marshall, *The Magic Circle of Rudolf II: Alchemy and Astrology in Renaissance Prague* (New York: Walker, 2006); and Eliska Fucíková et al., eds., *Rudolf II and Prague: The Court and the City* (London: Thames & Hudson, 1997), esp. the essay by Paula Findlen, "Cabinets, Collecting and Natural Philosophy," 209–19. On melancholia, Laurinda Dixon, *The Dark Side of Genius: The Melancholic Persona in Art, Ca. 1500–1700* (University Park: Pennsylvania State University Press, 2013); on collecting as cure, Francis Gage, "Exercise for Mind and Body: Giulio Mancini, Collecting, and the Beholding of Landscape Painting in the Seventeenth Century," *Renaissance Quarterly* 61 (2008): 1167–1207; on Kircher and natural history collectors, Paula Findlen, *Possessing Nature: Museums, Collecting, and Scientific Culture in Early Modern Italy* (Berkeley: University of California Press, 1994). On the Medici, Christopher Hibbert, *The House of Medici: Its Rise and Fall* (New York: Harper, 1974); on Savonarola, Lauro Martines, *Fire in the City: Savonarola and the Struggle for the Soul of Renaissance Florence* (Oxford: Oxford University Press, 2006).

On art, science, and the virtuoso in England, Craig Hanson, *The English Virtuoso: Art, Medicine and Antiquarianism in the Age of Empiricism* (Chicago: University of Chicago Press, 2009), Linda Peck, *Consuming Splendor: Society and Culture in Seventeenth-Century England* (Cambridge: Cambridge University Press, 2005), and Jerry Brotton, *The Sale of the Late King's Goods: Charles I and His Art Collection* (London: MacMillan, 2006); on Linnaeus and religion, Lisbet Koerner, *Linnaeus: Nature and Nation* (Cambridge, MA: Harvard University Press, 1999); on the Tulipmania, Anne Goldgar, *Tulipmania: Money, Honor, and Knowledge in the Dutch Golden Age* (Chicago: University of Chicago Press, 2007); on female curiosity, Line Cottegnies et al., eds., *Women and Curiosity in Early Modern England and France* (Leiden: Brill, 2016); on Sloane, James Delbourgo, *Collecting the World: Hans Sloane and the Origins of the British Museum* (Cambridge, MA: Belknap Press, 2017), and Michael Hunter, ed., *Magic and Mental Disorder: Sir Hans Sloane's Memoir of John Beaumont* (London: Robert Boyle Project, 2011).

CHAPTER FIVE: LIBERTINES AND TRINKET QUEENS

On Beckford in Paris, Anne Eschapasse, "William Beckford in Paris, 1788–1814: 'Le Faste Solitaire,'" in *William Beckford, 1760–1844: An Eye for the Magnificent*, ed. Derek Ostergard (New Haven, CT: Yale University Press, 2001), 99–116; on libertine philosophy and literature, Michel Feher, ed., *The Libertine Reader: Eroticism and Enlightenment in Eighteenth-Century France* (New York: Zone, 1998), and Lynn Hunt, *The Invention of Pornography: Obscenity and the Origins of Modernity, 1500–1800* (New York: Zone, 1996); on Christina, Susanna Åkerman, *Queen Christina of Sweden and Her Circle: The Transformation of a Seventeenth-Century Philosophical Libertine* (Leiden: Brill, 1991), Veronica Buckley, *Christina, Queen of Sweden: The Restless Life of a European Eccentric* (New York:

Harper, 2004), Veronica Biermann, "The Virtue of a King and the Desire of a Woman?: Mythological Representations in the Collection of Queen Christina," *Art History* 24 (2001): 213–30, and Erin Thompson, *Possession: The Curious History of Private Collectors from Antiquity to the Present* (New Haven, CT: Yale University Press, 2016); on Casanova, Lydia Flem, *Casanova: The Man Who Really Loved Women*, trans. Catherine Temerson (1995; New York: Farrar, Straus, and Giroux, 1997).

On Marie Antoinette and her world, Chantal Thomas, *The Wicked Queen: The Origins of the Myth of Marie-Antoinette*, trans. Julie Rose (1989; New York: Zone, 1999), Antonia Fraser, *Marie Antoinette: The Journey* (London: Weidenfeld and Nicolson, 2001), and Jennifer Jones, *Sexing la Mode: Gender, Fashion and Commercial Culture in Old Regime France* (Oxford: Berg, 2004); on Imelda Marcos, Gwenola Ricordeau, "Marie-Antoinette sous les tropiques: Imelda Marcos, sa collection de chaussures et la mémoire de la loi martiale," *Moussons: Recherche en sciences humaines sur l'Asie du Sud-Est* 25 (2015): 167–80; on Madame de Pompadour, Madame du Barry, Catherine the Great, and other female collectors since the eighteenth century, Charlotte Gere and Marina Vaizey, *Great Women Collectors* (London: Philip Wilson, 1999); on Catherine specifically, Ruth Dawson, *Catherine the Great and the Culture of Celebrity in the Eighteenth Century* (New York: Bloomsbury, 2022), and Vincent Carretta, "'Petticoats in Power': Catherine the Great in British Political Cartoons," *1650–1850: Aesthetics, Ideas, and Inquiries in Early Modern Era* 1 (1994): 23–81; on Hadice the Younger, Tülay Artan, "Eighteenth-Century Ottoman Princesses as Collectors: Chinese and European Porcelains in the Topkapı Palace Museum," *Ars Orientalis* 39 (2010): 113–47.

Thomas Keymer's edition of *Vathek* (Oxford: Oxford University Press, 2013) is based on the 1816 edition and has an excellent introduction and notes; Marina Warner, *Stranger Magic: Charmed States and the Arabian Nights* (Cambridge, MA: Belknap Press, 2012), esp. chap. 14. On Beckford's life, the essays in Ostergard, *William Beckford, 1760–1844*, esp. David Watkin, "Beckford, Soane and Hope: The Psychology of the Collector," 33–50, and Bet McLeod, "A Celebrated Collector," 155–76; Timothy Mowl, *William Beckford: Composing for Mozart* (London: John Murray, 1998); James Noggle, *The Temporality of Taste in Eighteenth-Century British Writing* (Oxford: Oxford University Press, 2012); and Robert Gemmett, ed., *The Consummate Collector: William Beckford's Letters to his Bookseller* (Norwich, UK: Michael Russell, 2000).

CHAPTER SIX: BIBLIOMANIA AND THE ROMANTIC COLLECTOR

On book collecting in general, Holbrook Jackson's *The Anatomy of Bibliomania* (1930; repr., Urbana: University of Illinois Press, 2001) is magisterially compendious; and Nicholas Basbanes, *A Gentle Madness: Bibliophiles, Bibliomanes and the Eternal Passion for Books* (New York: Henry Holt, 1995). On nineteenth-century bibliomania, Arnold Hunt, "Private Libraries in the Age of Bibliomania," in *The Cambridge History of Libraries in Britain and Ireland, Volume 2: 1640–1850*, ed. Giles Mandelbrote and K. A. Manley (Cambridge: Cambridge University Press 2006), 438–58; James Raven, "Debating Bibliomania and the Collection of Books in the Eighteenth Century," *Library & Information History*

29 (2013): 196–209; Alys Mostyn, "Leigh Hunt's 'World of Books': Bibliomania and the Fancy," *Romanticism* 21 (2015): 238–49; and Michael Robinson, "Ornamental Gentlemen: Thomas F. Dibdin, Romantic Bibliomania and Romantic Sexualities," *European Romantic Review* 22 (2011): 685–706. On Beau Brummell, Ian Kelly, *Beau Brummell: The Ultimate Dandy* (London: Hodder & Stoughton, 2005).

On the Romantic turn toward interiority and selfhood, Peter Gay, *The Naked Heart: The Bourgeois Experience, Victoria to Freud* (New York: Norton, 1995); on Victorian collecting, Jacqueline Yallop, *Magpies, Squirrels and Thieves: How the Victorians Collected the World* (London: Atlantic Books, 2011); on Sir Thomas Phillipps, A. N. L. Munby, *Portrait of an Obsession: The Life of Sir Thomas Phillipps, The World's Greatest Book Collector* (London: Constable, 1967); on Walter Scott, Nigel Leask, "Sir Walter Scott's *The Antiquary* and the Ossian Controversy," *Yearbook of English Studies* 47 (2017): 189–202, Shawn Malley, "Walter Scott's Romantic Archaeology: New/Old Abbotsford and 'The Antiquary,'" *Studies in Romanticism* 40 (2001): 233–51, Ann Rigney, "Things and the Archive: Scott's Materialist Legacy," *Scottish Literary Review* 7 (2015): 13–34, and Caroline McCracken-Flesher, "Anxiety in the Archive: From the Antiquary to the Absent Author," *Scottish Literary Review* 7 (2015): 75–94; Scott described Oldbuck's collections satirically in a fictionalized guide to his house called *Reliquiae Trotcosienses, or The Gabions of the late Jonathan Oldbuck Esq. of Monkbarns*, ed. Gerard Carruthers and Alison Lumsden (1893; repr., Edinburgh: Edinburgh University Press, 2004); on Charles Kirkpatrick Sharpe, Kelsey Williams, "The Cabinet of Charles Kirkpatrick Sharpe: An Essay in the Biographical Distillation of Affinities," *Rethinking History* 27 (2023): 750–79; on Balzac, Graham Robb, *Balzac: A Biography* (New York: Norton, 1994); and on collecting in France, Emma Bielecki, *The Collector in Nineteenth-Century French Literature: Representation, Identity, Knowledge* (New York: Peter Lang, 2012), and Janell Watson, *Literature and Material Culture from Balzac to Proust: The Collection and Consumption of Curiosities* (Cambridge: Cambridge University Press, 2000).

CHAPTER SEVEN: THE GLORY OF THE NATURALIST

General to this chapter are Robert Kohler, *All Creatures: Naturalists, Collectors and Biodiversity, 1850–1950* (Princeton, NJ: Princeton University Press, 2006); Richard Conniff, *The Species Seekers: Heroes, Fools and the Mad Pursuit of Life on Earth* (New York: Norton, 2010); Bruno Strasser, "Collecting Nature: Practices, Styles, and Narratives," *Osiris* 27 (2012): 303–40; Nicholas Jardine et al., eds., *Cultures of Natural History* (Cambridge: Cambridge University Press, 1996); Harriet Ritvo, *The Animal Estate: The English and Other Creatures in Victorian England* (Cambridge, MA: Harvard University Press, 1987).

On Romanticism and science, Andrew Cunningham and Nicholas Jardine, eds., *Romanticism and the Sciences* (Cambridge: Cambridge University Press, 1990); on Humboldt, Michael Dettelbach, "Global Physics and Aesthetic Empire: Humboldt's Physical Portrait of the Tropics," in *Visions of Empire: Voyages, Botany, and Representations of Nature*, ed. David Miller and Peter Hanns Reill (Cambridge: Cambridge University Press, 1996), 258–92, and Andrea Wulf, *The Invention of Nature: Alexander von Humboldt's New World* (New York: Knopf, 2015); on Darwin, Janet Browne, *Charles Darwin: A Biography*, 2 vols.

(Princeton, NJ: Princeton University Press, 1996, 2003); on French natural history, Emma Spary, *Utopia's Garden: French Natural History from Old Regime to Revolution* (Chicago: University of Chicago Press, 2000); on Elgin's curse, Gillen d'Arcy Wood, "Mourning the Marbles: the Strange Case of Lord Elgin's Nose," *Wordsworth Circle* 29 (1998): 171–77; on Wallace, James Costa, *Radical by Nature: The Revolutionary Life of Alfred Russel Wallace* (Princeton, NJ: Princeton University Press, 2023); on Annie Alexander, Susan Star and James Griesemer, "Institutional Ecology, 'Translations' and Boundary Objects: Amateurs and Professionals in Berkeley's Museum of Vertebrate Zoology, 1907–39," *Social Studies of Science* 19 (1989): 387–420; on Snethlage, Barbara and Richard Mearns, *The Bird Collectors* (San Diego: Academic Press, 1998); on Appun, Neil Whitehead, *Dark Shamans: Kanaima and the Poetics of Violent Death* (Durham, NC: Duke University Press, 2007).

CHAPTER EIGHT: DECADENTS AND DEADLY DANDIES

On Henry James and Gilded Age collecting in its broader context, T. J. Jackson Lears, *Fables of Abundance: A Cultural History of Advertising in America* (New York: Basic, 1994), Simone Francescato, *Collecting and Appreciating: Henry James and the Transformation of Aesthetics in the Age of Consumption* (Bern, Switzerland: Peter Lang, 2010), and Sergio Perosa, "Henry James and Unholy Art Acquisitions," *Cambridge Quarterly* 37 (2008): 150–63; on Isabella Stewart Gardner, Natalie Dykstra, *Chasing Beauty: The Life of Isabella Stewart Gardner* (New York: Mariner, 2024); on Berenson, Rachel Cohen, *Bernard Berenson: A Life in the Picture Trade* (New Haven, CT: Yale University Press, 2023); on domestic interiors, Charlotte Gere et al., *The House Beautiful: Oscar Wilde and the Aesthetic Interior* (London: Lund Humphries, 2000), Deborah Cohen, *Household Gods: The British and Their Possessions* (New Haven, CT: Yale University Press, 2006), and Anne Higonnet, *A Museum of One's Own: Private Collecting, Public Gift* (New York: Periscope, 2009).

For fin de siècle decadent culture, the writings of Philippe Jullian are magisterial if not unsurpassable in their range, penetration, and style (see below for specific references); Mario Praz, *The Romantic Agony*, trans. Angus Davidson (London: Oxford University Press, 1933) remains highly relevant; more recent studies of decadence include Barbara Spackman, *Decadent Genealogies: The Rhetoric of Sickness from Baudelaire to D'Annunzio* (Ithaca, NY: Cornell University Press, 1989), and David Weir, *Decadence and the Making of Modernism* (Amherst: University of Massachusetts Press, 1995); on Huysmans, Robert Baldick, *The Life of J.-K. Huysmans* (Gardena, CA: Dedalus, 2006); on Montesquiou, Philippe Jullian, *Prince of Aesthetes: Count Robert de Montesquiou, 1855–1921*, trans. John Haylock and Francis King (1967; New York: Viking, 1968); on French collecting, Emma Bielecki, *The Collector in Nineteenth-Century French Literature: Representation, Identity, Knowledge* (New York: Peter Lang, 2012), and Janell Watson, *Literature and Material Culture from Balzac to Proust: The Collection and Consumption of Curiosities* (Cambridge: Cambridge University Press, 2000); on D'Annunzio, Philippe Jullian, *D'Annunzio*, trans. Stephen Hardman (1971; New York: Viking, 1972), and Lucy Hughes-Hallett, *The Pike: Gabriele D'Annunzio—Poet, Seducer and Preacher of War* (London: Fourth Estate, 2013); on Wilde, Richard Ellmann, *Oscar Wilde* (New York: Knopf, 1988); on Schliemann, Cathy Gere, *Knossos and the Prophets of Modernism* (Chicago: University of Chicago Press, 2009).

CHAPTER NINE: THE INNER FIRE

On Kinsey, Donna Drucker, *The Classification of Sex: Alfred Kinsey and the Organization of Knowledge* (Pittsburgh: University of Pittsburgh Press, 2014), and Geoff Nicholson, *Sex Collectors: The Secret World of Consumers, Connoisseurs, Curators, Creators, Dealers, Bibliographers and Accumulators of "Erotica"* (New York: Simon & Schuster, 2006).

On Freud and collecting, John Forrester, *"Mille e Tre*: Freud and Collecting," in *The Cultures of Collecting*, ed. John Elsner and Roger Cardinal (Cambridge, MA: Harvard University Press, 1994), 224–51, Carlo Ginzburg, "Morelli, Freud and Sherlock Holmes: Clues and Scientific Method," *History Workshop* 9 (1980): 5–36, Lynn Gamwell and Richard Wells, eds., *Sigmund Freud and Art: His Personal Collection of Antiquities* (London: Freud Museum, 1989), and Ro Spankie, *Sigmund Freud's Desk: An Annotated Guide* (London: Freud Museum, 2015); on collecting and dreams, Sigmund Freud, *The Standard Edition of the Complete Psychological Works of Sigmund Freud*, 24 vols., ed. James Strachey, *Volume 5: The Interpretation of Dreams, and, On Dreams, 1900–1901* (London: Hogarth Press, 1958), 169–76, 282–84, 289–92; on psychoanalysis and collecting broadly, Werner Muensterberger, *Collecting, An Unruly Passion: Psychological Perspectives* (Princeton, NJ: Princeton University Press, 1993); and for Muensterberger's life, Lisa Zeitz, *Der Mann mit den Masken: Das Jahrhundertleben des Werner Muensterberger* [The man with the masks: Werner Muensterberger's century] (Munich: Berlin Verlag, 2013); Jean Baudrillard, "The System of Collecting" (1968), in Elsner and Cardinal, eds., *Cultures of Collecting*, 7–24, and Peter Subkowski, "On the Psychodynamics of Collecting," *International Journal of Psychoanalysis* 87 (2006): 383–401; on Freud and Freudianism, Peter Gay, *Freud: A Life for Our Time* (New York: Norton, 1988), Eli Zaretsky, *Secrets of the Soul: A Social and Cultural History of Psychoanalysis* (New York: Knopf, 2004), and Andreas Mayer, *Sites of the Unconscious: Hypnosis and the Emergence of the Psychoanalytic Setting*, trans. Christopher Barber (Chicago: University of Chicago Press, 2013). On kleptomania, Elaine Abelson, "The Invention of Kleptomania," *Signs* 15 (1989): 123–43.

On early twentieth-century women art collectors: Aline Saarinen, *The Proud Possessors: The Lives, Times and Tastes of Some Adventurous American Art Collectors* (New York: Random House, 1958); on Stein and subsequent women art collectors, Janet Bishop et al., eds., *The Steins Collect: Matisse, Picasso and the Parisian Avant-Garde* (San Francisco: SF MOMA, 2011); Dianne McLeod, *Enchanted Lives, Enchanted Objects: American Women Collectors and the Making of Culture, 1800–1940* (Berkeley: University of California Press, 2008); Mabel Dodge Luhan, *Intimate Memories: The Autobiography of Mabel Dodge Luhan*, ed. Lois Rudnick (Albuquerque: University of New Mexico Press, 1999); Ellen Hirschland and Nancy Ramage, *The Cone Sisters of Baltimore: Collecting at Full Tilt* (Evanston, IL: Northwestern University Press, 2008); on Peggy Guggenheim, Anton Gill, *Art Lover: A Biography of Peggy Guggenheim* (New York: Harper Perennial, 2002); and Guggenheim's autobiography, *Out of This Century: Confessions of an Art Addict* (New York: Universe Books, 1979).

CHAPTER TEN: SURREALISTS, NATIVE COLLECTORS, AND THE COLONIAL CURSE

On M. R. James, Patrick Murphy, *Medieval Studies and the Ghost Stories of M. R. James* (University Park: Pennsylvania State University Press, 2017); on curses, Zainab Bahrani, "Assault and Abduction: The Fate of the Royal Image in the Ancient Near East," *Art History* 18 (1995): 363–82; on the Koh-i-Noor diamond, William Dalrymple and Anita Anand, *Koh-i-Noor: The History of the World's Most Infamous Diamond* (London: Bloomsbury, 2017); on Tutankhamun's curse, Roger Luckhurst, *The Mummy's Curse: The True History of a Dark Fantasy* (Oxford: Oxford University Press, 2012); for Tintin and his background, Michael Farr, *Tintin: The Complete Companion* (London: John Murray, 2001).

On science and anthropological collecting, James Clifford, *The Predicament of Culture: Twentieth-Century Ethnography, Literature, and Art* (Cambridge, MA: Harvard University Press, 1988); Simon Schaffer, *From Physics to Anthropology and Back Again* (Cambridge: Prickly Pear Pamphlets, 1994); and Johannes Fabian, *Out of Our Minds: Reason and Madness in the Exploration of Central Africa* (Berkeley: University of California Press, 2000).

On surrealism, Louise Tythacott, *Surrealism and the Exotic* (New York: Routledge, 2003), and Katharine Conley, *Surrealist Ghostliness* (Lincoln: University of Nebraska Press, 2013); for Apollinaire, Guillaume Apollinaire, *Apollinaire on Art: Essays and Reviews, 1902–1918*, ed. LeRoy Breunig (New York: Viking, 1972); on Breton, Mark Pollizzotti, *Revolution of the Mind: The Life of André Breton* (New York: Farrar, Straus & Giroux, 1999), and Christina Rudosky, "Breton the Collector: A Surrealist Poetics of the Object (PhD diss., University of Colorado, 2015); on Breton's collections, "André Breton," https://www.andrebreton.fr (accessed October 12, 2024); and for Breton's writings, Franklin Rosemont, ed., *What Is Surrealism?: Selected Writings [of André Breton]* (New York: Pathfinder, 1978); on Leiris's life and work, Sally Price and Jean Jamin, "A Conversation with Michel Leiris," *Current Anthropology* 29 (1988): 157–74 and Clifford, *Predicament of Culture*; Leiris's autobiography is published as the series *Rules of the Game*, 4 vols., trans. Lydia Davis and Richard Sieburth (New Haven, CT: Yale University Press, 2017–24); on Benjamin, Howard Eiland and Michael Jennings, *Walter Benjamin: A Critical Life* (Cambridge, MA: Belknap Press, 2014), Ackbar Abbas, "Walter Benjamin's Collector: The Fate of Modern Experience," *New Literary History* 20 (1988): 217–37; for more on Benjamin on collecting, Esther Leslie, trans., and Ursula Marx et al., eds., *Walter Benjamin's Archive: Images, Texts, Signs* (London: Verso, 2007), and Howard Eiland and Kevin McLaughlin, trans., *The Arcades Project* (Cambridge, MA: Belknap Press, 1999); on Borges, William Egginton, *The Rigor of Angels: Borges, Heisenberg, Kant and the Ultimate Nature of Reality* (New York: Pantheon, 2023), and Alberto Manguel, *With Borges* (Toronto: Thomas Allen, 2004).

On George Hunt and native collecting generally, Margaret Bruchac, *Savage Kin: Indigenous Informants and American Anthropologists* (Tucson: University of Arizona Press, 2018); on Shotridge, Elizabeth Seaton, "The Native Collector: Louis Shotridge and the Contests of Possession," *Ethnography* 2 (2000): 35–61; and on Shotridge and the Penn Museum, see

"The Louis Shotridge Digital Archive," https://www.penn.museum/collections/shotridge/ (accessed September 8, 2024); on Boas, Ira Jacknis, "Franz Boas and Exhibits: On the Limitations of the Museum Method of Anthropology," in *Objects and Others: Essays on Museums and Material Culture*, ed. George Stocking, Jr. (Madison, WI: University of Wisconsin Press, 1985), 75–111; on Talayesva, Rebecca Lemov, "Anthropology's Most Documented Man, Ca. 1947: A Prefiguration of Big Data from the Big Social Science Era," *Osiris* 32 (2017): 21–42, and Don Talayesva, *Sun Chief: The Autobiography of a Hopi Indian* (New Haven, CT: Yale University Press, 1942); on Aby Warburg, Philippe-Alain Michaud, *Aby Warburg and the Image in Motion*, trans. Sophie Hawkes (1998; New York: Zone, 2004).

CHAPTER ELEVEN: HOW TO SAVE YOUR PORCELAIN

On Jewish collectors and antisemitism, Edmond de Waal, *The Hare with Amber Eyes: A Family's Century of Art and Loss* (New York: Farrar, Straus & Giroux, 2010), James McAuley, *The House of Fragile Things: Jewish Art Collectors and the Fall of France* (New Haven, CT: Yale University Press, 2021), and Hans Von Trotta, *Pollak's Arm*, trans. Elisabeth Lauffer (2021; New York: New Vessel, 2022); on the French context, Emma Bielecki, *The Collector in Nineteenth-Century French Literature: Representation, Identity, Knowledge* (New York: Peter Lang, 2012); on Nazi looting, Lynn Nicholas, *The Rape of Europa: The Fate of Europe's Treasures in the Third Reich and the Second World War* (New York: Knopf, 1994); on Nazi attitudes to the art market, Uwe Fleckner, "Marketing the Defamed: On the Contradictory Use of Provenances in the Third Reich," in *Provenance: An Alternate History of Art*, ed. Gail Feigenbaum and Inge Reist (Los Angeles: Getty, 2012), 137–53.

On antiquities collecting in China, including Duanfang and C. T. Loo, Karl Meyer and Shareen Blair Brysac, *The China Collectors: America's Century-Long Hunt for Asian Art Treasures* (New York: St. Martin's Press, 2015); on the Cultural Revolution, Frank Dikotter, *The Cultural Revolution: A People's History, 1962–1976* (London: Bloomsbury, 2016), and Denise Ho, *Curating Revolution: Politics on Display in Mao's China* (Cambridge: Cambridge University Press, 2017); on Shchukin, Natalya Semenova, *The Collector: The Story of Sergei Shchukin and His Lost Masterpieces*, trans. Anthony Roberts (New Haven, CT: Yale University Press, 2018), and Anne Odom and Wendy Salmond, eds., *Treasures into Tractors: The Selling of Russia's Cultural Heritage, 1918–1938* (Seattle: University of Washington Press, 2009); on Romania, Emanuela Grama, "Arbiters of Value: The Nationalization of Art and the Politics of Expertise in Early Socialist Romania," *East European Politics and Societies* 33 (2019): 656–76; on repatriation, Jeanette Greenfield, *The Return of Cultural Treasures*, 3rd ed. (Cambridge: Cambridge University Press, 2007); on Chatwin, Nicholas Shakespeare, *Bruce Chatwin: A Biography* (New York: Doubleday, 2000); for echoes of *Utz* and Chatwin's attitudes to collecting in the Chinese writer Lao She, Rey Chow, "Fateful Attachments: On Collecting, Fidelity and Lao She," *Critical Inquiry* 28 (2001): 286–304.

CHAPTER TWELVE: CROSSING THE CREEP THRESHOLD

For Bloch, Robert Bloch, *Once Around the Bloch: An Unauthorized Autobiography* (New York: Tor, 1993); on Fowles, including his collecting, Eileen Warburton, *John Fowles: A*

Life in Two Worlds (New York: Viking, 2004); on killing animals for science, Ben Minteer et al., "Avoiding (Re)Extinction," *Science* 344 (2014): 260–61, L. A. Rocha et al., "Specimen Collection: An Essential Tool," *Science* 344 (2014): 814–15, and Ben Minteer, *Fall of the Wild: Extinction, De-Extinction and the Ethics of Conservation* (New York: Columbia University Press, 2018); on Dahmer, Janet Warren et al., "The Collectors: Serial Sexual Offenders Who Preserve Evidence of Their Crimes," *Aggression and Violent Behavior* 18 (2013): 666–721, and J. Arturo Silva et al., "The Case of Jeffrey Dahmer: Sexual Serial Homicide from a Neuropsychiatric Developmental Perspective," *Journal of Forensic Science* 47 (2002): 1–13; Cary Wolfe and Jonathan Elmer, "Subject to Sacrifice: Ideology, Psychoanalysis and the Discourse of Species in Jonathan Demme's *Silence of the Lambs*," *Boundary* 2 (1995): 141–70; and Paul Gambino, *Morbid Curiosities: Collections of the Uncommon and Bizarre* (London: Laurence King, 2016); on murderabilia, Harold Schechter, *Murderabilia: A History of Crime in 100 Objects* (New York: Workman, 2023); on Nazi memorabilia, Michael Hughes, *The Anarchy of Nazi Memorabilia* (London: Routledge, 2021).

CHAPTER THIRTEEN: ALL HOARDERS NOW

Of general relevance to hoarding disorder (HD) and its cultural history in modern America is Scott Herring, *The Hoarders: Material Deviance in Modern American Culture* (Chicago: University of Chicago Press, 2014); for diagnostic descriptions, *DSM-5* (2013), https://www .ncbi.nlm.nih.gov/books/NBK519704/table/ch3.t29/, and ICD-11 (2018), https://icd.who .int/browse11/l-m/en#/http://id.who.int/icd/entity/1991016628, both accessed November 30, 2024; for diagnostic discussions of HD, Randy Frost and Gail Steketee, eds., *The Oxford Handbook of Hoarding and Acquiring* (Oxford: Oxford University Press, 2014); on collecting, hoarding, and neuroscience, Steven Anderson et al., "A Neural Basis for Collecting Behavior in Humans," *Brain* 128 (2005): 201–12, 201, Daniel Lord Smail, "Neurohistory in Action: Hoarding and the Human Past," *Isis* 105 (2014): 110–22, and Shirley Mueller, *Inside the Head of a Collector: Neuropsychological Forces at Play* (Seattle: Marquand, 2019); for examples of the extensive and growing literature on hoarding and psychology in different national contexts, Isabela Fontelle et al., "The Brazilian Portuguese Version of the Saving Inventory–Revised: Internal Consistency, Rest-Retest Reliability, and Validity of a Questionnaire to Assess Hoarding," *Psychological Reports* 106 (2010): 279–96, Kiara Timpano et al., "A Consideration of Hoarding Disorder Symptoms in China," *Comprehensive Psychiatry* 57 (2015): 36–45, and Fabio Gygi, "The Metamorphosis of Excess: 'Rubbish Houses' and the Imagined Trajectory of Things in Post-Bubble Japan," in *Consuming Life in Post-Bubble Japan: A Transdisciplinary Perspective*, ed. Katarzyna Cwiertka and Ewa Machotka (Amsterdam: Amsterdam University Press, 2018), 129–52.

For Robert Opie's Museum of Brands, " 'Unless you do these crazy things . . . ': An Interview with Robert Opie," in *The Cultures of Collecting*, ed. John Elsner and Roger Cardinal (Cambridge, MA: Harvard University Press, 1994), 25–48; the literature on Warhol is large, but some places to start are Victor Bockris, *Warhol: The Biography* (1989; repr., New York: Da Capo, 2003), and Blake Gopnik, *Warhol* (London: Allen Lane, 2020). Herring also has an excellent discussion of Warhol and hoarding in *The Hoarders*; for Pamuk's novel and museum in Istanbul, Orhan Pamuk, *The Museum of Innocence*, trans. Maureen Freely (2008; New York: Knopf, 2009), Orhan Pamuk, *The Innocence of Objects: The Museum of Innocence, Istanbul*, trans. Ekin Oklap (New York: Abrams, 2012), and Orhan Pamuk, *Istanbul: Memories and the City*, trans. Maureen Freely (2003; New York: Knopf, 2005).

EPILOGUE: THE GREAT COLLECTORS

Inge Reist, ed., *British Models of Art Collecting and the American Response: Reflections Across the Pond* (New York: Routledge, 2014); for Indian jewelry and the Al Thani collection, Martin Chapman and Amin Jaffer, eds., *East Meets West: Jewels of the Maharajas from the Al Thani Collection* (San Francisco: San Francisco Fine Arts Museum, 2018), and Amin Jaffer, *Beyond Extravagance: A Royal Collection of Gems and Jewels* (New York: Assouline, 2013); Nicole Angemi's "The Gross Room" may be found at https://theduramater.com/gross-room-join/ (accessed November 30, 2024); on Diversa in Hawaiʻi, Stefan Helmreich, *Alien Ocean: Anthropological Voyages in Microbial Seas* (Berkeley: University of California Press, 2009); for Indigidata, Sabrina Imbler, "Training the Next Generation of Indigenous Data Scientists," *New York Times*, June 29, 2021; on Mao Badges, Laurence Coderre, "The Curator, the Investor and the Dupe: Consumer Desire and Chinese Cultural Revolution Memorabilia," *Journal of Material Culture* 21 (2016): 429–47; on Fan Jianchuan's Cultural Revolution museum, Joshua Frank, "Collecting Insanity" (2014), https://www.youtube.com/watch?v=XNKlKu96_Vo (accessed November 30, 2024).

NOTES

PROLOGUE: LET THEM SEE WHAT KIND OF A PERSON I AM

1 All quotations from *Psycho* (Universal Pictures, 1960), dir. Alfred Hitchcock.
2 François Truffaut, *Hitchcock/Truffaut* (1966; rev. ed., New York: Simon & Schuster, 1985), 282.
3 John Dryden, *All for Love* (London, 1677), act II, scene I.
4 Michel Leiris, *Phantom Africa*, trans. Brent Edwards (1934; Kolkata: Seagull, 2017), 464.

CHAPTER ONE: STATUE LOVE

1 Cicero, *The Verrine Orations*, trans. L. H. G. Greenwood, 2 vols. (Cambridge, MA: Harvard University Press, 1928), 2:326 ("amentiam"), 2:339 ("covetous," "perverted").
2 Cicero, *Verrine Orations*, 2:433.
3 Cicero, *Verrine Orations*, 2:677 ("insane and immoral"), 2:418 ("Orcus").
4 Pliny the Elder, *Natural History,* in *The Art of Ancient Greece: Sources and Documents*, ed. J. J. Pollitt (1965; repr., Cambridge: Cambridge University Press, 1990), 84.
5 Suetonius, *The Lives of the Twelve Caesars*, trans. Alexander Thomson and T. Forester (London: Henry Bohn, 1855), 283.
6 Gustave Flaubert, *Notes de Voyages*, 1845, quoted in Kenneth Gross, *The Dream of the Moving Statue* (Ithaca, NY: Cornell University Press, 1992), 70, 215.
7 Paul Moreau, *Des Aberrations du Sens Génésique* (Paris: Asselin, 1880), 14 ("épileptique"), 16 ("alcoolique"), 25 ("aberrations"), translations mine.
8 Richard Krafft-Ebing, *Psychopathia Sexualis, with Especial Reference to Contrary Sexual Instinct: A Medico-Legal Study*, trans. Charles Chaddock (Philadelphia: F. A. Davis, 1893), 396.
9 Robert Graves, *I, Claudius* (1957; repr., New York: Vintage, 1989), 341; D. Thomas Benediktson, "Caligula's Madness: Madness or Interictal Temporal Lobe Epilepsy?," *Classical World* 82 (1989): 370–75; 375.

CHAPTER TWO: THE IDOLATER'S FOLLY

1 Exodus 20:4.

2 *The Qur'an*, trans. M. A. S. Abdel Haleem (Oxford: Oxford University Press, 2004), chap. 9, "Repentance," 119.

3 Radish blessing from the year 1499, quoted in Caroline Bynum, *Christian Materiality: An Essay on Religion in Medieval Europe* (New York: Zone, 1998), 147–48.

4 Guibert of Nogent, *Le Reliquie dei Santi* [Relics of the saints], trans. and ed. Matteo Salaroli (Turnhout, Belgium: Brepols, 2015), 70 ("two-headed"), 72 ("sacrilege"), 117 ("extreme folly"), translations mine.

5 *Abbot Suger on the Abbey Church of St. Denis and Its Art Treasures*, 2nd ed., trans. and ed. Erwin Panofsky and Gerda Panofsky-Soergel (Princeton, NJ: Princeton University Press, 2019), 62–65.

6 Geoffrey Chaucer, *The Complete Works of Geoffrey Chaucer: The Canterbury Tales— Text*, 2nd ed., ed. Walter Skeat (Oxford: Clarendon Press, 1900), 21 ("brimful" in *Prologue*), 303 ("money" and "avarice" in *The Pardoner's Tale*), English modernized.

7 Desiderius Erasmus, *In Praise of Folly* (1511), trans. Betty Radice, ed. A. H. T. Levi, in *Collected Works of Erasmus* (1974–), vol. 27, *Literary and Educational Writings* 5 (Toronto: University of Toronto Press, 1986), 149.

8 Erasmus, *In Praise of Folly*, 149.

9 Martin Luther, *Church Postils* (1522), quoted in Carlos Eire, *War Against the Idols: The Reformation of Worship from Erasmus to Calvin* (Cambridge: Cambridge University Press, 1986), 67–68.

10 Martin Luther, *Ninety-Five Theses* (1517), in *The Annotated Luther, Volume I: Roots of Reform*, trans. Charles Jacobs, ed. Timothy Wengert (Minneapolis, MN: Fortress Press, 2015), 46.

CHAPTER THREE: BEWARE THE UNOBSESSED

1 Confucius, quoted in Sunglim Kim, *Flowering Plums and Curio Cabinets: The Culture of Objects in Late Chosŏn Korean Art* (Seattle: University of Washington Press, 2018), 4, 241, n. 1; the *Zhuangzi* quoted in Wai-Yee Li, "The Collector, The Connoisseur and Late-Ming Sensibility," *T'oung Pao* 81 (1995): 269–302; 274.

2 Alvaro Semedo, *The History of That Great and Renowned Monarchy of China* (London, 1655), 23 ("naturally inclined"); Song Yingxing, quoted in Timothy Brook, *The Confusions of Pleasure: Commerce and Culture in Ming China* (Berkeley: University of California Press, 1998), 185 ("proper place").

3 Wen Zhenheng, *The Elegant Life of the Chinese Literati: From the Chinese Classic, Treatise on Superfluous Things—Finding Harmony and Joy in Everyday Objects*, trans. Tony Blishen (Shanghai: Shanghai Press, 2019), 13.

4 Judith Zeitlin, "The Petrified Heart: Obsession in Chinese Literature, Art, and Medicine," *Late Imperial China* 12 (1991): 1–26; 4.

5 Quoted in Zeitlin, "The Petrified Heart," 8 (Yuan, "no obsession"), 9 (Yuan, "self loving the self"), 8 (Zhang, "deep emotion").

6 Li Shizhen, quoted in Zeitlin, "The Petrified Heart," 17.
7 Cho Hŭiryong, quoted in Kim, *Flowering Plums*, 58.

CHAPTER FOUR: THE MAGUS AND THE MERCHANT

1 Archduchess Maria of Styria, quoted in Peter Marshall, *The Theatre of the World: Alchemy, Astrology and Magic in Renaissance Prague* (New York: Walker, 2006), 85.
2 Manfredi, 1604, quoted in Paula Findlen, "Cabinets, Collecting and Natural Philosophy," in *Rudolf II and Prague: The Court and the City*, ed. Eliska Fucíková et al. (London: Thames & Hudson, 1997), 209–19, 211 ("motionless"); Spinelli, 1600, quoted in Marshall, *Theatre of the World*, 194 ("bewitched" and "bidding"), 198 ("possessed").
3 Frances Yates, *The Rosicrucian Enlightenment* (1972; repr., London: Taylor & Francis, 2003), 26; Bruce Chatwin, *Utz* (1988; repr., London: Vintage, 2005), 12; Werner Muensterberger, *Collecting, An Unruly Passion: Psychological Perspectives* (Princeton, NJ: Princeton University Press, 1993), 193 ("anal-obsessive"), 195 ("melancholic voyeur," "depression").
4 Christopher Marlowe, *Doctor Faustus: The A-Text*, ed. David Ormerod and Christopher Wortham (Nedlands: University of Western Australia Press, 1985), 99 ("conjuring books"), 137 ("danger"), 63 ("spells").
5 Galileo to Kepler, 1610, quoted in Paula Findlen, *Possessing Nature: Museums, Collecting and Scientific Culture in Early Modern Italy* (Berkeley: University of California Press, 1994), 344.
6 Prynne, quoted in Jerry Brotton, *The Sale of the Late King's Goods: Charles I and His Art Collection* (London: Pan MacMillan, 2007), 143.
7 Trevor Cooper, *The Journal of William Dowsing: Iconoclasm in East Anglia During the English Civil War* (Woodbridge, UK: Boydell Press, 2001), 239 ("cleansed"); and Brotton, *Late King's Goods*, 239 ("Tyrannus").
8 Jonathan Sawday, "The Leiden Anatomy Theatre as a Source for Davenant's 'Cabinet of Death' in *Gondibert*," *Notes and Queries* 30 (1983): 437–39; Arthur MacGregor, *Curiosity and Enlightenment: Collectors and Collections from the Sixteenth to the Nineteenth Century* (New Haven, CT: Yale University Press, 2007), 161 ("macabre antithesis").
9 Thomas Shadwell, *The Virtuoso*, ed. Marjorie Nicolson and David Rodes (1676; repr., Lincoln: University of Nebraska Press, 1966), 47.
10 Judith Drake, *An Essay in Defence of the Female Sex* (London, 1696), in Mary Astell, *A Serious Proposal to the Ladies, Parts I and II*, ed. Patricia Springborg (1694; Peterborough, ON: Broadview, 2002), 237.
11 William King, *The Transactioneer* (London, 1700) and Horace Walpole, 1753, quoted in James Delbourgo, *Collecting the World: Hans Sloane and the Origins of the British Museum* (Cambridge, MA: Belknap Press, 2017), 166 and 313.
12 Sloane, 1740, in *Magic and Mental Disorder: Sir Hans Sloane's Memoir of John Beaumont*, ed. Michael Hunter (London: Robert Boyle Project, 2011), 12.
13 Edward Miller, *That Noble Cabinet: A History of the British Museum* (London: Deutsch, 1973), front flap ("flamboyant eccentric"); museum labels quoted in Del-

bourgo, *Collecting the World*, xxvi ("fanatical"); " 'Magic' Chest [Found] Among Rubbish: Old Remedies of a Queen's Physician," *Daily Mail*, October 11, 1935.

CHAPTER FIVE: LIBERTINES AND TRINKET QUEENS

1 Beckford, 1784, quoted in Anne Eschapasse, "William Beckford in Paris, 1788–1814: *'Le Faste Solitaire*,' " in *William Beckford, 1760-1844: An Eye for the Magnificent*, ed. Derek Ostergard (New Haven, CT: Yale University Press, 2001), 99–116, 104.

2 Quoted in Eschapasse, "William Beckford in Paris," 107.

3 *A Collection of the State Papers of John Thurloe*, ed. Thomas Birch (London, 1742), 546.

4 *Istoria degli intrighi galanti della Regina Cristina di Svezia*, 1697, quoted in Veronica Biermann, "The Virtue of a King and the Desire of a Woman?: Mythological Representations in the Collection of Queen Christina," *Art History* 24 (2001): 213–30, 222 ("advantages of both sexes"); Anonymous, *Recueil de quelques pièces*, 1668, quoted in Susanna Åkerman, *Queen Christina of Sweden and Her Circle: The Transformation of a Seventeenth-Century Philosophical Libertine* (Leiden: Brill, 1991), 305 ("see these paintings").

5 Jacques Lacombe, *The History of Christina, Queen of Sweden* (London, 1766), 95.

6 Lorenzo Da Ponte, *Mozart's Don Giovanni*, trans. Ellen Bleiler (New York: Dover, 1964), 18–20, translations adapted by author.

7 Chantal Thomas, *The Wicked Queen: The Origins of the Myth of Marie-Antoinette*, trans. Julie Rose (1989; New York: Zone, 1999), 95 ("trinket queen").

8 *Description of the Royal Menagerie of Living Animals* and *The Aristocratic League, or the French Catalinas*, quoted in Thomas, *Wicked Queen*, 240 ("beasts") and 230 ("sofas"), respectively.

9 William Anderson, *Sketches of the History and Present State of the Russian Empire* (London, 1815), 370.

10 Gwenola Ricordeau, "Marie-Antoinette sous les tropiques: Imelda Marcos, sa collection de chaussures et la mémoire de la Loi martiale," *Moussons: Recherche en sciences humaines sur l'Asie du Sud-Est* 25 (2015): 167–80.

11 William Beckford, *Vathek*, ed. Thomas Keymer (1816 ed.; repr., Oxford: Oxford University Press, 2013), 3, 4.

12 Beckford, *Vathek*, 4–5.

13 Beckford, *Vathek*, 8.

14 Beckford, *Vathek*, 8.

15 Beckford, *Vathek*, 45, 93, 94.

16 Meister, 1791, quoted in Timothy Mowl, *William Beckford: Composing for Mozart* (London: John Murray, 1998), 201–2.

17 Mowl, *William Beckford*, 279 ("I do not know"); William Beckford, *Memoirs of William Beckford of Fonthill, Author of "Vathek,"* 2 vols. (London, 1859), 2:332 ("Lausanne"); James Noggle, *The Temporality of Taste in Eighteenth-Century British Writing* (Oxford: Oxford University Press, 2012), 190 ("rages").

18 Mowl, *William Beckford*, 280 ("fatal"); Robert Gemmett, *William Beckford's Fonthill: Architecture, Landscape and the Arts* (Oxford: Fonthill Media, 2016), 71 ("spider").

CHAPTER SIX: BIBLIOMANIA AND THE ROMANTIC COLLECTOR

1 Lord Chesterfield to his son, March 19, 1750, in *Lord Chesterfield's Letters*, ed. David Roberts (Oxford: Oxford University Press, 2008), 201.

2 Thomas Dibdin, *Bibliomania; or Book-Madness; A Bibliographical Romance* (London, 1842).

3 Dibdin, *Bibliomania*, 3 ("excessive attachment"), 15 ("downright"), 11 ("male sex" and "higher and middling").

4 Quotations on Heber in John Michell, *Eccentric Lives and Peculiar Notions* (San Diego: Harcourt, Brace, Jovanovich, 1984), 155; Bagford quotations in Dibdin, *Bibliomania*, 10.

5 Dibdin, *Bibliomania*, 43 ("passion"), 46 ("merely to please"), 54 ("true editions").

6 Chesterfield to his son, March 19, 1750, in *Lord Chesterfield's Letters*, 201.

7 Deidre Lynch, *Loving Literature: A Cultural History* (Chicago: University of Chicago Press, 2015), 103–45 ("Wedded to Books"); Hunt quoted in Alys Mostyn, "Leigh Hunt's 'World of Books': Bibliomania and the Fancy," *Romanticism* 21 (2015): 238–49, 242.

8 Holbrook Jackson, *The Anatomy of Bibliomania* (1930; repr., Urbana: University of Illinois Press, 2001), 46 ("bibliophily"), 535 ("bibliotaphs"), 216 ("bibliolatry"); Holbrook Jackson, *The Anatomy of Bibliomania*, 2 vols. (London, original 1930 ed.), 2:273 ("book please").

9 Jackson, *Bibliomania*, Illinois 2001 ed., 566 ("bibliosanity"), 524 ("hypnotized"), 166 ("book-hunger"), 580 ("book-ghouls"), 511 ("sweet madness" and "soothing affliction"); 1930 ed., 2:643 ("water").

10 Jackson, *Anatomy of Bibliomania*, 2001 ed., 359 ("biblioklepts"), 524 ("tiger").

11 Gustave Flaubert, "Bibliomania," in *A Passion for Books: A Book-Lover's Treasury of Stories, Essays, Humor, Lore and Lists on Collecting, Reading, Borrowing, Lending, Caring for and Appreciating Books*, ed. Harold Rabinowitz and Rob Kaplan (New York: Times Books, 1999), 76.

12 Phillipps, 1869, quoted in A. N. L. Munby, *Portrait of an Obsession: The Life of Sir Thomas Phillipps, The World's Greatest Book Collector* (London: Constable, 1967), 237.

13 Munby, *Portrait of an Obsession*, 150 ("ardour"), 26 ("villainous"); A. N. L. Munby, ed., *The Catalogues of Manuscripts and Printed Books of Sir Thomas Phillipps, Their Composition and Distribution* (Cambridge: Cambridge University Press, 1951), 18 ("vello-maniac").

14 Munby, *Portrait of an Obsession*, 71.

15 Munby, *Portrait of an Obsession*, 185 ("sickening"), 239 ("no heart").

16 Munby, *Portrait of an Obsession*, 141 ("cracked"), 237 ("book-buying"), 89 ("bibliomaniacally").

17 A. N. L. Munby, *The Formation of the Phillipps Library: From 1841 to 1872*, 2 vols. (Cambridge: Cambridge University Press, 1954–56), 1:169.

18 Sir Walter Scott, *The Antiquary* [*Waverley Novels, Volume 5*] (1816; repr., London, 1895), 32–34.

19 Scott, *The Antiquary*, 38 ("force of money" and "ballads"), 40 ("dilated").

20 "Charles Kirkpatrick Sharpe, A Reminiscence," *Gentleman's Magazine* 227 (1869): 158–64, 159 ("queer and witty"); "Charles Kirkpatrick Sharpe," *Cornhill Magazine* 21 (1870): 319–32 [first printed as John Hill-Burton, "The Book-Hunter," in *Blackwood's Edinburgh Magazine* 89 (1861): 643–64], 319 ("charmingly antiquated"); "Sharpe," *Gentleman's Magazine*, 160 ("effeminate"), 158 ("clinging").

21 "Sharpe," *Gentleman's Magazine*, 159 ("prevailing"), 161 ("fanciful and facetious"), 158 ("sealed book").

22 "Sharpe," *Gentleman's Magazine*, 161.

23 "Sharpe," *Cornhill Magazine*, 320.

24 "Sharpe," *Cornhill Magazine*, 320.

25 Balzac, letter of August 4, 1846, *Honoré de Balzac: Letters to Madame Hanska*, trans. Katharine Prescott Wormeley (Boston, 1900), 732 ("I shall win"); Graham Robb, *Balzac: A Biography* (New York: Norton, 1994), 367 ("demon").

26 Honoré de Balzac, *Cousin Pons*, trans. Herbert Hunt (London: Penguin, 1968), 25, 27.

27 Balzac, *Cousin Pons*, 19, 21, 142, 146.

28 Balzac, *Cousin Pons*, 331.

CHAPTER SEVEN: THE GLORY OF THE NATURALIST

1 Charles Kingsley, *Glaucus, or, The Wonders of the Shore* (1855), quoted in Richard Conniff, *The Species Seekers: Heroes, Fools and the Mad Pursuit of Life on Earth* (New York: Norton, 2010), 12.

2 J. D. Bernal, *The Social Importance of Science* (London: Routledge, 1939), 9, has the line as "Rutherford used to divide science into physics and stamp collecting"; for the Hunt quotation, see chap. 8, n. 7.

3 Francis Bacon, *New Atlantis*, in *New Atlantis and The Great Instauration*, 2nd. ed., ed. Jerry Weinberger (Oxford: Wiley-Blackwell, 2016), 108, 109.

4 James Jurin, 1727, quoted in James Delbourgo, *Collecting the World: Hans Sloane and the Origins of the British Museum* (Cambridge, MA: Belknap Press, 2017), 195.

5 Alexander von Humboldt, *Cosmos: Sketch of a Physical Description of the Universe*, ed. Edward Sabine, 2 vols. (1846; repr., Cambridge: Cambridge University Press, 2010), 1:xvii, xviii ("irresistible impulse," "mutual connection"), 21 ("mere accumulation," "generalization," "feelings").

6 Humboldt to Karl August Varnhagen von Ense, October 27, 1834, in *Letters of Alexander von Humboldt, Written Between the Years 1827 and 1858, to Varnhagen von Ense*, 3rd. ed. (London, 1860), 15; Poe, quoted in John Ingram, *Edgar Allan Poe: His Life, Letters and Opinions*, 2 vols. (London, 1880), 2:146.

7 Charles Darwin, *The Autobiography of Charles Darwin, 1809–1882*, ed. Nora Barlow (1887; repr., New York: Norton, 1958), 23 ("innate"), 63 ("no poet"); Janet Browne, *Charles Darwin: A Biography, Volume 1—Voyaging* (New York: Knopf, 1995), 110 ("bliss").

8 Charles Darwin, *The Beagle Record: Selections from the Original Pictorial Records and Written Accounts of the Voyage of HMS Beagle*, ed. Richard Keynes (Cambridge:

Cambridge University Press, 1979), 41 ("rare union"); Charles Darwin, *The Voyage of the Beagle* (1839; repr., London: Penguin, 1989), 77 ("crawl[ed] . . . specimen").

9 Darwin, *Autobiography*, 45 ("consulting"), 79 ("pleasure of observing. . .").

10 Darwin, *Autobiography*, 99 ("collecting facts"), 119 ("true Baconian principles").

11 Darwin, *Autobiography*, 145 ("industry . . . invention"), 139 ("curious and lamentable loss"), 138 ("intense delight . . . music"), 139 ("my mind").

12 Darwin, *Autobiography*, 139.

13 Edmund Gosse, *Father and Son: A Study of Two Temperaments* (1907; repr., London: Penguin, 1989), 113 ("humble slave"), 123 ("failure in theorizing"), 113 ("mind so acute," "collector of facts"), 123 ("broad generalizations").

14 Andrew McClellan, *Inventing the Louvre: Art, Politics and the Origins of the Modern Museum in Eighteenth-Century Paris* (Berkeley: University of California Press, 1994), 123 ("Rome," quotation adapted by author); Antoine Quatremère de Quincy, "Letters on the Plan to Abduct the Monuments of Italy" (1796), in *Letters to Miranda and Canova on the Abduction of Antiquities from Rome and Athens*, trans. Chris Miller and David Gilks (Los Angeles: Getty Research Institute, 2012), 100 ("Verrine lust"), 116 ("genius of tyranny"), 111 ("dismemberment").

15 Ardeta Gjikola, "The Formation of a Taste Judgment: How Benjamin R. Haydon Came to Value, Observe and Evaluate the Elgin Marbles," *British Journal for the History of Science Themes* 7 (2022): 157–80, 158.

16 George Gordon, Lord Byron, "Childe Harold's Pilgrimage," *Poetical Works of Lord Byron*, 3 vols. (London, 1886), 1:285 ("barren . . ."); Gillen D'Arcy Wood, "Mourning the Marbles: The Strange Case of Lord Elgin's Nose," *Wordsworth Circle* 29 (1998): 171–77, 171 ("noseless," attributed to Byron).

17 Darwin, *Voyage of the Beagle*, 216.

18 Jones, quoted in Raymond Stearns, *James Petiver: Promoter of Natural Science, c. 1663–1718* (Worcester, MA: American Antiquarian Society, 1952), 263; Tobin, quoted in Jennifer Newell, *Trading Nature: Tahitians, Europeans and Ecological Exchange* (Honolulu: University of Hawai'i Press, 2010), 68; Ernest Henry Wilson, *A Naturalist in Western China: With Vasculum, Camera and Gun—Volume 1* (London, 1913), 86.

19 Alfred Russel Wallace, *The Annotated Malay Archipelago*, ed. John Van Wyhe (1869; repr., Singapore: National University of Singapore, 2015), 312 ("dogs barked . . . monster").

20 Wallace, *Annotated Malay Archipelago*, 411 ("trembled"), 86 ("no less than"), 607 ("penetrat[ed]").

21 Wallace, *The Annotated Malay Archipelago*, 524 ("utterly beyond . . . secret"); and Wallace, quoted in Conniff, *Species Seekers*, 262 ("conjuror").

22 Alfred Russel Wallace, *The Wonderful Century: Its Successes and Failures* (New York, 1898), 369, 378.

23 Chapman, quoted in Robert Kohler, *All Creatures: Naturalists, Collectors and Biodiversity, 1850–1950* (Princeton, NJ: Princeton University Press, 2006), 191 ("this miserable collecting . . . cents"); W. B. Grove, quoted in David Allen, *The Naturalist in Britain: A Social History* (1976; repr., Princeton, NJ: Princeton University Press, 1994), 174 ("glory of the field naturalist").

24 Gosse, *Father and Son*, 125.

25 All quotations from Guy de Maupassant, "Au Muséum d'Histoire Naturelle" (1884), in *A Selection of the Chroniques, 1881–87*, ed. Adrian Ritchie (New York: Peter Lang, 2002), 27–34, translations adapted by author.

26 Joseph Conrad, *Heart of Darkness* (1899; repr., London: Penguin, 2017), 12.

CHAPTER EIGHT: DECADENTS AND DEADLY DANDIES

1 Joris-Karl Huysmans, *A Rebours*, trans. Robert Baldick (1884; Penguin: London, 1956), 49.

2 Charles Baudelaire, *Paris Spleen*, trans. Louise Varèse (1869; New York: New Directions, 1947), 74.

3 Charles Baudelaire, *The Flowers of Evil*, trans. James McGowan (1857; Oxford: Oxford University Press, 1993), 5 ("swarming . . . charms"), 157 ("wound," translation adapted by author).

4 *The Collected Works of Paul Valéry: Masters and Friends*, trans. Martin Turnell (Princeton, NJ: Princeton University Press, 1956), 267.

5 Bonnaffé, 1878, quoted in Emma Bielecki, *The Collector in Nineteenth-Century French Literature: Representation, Identity, Knowledge* (New York: Peter Lang, 2012), 6 (author's translation).

6 Friedrich Nietzsche, "On the Uses and Disadvantages of History for Life" (1874), in *Untimely Meditations*, trans. R. J. Hollingdale (Cambridge: Cambridge University Press, 1997), 79 ("walking encyclopaedias"), 75 ("blind rage").

7 William James, *The Principles of Psychology*, 2 vols. (New York, 1890), 1:293 ("instinctive . . . selves"), 683 ("annihilation"), 292 ("material self"); Thorstein Veblen, *The Theory of the Leisure Class: An Economic Study of Institutions* (New York, 1899), chap. 4.

8 Max Nordau, *Degeneration*, trans. unknown (1892; New York, 1895), 11 ("everything . . . bewildering"), 27 ("aimless"), 11 ("discrepant"), 27 ("purchases").

9 Sergio Perosa, "Henry James and Unholy Art Acquisitions," *Cambridge Quarterly* 37 (2008): 150–63, 153 ("Cleopatra"); Mary Berenson, *Mary Berenson: A Self Portrait from her Letters and Diaries*, ed. Barbara Strachey and Jayne Samuels (London: Hamish Hamilton, 1983), 237 ("something horrible").

10 Berenson, *Mary Berenson*, 110 ("squillionaires"); Cole Porter, "Blue Boy Blues," quoted in Shelley Bennett, *The Art of Wealth: The Huntingtons in the Gilded Age* (San Marino, CA: Huntington Library, 2013), 240.

11 Archer Huntington to his sister Caroline, 1944, quoted in Bennett, *The Huntingtons*, 293.

12 Duveen to Henry Huntington, quoted in Bennett, *The Huntingtons*, 282.

13 James quoted in Perosa, "Unholy Art Acquisitions," 153 ("barbarians"), 154 ("money in the air"), 155 ("rapine").

14 Henry James, *The Portrait of a Lady* (1881; repr., Oxford: Oxford University Press, 2009), 304 ("figure"); Henry James, *The Princess Casamassima* (1886), in Henry James, *Novels, 1886–1890* (New York: Library of America, 1989), 353 ("rapacities of the past").

15 Henry James, *The Spoils of Poynton* (1897; repr., London: Penguin, 1987), 53 ("living

things . . . *us*"); Henry James, *The Outcry* (1911; repr., New York Review of Books, 2002), 60 ("*ideally* expensive").

16 Nordau, *Degeneration*, 305 ("drivel"), 302 ("anaemic").

17 Huysmans, 1890, quoted in Robert Baldick, *The Life of J.-K. Huysmans* (Gardena, CA: Dedalus, 2006), 226–27.

18 *The Road from Decadence: From Brothel to Cloister—Selected Letters of J. K. Huysmans*, ed. and trans. Barbara Beaumont (London: Athlone, 1989), 47.

19 Quoted in Philippe Jullian, *Prince of Aesthetes: Count Robert de Montesquiou, 1855–1921*, trans. John Haylock and Francis King (1967; New York: Viking, 1968), 47.

20 Huysmans, *A Rebours*, 22 ("nature"), 20 ("embers").

21 Huysmans, *A Rebours*, 230 ("jovial bourgeois"), 198 ("decayed nobility"), 199 ("commercialism"), 203 ("suppression").

22 Emil Goudeau in *L'Echo de Paris*, 1884, excerpted by Baldick in Huysmans, *A Rebours*, 223.

23 D'Annunzio, 1931, quoted in Lucy Hughes-Hallett, *The Pike: Gabriele D'Annunzio—Poet, Seducer and Preacher of War* (London: Fourth Estate, 2013), 632 ("three wonders"); Barbara Spackmann, *Decadent Genealogies: The Rhetoric of Sickness from Baudelaire to D'Annunzio* (Ithaca, NY: Cornell University Press, 1989), 9 ("disease"); Philippe Jullian, *D'Annunzio,* trans. Stephen Hardman (1971; New York: Viking, 1972), 54 ("product of an illness").

24 D'Annunzio quoted in Jullian, *D'Annunzio*, 77 ("divans"); Mario Praz, *The Romantic Agony*, trans. Angus Davidson (London: Oxford University Press, 1933), 362 ("lust").

25 Gabriele D'Annunzio, *Pleasure*, trans. Lara Rafaelli (1889; London: Penguin, 2013), 34 ("intellectual race"), 33 ("gray democratic flood"), 62 ("mania"), 52 ("vase").

26 D'Annunzio, *Pleasure*, 63 ("particle . . . magnetic"), 66 ("love my house"), 18 ("diaphanous . . . palpitation"), 47 ("scintillate"), 56 ("would have liked to surround").

27 D'Annunzio, *Pleasure*, 47 ("champagne"), 48 ("moistened"), 49 ("courtesan . . . fantasies").

28 D'Annunzio, *Pleasure*, 307 ("my very life"), 305 ("agitated"), 323 ("arms of Death").

29 Wilde, quoted in Richard Ellmann, *Oscar Wilde* (New York: Knopf, 1988), 229.

30 Oscar Wilde, *The Picture of Dorian Gray*, ed. Robert Mighall (1890; repr., London: Penguin, 2003), 121 ("curious jewelled style"), 123 ("prefiguring type"), 133–34 ("dainty Delhi muslins").

31 Wilde, *Picture of Dorian Gray*, 134.

32 Wilde, *Picture of Dorian Gray*, 137 ("complex . . . grace"), 138 ("there were times").

33 Wilde, *Picture of Dorian Gray*, 65.

34 Wilde, *Picture of Dorian Gray*, 151 ("worship"), 115 ("not that mere").

CHAPTER NINE: THE INNER FIRE

1 Robert Morison, quoted in Geoff Nicholson, *Sex Collectors: The Secret World of Consumers, Connoisseurs, Curators, Creators, Dealers, Bibliographers and Accumulators of "Erotica"* (New York: Simon & Schuster, 2006), 225 ("very vigorous drive"); Edgar Anderson, 1961, quoted in Donna Drucker, *The Classification of Sex: Alfred Kinsey*

and the Organization of Knowledge (Pittsburgh: University of Pittsburgh Press, 2014), 29 ("inner drive").

2 Freud, 1896, quoted in John Forrester, *"Mille e Tre*: Freud and Collecting," in *The Cultures of Collecting*, ed. John Elsner and Roger Cardinal (Cambridge, MA: Harvard University Press, 1994), 224–51, 232.

3 H.D. [Hilda Doolittle], *Tribute to Freud* (1956; repr., New York: New Directions, 2012), 68.

4 H.D. *Tribute to Freud*, 14.

5 Freud, 1896, quoted in John Forrester, *Dispatches from the Freud Wars: Psychoanalysis and Its Passions* (Cambridge, MA: Harvard University Press, 1997), 110.

6 Freud to William Fliess, January 24, 1895, in *The Complete Letters of Sigmund Freud to Wilhelm Fleiss*, ed. Jeffrey Masson (Cambridge, MA: Belknap Press, 1985), 110 ("snuffboxes . . . equivalents"); *The Revised Standard Edition of the Complete Psychological Works of Sigmund Freud*, trans. James Strachey, rev. Mark Solms, 24 vols. (London: Rowman & Littlefield, 2024), 156–57 ("psychical displacement").

7 Freud, 1908, quoted in Forrester, *"Mille e Tre,"* 236 ("libido . . . things").

8 Sigmund Freud, *Civilization and Its Discontents*, trans. James Strachey (1929; New York: Norton, 2010), 95.

9 Sigmund Freud, "Character and Anal Erotism" (1908), in *The Complete Psychological Works of Sigmund Freud*, vol. 9, *Jensen's 'Gradiva' and Other Works* (London: Vintage, 2001), 169 ("orderly"), 174 ("faeces of hell").

10 Karl Abraham, "The Psycho-Sexual Differences Between Hysteria and Dementia Praecox" (1908), in *Selected Papers, with an Introductory Memoir by Ernest Jones*, trans. Douglas Bryan and Alex Strachey (1927; London: Hogarth Press, 1968), 66–67.

11 Abraham, "The Psycho-Sexual Differences," 67.

12 Ernest Jones, "Anal Erotic Character Traits" (1912), in *Papers on Psychoanalysis* (London, 1923), quoted in Ruth Formanek, "Why They Collect: Collectors Reveal Their Motivations," in *Interpreting Objects and Collections*, ed. Susan Pearce (London: Routledge, 1994), 327–35, 328.

13 Karl Abraham, "A Short Study of the Development of the Libido, Viewed in the Light of Mental Disorders" (1924), in *Selected Papers*, 481 ("cannibalistic . . . development"), 492 ("obsessional neuroses"), 488 ("primitive people").

14 Otto Fenichel, "Trophy and Triumph: A Clinical Study" (1939), in *The Collected Papers of Otto Fenichel*, ed. Hannah Fenichel and David Rapaport, 2 vols. (New York: Norton, 1953–54), 2:148 ("sits"), 149 ("I have acquired something").

15 Fenichel, "Trophy and Triumph," 152 ("collections of trophies . . . incorporate them").

16 W. H. Auden, *The Complete Works of W. H. Auden: Poems*, vol. 1, *1927–1939* (Princeton, NJ: Princeton University Press, 2022), 379.

17 Fenichel, "Trophy and Triumph," 149.

18 "The Mad Collector," *Famous Crimes* (London, n.d.), vol. 8, no. 99: 126, in Nineteenth Century Collections Online.

19 Abraham, "A Short Study," 483 ("female castration"), 484 ("enema . . . possess").

20 Claribel Cone, quoted in Dianne McLeod, *Enchanted Lives, Enchanted Objects: American Women Collectors and the Making of Culture, 1800-1940* (Berkeley: Univer-

sity of California Press, 2008), 205 ("craving . . . foolishness"); 1918, Mary Gabriel, *The Art of Acquiring: A Portrait of Etta and Claribel Cone* (Baltimore: Bancroft Press, 2002), 115 ("I find . . . consume you").

21 Mabel Dodge Luhan, *Intimate Memories: The Autobiography of Mabel Dodge Luhan*, ed. Lois Rudnick (Albuquerque: University of New Mexico Press, 1999), 79.

22 Mary McCarthy, "The Cicerone" (1948), quoted in Frances Kiernan, *Seeing Mary Plain: The Life of Mary McCarthy* (New York: Norton, 2000), 281.

23 Jean Baudrillard, "The System of Collecting" (1968), in *Cultures of Collecting*, ed. Elsner and Cardinal, 7–24, 13.

24 Baudrillard, "System of Collecting," 10 ("harem . . . seraglio"), 11 ("neurotic"); Norman Weiner, "On Bibliomania," *Psychoanalytic Quarterly* 35 (1966): 217–32, 231.

25 Baudrillard, "System of Collecting," 9 ("sublimity"), 24 ("depleted humanity").

26 Werner Muensterberger, *Collecting: An Unruly Passion: Psychological Perspectives* (Princeton, NJ: Princeton University Press, 1993), 59.

27 Muensterberger, *Collecting*, 60 ("subliminal nexus"), 57 ("archaic need").

28 Muensterberger, *Collecting*, 200 ("peace of mind"), 197 ("in search of himself").

29 Muensterberger, *Collecting*, 193 ("progressive paranoid . . . anal-obsessive"), 195 ("reassurance").

30 *The Seven Year Itch* (20th-Century Fox, 1955), dir. Billy Wilder.

CHAPTER TEN: SURREALISTS, NATIVE COLLECTORS, AND THE COLONIAL CURSE

1 M. R. James, *Complete Ghost Stories* (London: MacMillan Collector's Library, 2017), 21 ("dispute"), 16 ("spiders").

2 Ninurta temple stela quoted in Zainab Bahrani, "Assault and Abduction: The Fate of the Royal Image in the Ancient Near East," *Art History* 18 (1995): 363–82, 379.

3 Augustus Pitt Rivers, "On the Principles of Classification Adopted in the Arrangement of His Anthropological Collection," *Journal of the Anthropological Institute of Great Britain and Ireland* 4 (1875): 293–95 ("miscellaneous . . . arranged"); Augustus Pitt Rivers, "Typological Museums, as Exemplified by the Pitt Rivers Museum at Oxford," *Journal of the Society of Arts* 40 (1891): 115–17 ("typological museums"); Leonard Woolley, *Digging up the Past* (1930; 2nd ed., London: Penguin, 1954), 18 ("casual digger . . . scientific worker"), 136 ("powers of synthesis").

4 André Breton and Philippe Soupault, *Magnetic Fields*, trans. David Gascoyne (London: Atlas, 1985), 25 ("boring"); André Breton, "Manifesto of Surrealism" (1924), in *100 Artists' Manifestos from the Futurists to the Stuckists*, ed. Alex Danchev (London: Penguin, 2011), 243 ("reign of logic"), 244 ("absolute rationalism . . . superstition"), 243 ("secrets of the insane"), 247 ("only the marvelous . . . *surreality*").

5 Breton, "Manifesto of Surrealism," 247; 1938 quotation in André Breton, *What Is Surrealism?: Selected Writings [of André Breton]*, ed. Franklin Rosemont (New York: Pathfinder, 1978), book 1:228.

6 André Breton, *Nadja*, trans. Richard Howard (1928; New York: Grove, 1988), 15–16.

7 André Breton, "Océanie," trans. Christina Rudosky (Paris: Galerie Andrée Olive,

1948), https://www.andrebreton.fr/en/work/56600100995880 (accessed November 30, 2024).

8 Michel Leiris, *Phantom Africa*, trans. Brent Edwards (1934; Kolkata: Seagull, 2017), 514 ("wacky . . . birds"), 203 ("mad laughter"), 293 ("ultra-comic animals").

9 Leiris, *Phantom Africa*, 163 ("without remorse . . . grandiose"), 161 ("stolen fire").

10 Leiris, *Phantom Africa*, 163 ("vicious circle . . . pillage them"), 498 ("at the edge of something").

11 Michel Leiris, *Manhood: A Journey from Childhood into the Fierce Order of Virility*, trans. Richard Howard (1939; Chicago: University of Chicago Press, 1992), 35.

12 Sally Price and Jean Jamin, "A Conversation with Michel Leiris," *Current Anthropology* 29 (1988): 157–74, 170 ("wrong"), 159 ("down with France," "rebellion").

13 Walter Benjamin, "Unpacking My Library: A Talk About Collecting" (1931), in *Illuminations*, trans. Harry Zohn (New York: Schocken, 1969), 59–67, 60 ("true collector . . . magic encyclopedia"), 66 ("behind the times"), 67 ("disappear inside"), 60 ("enchantment").

14 Benjamin, "Unpacking My Library," 61 ("renewal"), 60 ("passion"), 67 ("he who lives").

15 Jorge Luis Borges, "The Analytical Philosophy of John Wilkins" (1942), in *Other Inquisitions, 1937–1952*, trans. Ruth Simms (1952; Austin: University of Texas Press, 1993), 101–5, 103.

16 Jorge Luis Borges, "The Library of Babel" (1941), in *Collected Fictions*, trans. Andrew Hurley (New York: Viking, 1998), 112–18, 113 ("imperfect librarian"), 112 ("catalogue of catalogues").

17 Borges, "The Library of Babel," 118.

18 Quoted in Richard and Sally Price, *Equatoria* (New York: Routledge, 1992), 150.

19 Quoted in Margaret Bruchac, *Savage Kin: Indigenous Informants and American Anthropologists* (Tucson: University of Arizona Press, 2018), 20.

20 Quoted in Elizabeth Seaton, "The Native Collector: Louis Shotridge and the Contests of Possession," *Ethnography* 2 (2000): 35–61, 54.

21 Quoted in Seaton, "The Native Collector," 53.

22 Rebecca Lemov, "Anthropology's Most Documented Man, Ca. 1947: A Prefiguration of Big Data from the Big Social Science Era," *Osiris* 32 (2017): 21–42.

23 Breton, 1959, in *What Is Surrealism?*, book 2: 459.

24 Don Talayesva, *Sun Chief: The Autobiography of a Hopi Indian* (New Haven, CT: Yale University Press, 1942), 374 ("damned missionary"), 252 ("wicked"), 41 ("our gods were no good"), 252 ("graven images").

25 Hergé, *The Seven Crystal Balls*, trans. Leslie Lonsdale-Cooper and Michael Turner (1948; London: Methuen, 1962), 1.

26 Aimé Césaire, *Discourse on Colonialism*, trans. Joan Pinkham (1955; New York: Monthly Review Press), 71–72.

CHAPTER ELEVEN: HOW TO SAVE YOUR PORCELAIN

1 Nien Cheng, *Life and Death in Shanghai* (New York: Grove, 1986), 76 ("rich and lazy").

2 Cheng, *Life and Death*, 75.

3 Cheng, *Life and Death*, 74–75.

4 The *Journal* of Edmond and Jules Goncourt, quoted in James McAuley, *The House of Fragile Things: Jewish Art Collectors and the Fall of France* (New Haven, CT: Yale University Press, 2021), 28.

5 Drumont quoted in McAuley, *House of Fragile Things*, 61 ("love ... store"), 14 ("heartbreaking").

6 Goncourt and Daudet quoted in McAuley, *House of Fragile Things*, 211 ("falseness," orig. "fausseté") and 48 ("truncated").

7 Marcel Proust, *Remembrance of Things Past, Volume 2: The Guermantes Way and Cities of the Plain*, trans. C. K. Scott Moncrieff (1920; New York: Knopf, 1982), 702.

8 "Hitler Forbids Art Not Obvious to All; Says Works Not Immediately Comprehensible to Average German Will Be Banned," *New York Times*, July 19, 1937; textual descriptions from the 1937 "Degenerate Art" exhibition quoted in Lynn Nicholas, *The Rape of Europa: The Fate of Europe's Treasures in the Third Reich and the Second World War* (New York: Knopf, 1994), 21 ("Jewish trash"), 22 ("total madness").

9 Nicholas, *Rape of Europa*, 23 ("safeguard").

10 "Art Is Long," *New York Times*, December 26, 1943.

11 Douglas and Elizabeth Rigby, "Dictators and the Gentle Art of Collecting," *American Scholar* 11 (1942): 168–80, 168 ("tranquil ... ruthless"), 171 ("destroyer-collector").

12 Rigby, "Dictators," 180.

13 Rigby, "Dictators," 178 ("hawk and pigeon"), 169 ("ancient breed"), 173 ("Gestapo").

14 Hannah Arendt, *Eichmann in Jerusalem: A Report on the Banality of Evil* (1963; repr., London: Penguin, 2006), 45.

15 Loo, quoted in Karl Meyer and Shareen Blair Brysac, *The China Collectors: America's Century-Long Hunt for Asian Art Treasures* (New York: St. Martin's Press, 2015), 100.

16 Ji Xianlin, *The Cowshed: Memories of the Chinese Cultural Revolution*, trans. Chenxin Jiang (1998; New York: New York Review of Books, 2016), 19 ("black clay figurine"), 66 ("incorrigible").

17 Cheng, *Life and Death*, 76 ("class enemies"), 507 ("bloodsuckers").

18 Decree 672, USSR Council of Ministers, quoted in Natalya Semenova, *The Collector: The Story of Sergei Shchukin and His Lost Masterpieces*, trans. Anthony Roberts (New Haven, CT: Yale University Press, 2018), 246.

19 Romanian Ministry of Arts, 1948, quoted in Emanuela Grama, "Arbiters of Value: The Nationalization of Art and the Politics of Expertise in Early Socialist Romania," *East European Politics and Societies* 33 (2019): 656–76, 658.

20 "The Nomadic Alternative" (1969–70) and "The Morality of Things" (1973) are essays collected in Bruce Chatwin, *Anatomy of Restlessness: Selected Writings, 1969–1989* (New York: Viking, 1996), quoted in Nicholas Shakespeare, *Bruce Chatwin: A Biography* (New York: Doubleday, 2000), 110 and excerpted here.

21 Bruce Chatwin, *Utz* (1988; repr., London: Penguin, 1989), 12.

22 Chatwin, *Utz*, 104 ("porcelain-mania"), 114 ("world of little figures," emphasis added).

23 Chatwin, *Utz*, 26.

24 Chatwin, *Utz*, 20.

CHAPTER TWELVE: CROSSING THE CREEP THRESHOLD

1 *The Most Dangerous Game* (R.K.O. Pictures, 1932), dir. Ernest Schoedsack and Irving Pichel.

2 Richard Krafft-Ebing, *Psychopathia Sexualis, with Especial Reference to Contrary Sexual Instinct: A Medico-Legal Study*, trans. Charles Chaddock (Philadelphia: F. A. Davis, 1893), 163–64 ("hair-despoiler . . . booty"), 74 ("girl-cutter").

3 Robert Bloch, *Once Around the Bloch: An Unauthorized Autobiography* (New York: Tor, 1993), 228.

4 Robert Bloch, *Three Complete Novels: Psycho* [1959], *Psycho II and Psycho House* (New York: Random House, 1993), 7.

5 François Truffaut, *Hitchcock/Truffaut* (1966; rev. ed., New York: Simon & Schuster, 1985), 282.

6 *Psycho* (Universal Pictures, 1960), dir. Alfred Hitchcock.

7 John Fowles, *The Collector* (London: Jonathan Cape, 1963), 54 ("how many"), 135 ("fellow-victims"), 55 ("I hate scientists"), 171 ("great dead thing"), 129 ("anti-life").

8 Fowles, *The Collector*, 79.

9 Fowles, *The Collector*, 135.

10 Fowles, *The Collector*, 128 ("sexless"), 60 ("queer").

11 Fowles, *The Collector*, 141.

12 Kirk Johnson, "The Ornithologist the Internet Called a Murderer," *New York Times*, June 15, 2018.

13 Johnson, "The Ornithologist."

14 " 'The Collector' Spurs Abduction," *Washington Post/Times Herald*, November 12, 1966.

15 Quoted in Lionel Dahmer, *A Father's Story: One Man's Anguish at Confronting the Evil in His Son* (New York: Little, Brown, 1994), 126.

16 Janet Warren et al., "The Collectors: Serial Sexual Offenders Who Preserve Evidence of Their Crimes," *Aggression and Violent Behavior* 18 (2013): 666–721, 669.

17 Dahmer, *Father's Story*, 216.

18 J. Arturo Silva et al., "The Case of Jeffrey Dahmer: Sexual Serial Homicide from a Neuropsychiatric Developmental Perspective," *Journal of Forensic Science* 47 (2002): 1–13, 2; Warren et al., "The Collectors," 672.

19 Benjamin, quoted in Warren et al., "The Collectors," 669 ("lives in"); 671 ("collecting impulse").

20 Thomas Harris, *The Silence of the Lambs* (New York: St. Martin's Press, 1988), 163.

21 Harris, *Silence of the Lambs*, 163.

22 Bret Easton Ellis, *American Psycho* (New York: Vintage, 1991), 197 ("murders and acquisitions"), 228 ("fit in").

23 Ellis, *American Psycho*, 130.

24 Ellis, *American Psycho*, 186.

25 Paul Gambino, *Morbid Curiosities: Collections of the Uncommon and Bizarre* (London: Laurence King, 2016), 6 ("macabre"), 7 ("monsters").

26 Gambino, *Morbid Curiosities*, 10.

27 Gambino, *Morbid Curiosities*, 194.

28 Gambino, *Morbid Curiosities*, 116.

29 Gambino, *Morbid Curiosities*, 138 (Kump: "either I have a very high creep threshold, or I'm a true sociopath").

30 Gambino, *Morbid Curiosities*, 116.

CHAPTER THIRTEEN: ALL HOARDERS NOW

1 Adolf Ziegler, 1937, quoted in Lynn Nicholas, *The Rape of Europa: The Fate of Europe's Treasures in the Third Reich and the Second World War* (New York: Knopf, 1994), 21.

2 Karl Abraham, "Contributions to the Theory of the Anal Character" (1921), in *Selected Papers of Karl Abraham*, trans. Douglas Bryan and Alix Strachey (London: Hogarth Press, 1927), 386.

3 *Citizen Kane* (R. K. O. Pictures, 1941), dir. Orson Welles.

4 *Citizen Kane* (R. K. O. Pictures).

5 "Monitor: Orson Welles," *Monitor* (BBC Television, 1960), https://www.youtube.com/watch?v=kQpLmVzT_YA (accessed November 30, 2024).

6 Andy Warhol, *The Philosophy of Andy Warhol: From A to B and Back Again* (New York: Harcourt, 1975), 152–53.

7 Warhol, *Philosophy of Andy Warhol*, 145.

8 Pivar, quoted in Victor Bockris, *Warhol: The Biography* (1989; repr., New York: Da Capo, 2003), 439–40; Greenspan, quoted in Scott Herring, *The Hoarders: Material Deviance in Modern American Culture* (Chicago: University of Chicago Press, 2014), 52.

9 Richardson, quoted in Bockris, *Warhol*, 394.

10 1993 interview with Harrison in *Empire Magazine* reprinted as "Ward Harrison, Celebrity Scavenger," in Susan Pearce and Paul Martin, eds., *The Collector's Voice: Critical Readings in the Practice of Collecting, Volume 4—Contemporary Voices* (Burlington, VT: Ashgate, 2002), 291–94.

11 *DSM-5* (2013). https://www.ncbi.nlm.nih.gov/books/NBK519704/table/ch3.t29/ (accessed November 30, 2024).

12 ICD-11 (2018). https://icd.who.int/browse11/l-m/en#/http://id.who.int/icd/entity/1991016628 (accessed November 30, 2024).

13 ICD-11 (2018).

14 Steven Anderson et al., "A Neural Basis for Collecting Behavior in Humans," *Brain* 128 (2005): 201–12; 201.

15 Anderson et al., "Neural Basis for Collecting Behavior," 202.

16 Anderson et al., "Neural Basis for Collecting Behavior," 201.

17 Shirley Mueller, *Inside the Head of a Collector: Neuropsychological Forces at Play* (Seattle: Marquand, 2019), 115–19.

18 Elizabeth Gettelman, "We're All Hoarders Now: A Nation of Pack Rats Struggles to Store Its Junk," *Mother Jones*, July 5, 2007; "Hoarder Extraordinaire: The Life and Curiosity of Hans Sloane," *The Economist*, June 8, 2017.

19 Orhan Pamuk, *The Museum of Innocence*, trans. Maureen Freely (2008; New York: Knopf, 2009), 157.
20 Pamuk, *Museum of Innocence*, 525.

EPILOGUE: THE GREAT COLLECTORS

1 Quotations based on notes on presentations taken by the author.
2 *Psycho* (Universal Pictures, 1960), dir. Alfred Hitchcock.
3 See chap. 13, n. 19.

INDEX